Defenses of the Imagination

BOOKS BY ROBERT ALTER

Partial Magic: The Novel as a Self-Conscious Genre
Modern Hebrew Literature
After the Tradition
Fielding and the Nature of the Novel
Rogue's Progress: Studies in the Picaresque Novel

Robert Alter
Defenses of
the Imagination
Jewish Writers
and Modern
Historical Crisis

The Jewish Publication Society of America
Philadelphia 5738/1977

Copyright © 1977 by The Jewish Publication Society of America
First edition   All rights reserved
ISBN 0–8276–0097–6
Library of Congress catalog card no. 77–87244
Manufactured in the United States of America

Designed by Adrianne Onderdonk Dudden

For Ted and Ruth

Acknowledgments

All but three of these essays originally appeared in *Commentary*, from 1969 to 1977, and I am grateful to the editors of that magazine for their continued encouragement of my work as well as for their kindness in granting me rights to the material. I would like to thank the Harvard University Press for permission to reprint "Jewish Humor and the Domestication of Myth," which first appeared in *Veins of Humor*, Harvard English Studies, no. 3, edited by Harry Levin (Cambridge, Mass., copyright © 1972 by the President and Fellows of Harvard College). Thanks are also extended to *Triquarterly* magazine and to The Jewish Publication Society of America, co-publishers of *Contemporary Israeli Literature* (1977), in which "A Problem of Horizons" appeared as the Afterword. "Agnon's Mediterranean Myth" was initially presented in a shorter version at the meeting of the International Comparative Literature Association in Bordeaux in 1970, and it appears in print here for the first time in this country.

The unity of any event and the integrity of the world are guaranteed merely by enigmatic, although visible, symbols, which are necessary because without them the visible world would fall asunder into unnameable, bodiless, dry layers of cold and transparent ash.
—Hermann Broch
The Sleepwalkers

Defenses of the Imagination

Children of a dark century, we tend to look into our literature as in a glass darkly. The glass itself, in our most recurrent images of it, is thought of as cracked and splintered and skewed so that through its own violent fashioning it may mirror more faithfully the twisted confusion of faces that modern reality has assumed. If we ask ourselves how writers have been able to go on making poems and plays and novels while mankind runs amok, irresistibly bent, it often seems, on the simultaneous destruction of its own past and its own future, our most common answer is that literature has served as a uniquely sensitive seismograph of the age's disasters, or, indeed, as a warning-system for disasters still to come. There is of course much justice in this answer, and it could hardly be otherwise: unless literature were no more than an escape from reality into self-caressing fantasy, it would somehow have to body forth the historical darkness through which we

3

all grope. But if, as Saul Bellow was arguing persuasively not long ago, the apocalyptic stance among writers has declined through constant repetition into an empty gesture of piety, one may also wonder whether criticism itself has not perpetuated a similar cliché on the level of interpretation in so often describing the role of the modern writer as a conjurer with apocalypses. For well over half a century, poets and novelists have conspicuously used the resources of their art to lay bare the death's-heads and dry-rot of a crumbling world, but there also persists among them a powerful impulse simply to make beautiful things, even in the valley of the shadow of apocalypse, and the nature of that impulse deserves some reflection.

If much of the major literature of our century has turned upon some historical or moral abyss, it is also true that literature in this period has been turned in upon itself to an unprecedented degree. *The Trial, Women in Love,* and *The Sound and the Fury* are, of course, exemplary works of the years of deepening inner trouble that followed World War I, but just as exemplary, in a very different way, are Valéry's *Le Cimetière marin,* Wallace Stevens's *Harmonium,* Joyce's *Ulysses;* and the Thomas Mann who wrote *The Magic Mountain* in these years would also work, both early and late in his career, on *Felix Krull,* a radiant portrait of the artist as protean master of experience. Mann's example should suggest that the impulse to look into the depths has often been intertwined with the impulse of the artist to reflect on the processes of making art. Proust's patient evocation of the growth of an artist's consciousness through time concludes with a whole cultural order in ruins and the reverberation of German bombs in the salons of the Faubourg Saint-Germain. Conversely, Sartre's *Nausea,* which begins with a traumatic exposure of its protagonist to the formless abyss of the absurd, ends on a resolution to transcend meaningless existence by, of all things, writing a novel.

There are, to be sure, certain escapist or elitist tendencies in this recurrent preoccupation of modern writers with art as the subject of art. To cite a relatively recent example, the French New Novel of the fifties and early sixties, for all the insistence of its manifestoes that it sought to confront a world stripped of predetermined value, represented a retreat of the imagination from history after four decades of historical trauma, and thus reduced the novel to a laboratory of narrative technique. Elsewhere, however, literary art has often been driven to reflect on itself out of the deepest inner necessity, recapitulating its own past through complex strategies of allusion, imitation, and parody; brooding over its own nature and ends; exploring its connections with all that is not art —in order to make literature still possible in a world that threatens to overwhelm it, and through the assertion of literature's prerogatives to keep alive as well the idea of a more humanly livable world.

The two major works of Hermann Broch offer an instructive paradigm of this dialectical relationship between the literary consciousness of history and the literary consciousness of art. His trilogy, *The Sleepwalkers*, written in Austria on the eve of Hitler's ascent to power, moves step by careful step, from 1888 to 1918, toward what Broch himself calls the "disintegration of values" of European civilization. The darkening historical landscape is appropriately reflected in the shifts of narrative texture from one part of the novel to the next. The poignant muted lyricism of the 1888 section gives way in the middle volume, set in 1903, to a harsher satirical mode of representation in which a discursively meditative narrator views the sexual and commercial shenanigans of the characters as despairing acts of creatures hungering for an unattainable salvation. The last volume, set in the closing months of World War I, is deliberately disjointed, moving back and forth nervously among different, barely related stories, interweaving verse-narrative with the prose, interpolating chapters of a historical-philosophical essay on the decay of European values in the modern age. It is Broch's contention here that with the breakdown of an overarching system of values, competing "partial systems," representing different techniques, interests, spheres of life, tend to absolutize their own values and thus to translate destructive unreason into social and political action on an unprecedented scale. "There arises a specific commercial kind of thinking, or a specific military kind of thinking, each of which strives toward ruthless and consistent absoluteness, each of which constructs a deductive *schema* of plausibility to suit itself, each of which has its 'theology' or its 'private theology.'" Forty years after the writing of these words, they seem at least one likely way of explaining the various kinds of mentality that could invent a Final Solution, a global strategy of overkill, and "plausible" scenarios for the pacification of Southeast Asia. Yet the very sharpness of Broch's analysis has the effect of cutting the ground from under him as a novelist. Like most ambitious writers, Broch clearly wants to make literature work as an art of the whole—pulling all characters and events into an orchestrated system of values, seeing individual lives and life at large in a unified field of vision. But how can an art of the whole function among the broken pieces of an age of partial systems? Not at all, one is led to infer from the end of *The Sleepwalkers*, where the novel, caught in the toils of imitative form, seems to confess the inability of the literary imagination to produce coherence in an incoherent world.

I have underscored the predicament of the novel-form implicit in *The Sleepwalkers* because it helps make clear why Broch's later work, *The Death of Virgil*, is both a logical development in his own career and, for all its seeming peculiarity, part of an important current in twentieth-century literature. Viewed superficially, the writing of such a book looks like an act of mere withdrawal: a major European novelist, in exile in America, at the very moment when his native continent is in flames, turns his back on two thousand years of history to re-create in an elaborate poetic novel the death of a Roman poet. Obviously, there are many ways of talking about so anomalous a book: as the longest lyric poem in the German language, as the closest approximation in fiction to the formal effects of music, or—in connection with the predicament of the novel raised by *The Sleepwalkers*—as a threatened literary art undertaking a sweeping review of its own resources and limits, of its own ontological grounds. The choice of the historical setting, then, is doubly apt, because it allows the writer to focus on an archetype of the European poet with an intense introspective purity, and because the whole novel thus implies the relationship between the act of writing and the cultural past that is so central to the problematics of literature in an age of disintegrating values.

Broch is careful not to project too crudely the troubles of his own time onto Virgil's, but, like Yeats, he thinks of history as a series of two-thousand-year cycles, and so can see a structural correspondence between Virgil's age and ours as periods of critical transition. Accordingly, he suggests that already for Virgil poetic invention had become a self-conscious, self-skeptical act; that the Latin poet was already isolated from the people, the people itself become a potentially anarchic mob; that great political forces were changing the face of the known world and making imperious demands on the writer to be their voice. "Oh, Augustus," Virgil calls out at one point in his long colloquy with the emperor, "the ground is shaking . . . nothing shook for Homer or his heroes."

What is perhaps most impressive about Broch's oceanic meditation on poetry is the way it avoids easy resolutions, swinging back and forth in great dialectic movements between doubt and affirmation. The dying Virgil knows how the calling of poetry has kept him apart from other men, always self-bent on the fashioning of his own edifice of fame, but as an artist he will not relinquish the idea of "an affiliation with the human community, which was the aim of real art in its aspiration toward humanity," and his own luminous poetic consciousness in this novel of the living and the dead finally demonstrates how art can reach outward from the prison of the self to embrace mankind. Virgil is haunted by a still more troubling fear that his whole life has been only a game with words, that all words can do is to embellish, imperfectly duplicate, and thus falsify reality. "Nothing unreal is allowed to survive," he announces to his dismayed friends in order to explain his decision to burn the *Aeneid*. The major part of the novel is caught up in the backward and forward surge of debate over this harsh resolution. In the end, Virgil leaves the manuscript of the *Aeneid* in Caesar's possession, whether out of uncertainty, or inclination to compromise, or sheer fatigue, or some glimmering hope that his epic may not after all be entirely unreal.

Language, the dying poet perceives, is an instrument of treacherous duplicity, forever tempting us to take the resonant word for the thing itself. Yet if all reality, as Virgil tells Augustus, "is but the growth of perception," language remains the necessary medium for the realization of perception, and cadenced language shaped into images is our chief means of making the world around us real, binding the fragments of transient experience into a ring of lasting significance: "Human life was thus image-graced and image-cursed; it could comprehend itself only through images, the images were not to be banished, they had been with us since the herd-beginning, they were anterior to and mightier than our thinking, they were timeless, containing past and future, they were a twofold dream-memory and they were more powerful than we."

Perhaps it begins to be clear why this self-consciously "literary" novel was no self-indulgence for Broch. He began working on it not long before his months of imprisonment by the Nazis and his subsequent departure from Austria in 1938, and his very choice of this subject at that time and place suggests how the nightmare of history has driven much modern literature back upon itself, led it to rehearse the process of literary creation in order to discover what use literary creation might conceivably have in a world of nightmares. The chief use of literature that emerges from *The Death of Virgil* is as the one road of escape from what Broch calls the "herd-experience"—that primordial condition in which each individual creature cowers before the menace of death in his animal aloneness, crowding against the bodies around him for the surface warmth and solace of sheer physical closeness. Language, as the unique human instrument, and poetry, as the most complex ordering of language, lift man beyond the herd by placing his consciousness in touch with others, with the collective consciousness of mankind, with the shared human experience of the past back to its evolutionary beginnings, through all these allowing man to project an image of the future out of his trapped moments of existential dread. Sounds and colors and shapes have a timeless quality, always present as materials for the artist, but language is the one artistic medium that develops perceptibly through historical time, bearing the marks of past uses upon it, and thus literature is before all the others the memory-laden art, the one that resumes its past in the very act of exploiting its full resources for the expression of the present. In "An Apology for Literature" (*Commentary*, July 1971), Paul Goodman formulated this essential operation of the literary imagination with a fine lucidity: "Man is the animal who makes himself and the one who is made by his culture. Literature repeats the meaning and revives the spirit of past makings, so they are not dead weight, by using them again in a making that is occurring now." The possession of a past, then, is a necessary condition for the imagining of the future; the vaster and more varied the past, the richer the possibilities of the future will be.

Viewed in these terms, the very end of *The Death of Virgil* is not an outrageous self-assertion of poetry but a resonant culmination of Virgil's long inner journey. The poet's fantastically restless, image-spawning mind having explored the far reaches of personal and collective memory, Broch creates for him an apotheosis which fuses the Western literary memory of two great moments of creation, the first chapter of Genesis and the first chapter of John, memory thus triumphantly passing into renewal. The Logos here is not an embodiment or intermediary of the Divinity but is in itself the generating nub of existence, the image of the fulfilled perfection of language making reality, toward which all the imperfections of earthly poetry aspire: "The word hovered over the universe, over the nothing, floating beyond the expressible as well as the inexpressible, and he, caught under and amidst the roaring, he floated on with the word . . . ; it was the word beyond speech." It is characteristic of Broch that this assumption of the poet into eternity did not end his own inner dialogue on the worth of literature. Haunted by the revelations of the Nazi horrors, he resolved in his last years to abandon literature for the direct action of politics and the chaste precision of mathematics. Nevertheless, circumstances led him to rewrite for publication two earlier works, *The Tempter* and *The Innocent*, and it seems clear that there was some inner necessity as well that impelled him again to the making of fiction.

The novels of Vladimir Nabokov offer a suggestive complement to Broch precisely because the two writers are so obviously antithetical in the way they approach history and art—Nabokov playfully elusive and ironic where Broch is argumentative or grandly assertive, Nabokov coolly dismissing (in the afterword to *Lolita*) all manifestations of the Literature of Ideas that is Broch's natural medium. On the surface, Nabokov might seem to be a preeminent example of the escapist tendency in twentieth-century literature, and, indeed, one study of his English novels has adopted the unfortunate title, *Escape into Aesthetics*. Art and the artist are, in varying ways, the subject of all his novels, and his self-conscious fictions reflect infinitely greater interest in the history of the novel than in history as such, from the ingenious parody of *Madame Bovary* in *King, Queen, Knave* down to the great composite parody of the genre's development in *Ada*. Nevertheless, I would contend that the awareness of history significantly shapes Nabokov's perception of art in most of his work since the early 1930s, and that his art-centered literary enterprise must finally be seen as a rescue operation on behalf of human consciousness in a world variously contrived to obliterate such consciousness. Stalking after the figure of the artist in many of Nabokov's fictions is some embodiment of Yakob Gradus, the imaginary and all-too-real assassin of *Pale Fire*, who is the perfect modern political man—the mindless instrument of his ideological masters, humanity reduced to an ambulating fleshly extension of the finger on the trigger, a creature of pure anti-imagination.

In this regard, Nabokov's two novels set in totalitarian states, *Invitation to a Beheading*, written in Berlin in 1935, and *Bend Sinister*, written immediately after World War II in this country, constitute an instructive test-case of his relationship to history, and of the general effort of the modern literary imagination to affirm its own abiding validity. Both books are formally constituted as novels about the construction of novels; in both, the protagonist is a kind of writer whose vivid inner life is about to be extinguished by a totalitarian regime that properly regards him as the ultimate subversive. Totalitarianism is seen in both novels as an insidious, not-quite-credible farce, rendered in a weird slapstick mode that surprisingly touches to the quick of the totalitarian principle by showing its crude mechanical reduction of the variety of human life, the wooden rigidity and crassness of its attempt everywhere to manipulate what cannot be manipulated. In such a world, the figure of the artist emerges as the most steadfast representative of mankind, and the act of imagination, far from being an aesthetic luxury, is the means by which humanity makes itself human and keeps itself human.

One of the most damaging effects of the imperious insistence of political life in recent decades has been an expectation that writers should respond directly to the political sphere, in its own terms; and in this respect it is noteworthy that neither Cincinnatus in *Invitation to a Beheading* nor Krug in *Bend Sinister* has any interest in writing about the totalitarian state which seeks to destroy him. Instead, both Cincinnatus the diarist and Krug the philosopher ponder the mystery of their own irreducible selfhood, the outrageous fact of mortality, the myriad ways in which circumscribed, inexhaustible consciousness constructs reality. Thus, the book Cincinnatus dreams of writing, which he adumbrates in his prison-cell diary, is not a denunciation of his stupid captors but a way to express the aching wonder of being a man, as men have done with artfully-ordered words since the shadowy beginnings of literary culture: "I issue from such burning blackness, I spin like a top, with such propelling force, such tongues of flame, that to this day I occasionally feel . . . that primordial palpitation of mine, that first branding contact, the mainspring of my 'I.' " And just a moment earlier, Cincinnatus sums up his aspiration: "I have lived an agonizing life, and I would like to describe that agony to you."

Literary allusion, as I have already intimated, has a peculiar centrality in much of the serious literature of our century. The frequency and complexity of allusion in writers like Nabokov, Joyce, Mann, Yeats, Eliot, Stevens, Borges, even Faulkner, are probably unprecedented, at least since the time of Dryden and Pope. In contrast, moreover, to the neoclassical writers, who could assume the literary past as a common point of departure, however ironically it might then be used, these moderns give the appearance of laboriously working through a vanishing or esoteric past, reconstituting it by an act of determined will, musing over the enigma of its pastness, variously using it to flesh out an otherwise hallucinatory present. Allusions can, of course, serve to reinforce a cultural elitism, but in Nabokov they generally act both to heighten a sense of play and to sharpen the focus of critical self-consciousness in the work of art. Literature, he constantly reminds us, is condemned to work with the models, conventions, and techniques of its own past; his parodistic invocation of past models turns them into objects of critical scrutiny even as they operate to evoke an imaginable world out of mere paper and print. In the second of Nabokov's two "political" novels, where the allusions are far more abundant and specific, they serve an implicitly thematic purpose. At first thought, it may seem gratuitously playful to mark a somber totalitarian landscape with references to and quotations from Mallarmé, Melville, Joyce, Flaubert, Maupassant, and a motley variety of other writers, but it is through such allusions that authorial intelligence—"the anthropomorphic deity" is Nabokov's phrase for it—asserts its power to move freely in a realm outside the totalitarian prison world, to exhibit a lively and witty awareness of imaginative possibilities transcending the field-gray uniforms, underground torture chambers, and other hackneyed formulas of the police state.

From this thematic viewpoint, it makes special sense that the central allusion in this novel is to one of the richest and most ultimately mystifying achievements of Western literature, *Hamlet,* with the figure of Shakespeare as poet of the ages looming like some monumental wraith through the half-lights of Adam Krug's bedeviled world. Perhaps with a gesture of obeisance to the library scene in *Ulysses,* Nabokov devotes an entire chapter, at the midpoint of the novel, to a discussion of the meanings of *Hamlet* and the elusive identity of Shakespeare, who emerges as the perfect paradigm of the Nabokovian artist-figure ("His name is protean. He begets doubles at every corner. . . . Who is he? William X, cunningly composed of two left arms and a mask"). In order to bring the police state in proper relation to Shakespeare, Nabokov treats us to several pages of a Marxist-National-Socialist-populist-mechanist reading of *Hamlet.* (The real hero is Fortinbras, Denmark is a decadent democracy "criminally misruled by degenerate King Hamlet and Judeo-Latin Claudius," the greatness of the plot is in the historically significant working out of mass justice, and so forth.) Against this, Krug's friend Ember, who is translating *Hamlet,* conjures up a possible film scenario of the opening scene that shows a ripe baroque inventiveness, finally pushing its own excesses into an open spoof of film convention, yet demonstrating how a responsive imagination has been moved into sudden life by a great imagination of the past. Ember then proceeds to recite to Krug a sample of his own translation of *Hamlet* into their native Germano-Slavic tongue while the philosopher contemplates the twin mysteries of creation and translation:

Nature had once produced an Englishman whose domed head had been a hive of words; a man who had only to breathe on any particle of his stupendous vocabulary to have that particle live and expand and throw out tremulous tentacles until it became a complex image with a pulsing brain and correlated limbs. Three centuries later, another man, in another country, was trying to render these rhythms and metaphors in a different tongue. This process entailed a prodigious amount of labor, for the necessity of which no real reason could be given.

Shakespeare, as archetypal poet, is an inexplicable but ultimate fact of our shared existence in culture. A creature in nature, with a shell of skull-bone encasing gray matter like any other man, he could achieve such prodigies with words, themselves mere constructs of convention, that to explain what he did one is forced to invoke theological metaphors of creation and breathing life into inert things. Other life lives simply because it is born, one with the "herd-beginnings," living from moment to encapsulated moment in an unreflective present. Human life, because it possesses consciousness and memory, because consciousness generates language as its necessary instrument, must continually make more life through these uniquely human means if it is not to begin going dead. Nabokov sees that the most murderous aspect of totalitarianism is not the killing of people but the systematic extinguishing of consciousness—through social institutions, language-rules, pseudo-art, and simple terror—which could some day leave no survivors. Shakespeare's potent presence, then, in the minds of two citizens of this police state, becomes an aperture looking out "to another world of tenderness, brightness and beauty," as Nabokov wrote of a rather different device of authorial intervention in his 1963 introduction to *Bend Sinister*.

One should note that the most appropriate response to a presence like Shakespeare's is the desire to translate him, however futile and "unnecessary" the effort. Translation is one of the great recurring concerns of Nabokov's fiction, literal translation and translation in a series of related metaphoric applications. Each individual experience of a literary work is in effect a form of translation, the actual conversion of a text into the words of another language being only the most gross, and often painful, illustration of a process that goes on constantly at other levels. Thus, the commentary in *Pale Fire*, which itself devotes some attention to Zemblan translations of Shakespeare, is an extreme instance of a fantastic "translation" of John Shade's poem, flamboyantly demonstrating how a writer's work must always exist through the active mediation of someone else's imagination. Original literary composition is also a kind of translation—if one likes, a translation of immediate experience into words; in any case, a translation of earlier literature into the author's own idiom and mode of perception through his need as a writer to absorb and remake the literary past. To cite one central example that remains for Nabokov a crowning achievement of modern fiction, Joyce's *Ulysses* is not an imitation, not, according to the usual limiting acceptation of the word, a parody, but, in the sense I have described, a bold translation of Homer and the Bible, Swift and Fielding, Dickens, Flaubert, and many others. Ember's dedication to translating *Hamlet* under a regime that thinks of a machine as the ideal writing instrument means a stubborn commitment to sustaining the precious life of consciousness by remaking a past embodiment of it for the present time and place. Behind Ember stands Nabokov the artificer, affirming the high prerogatives of art by transmuting totalitarian terrors into the stuff of an ironically intelligent novel of flaunted artifice, where a poised perfection of style is the token of a state of grace, proving the power of plastic imagination to transcend the pervasive deathliness of the totalitarian world. Literature, then, turns out to be not an escape from history but the last line of man's defense against a history gone wild.

As in many other matters of cultural history, the Jews constitute an especially peculiar, troublesome, and finally in-

structive case for the understanding of this general phenomenon. There are good and manifest reasons for writers with a
deep Jewish consciousness to be suspicious of the saving
power of art. The Jews have had no tradition of aesthetics as
an autonomous realm, no historically-rooted notions of the
poet as hero and guide. Some Jewish writers seem vaguely
uncomfortable with the very idea of artistic originality, even
as they aspire to it, as though it were something they had
filched from European Romanticism without ever being quite
sure of the genuineness of the article. Recalling a heritage
that stressed sharpness of exegesis and legal argument,
moral wisdom grounded in belief, Jews have generally found
chill comfort in art as they saw themselves flung into the maw
of modern history, too often its principal victims. In their
vulnerable position of exposure and deracination, Jews have
frequently proved to be the modernists par excellence, but, at
least in some notable instances, they retain a lingering suspicion that the whole dramatic agony of modernity is not worth
the candle, that there is something perhaps bogus and certainly futile in the effort to be authentically modern through
a heroism of the imagination. It may be that Kafka's ultimate
Jewish gesture is his deathbed instruction to Max Brod to
burn his writings. "Nothing unreal is allowed to survive," and
for Kafka the construction of mere stories without a *Wahr-
heitsgrund*, a substratum of truth theologically confirmed,
must have finally seemed a deceptive play with alluring un-
realities. (It is not surprising that Broch, a Jew converted to
Catholicism, should comment on Kafka's last resolution with
finely perceptive empathy.) No one has grasped this aspect of
Kafka more firmly than Walter Benjamin, and Benjamin's
own attitude toward modern literature in general exhibits a
strange doubleness, richly responsive to its innovative daring
and apprehensive of its possible factitiousness. Seeing the
atrophy of experience as a basic process of modern history,
he is not really willing to accept the adequacy of a merely
literary response to this radical devolution. The controlled
note of skeptical pessimism in his description of Proust's
effort to recreate verbally the life of the imagination is characteristic: "*A la Recherche du temps perdu* may be regarded
as an attempt to produce experience synthetically, as Bergson

imagines it, under today's conditions, for there is less and less hope that it will come into being naturally."

The pressing dilemmas of history and art felt by the modern writer are likely to be sharpened if he is a Jew, and become even more acute if he writes in Hebrew. The unique history of the Hebrew language and its modern literary revival make Hebrew at once an anomaly among modern literatures and a paradigm—illuminating through its very extremeness—of literature trying to cope with the maelstrom of modernity. If, as I have suggested, language is the memory-laden medium, the Hebrew language is so thoroughly suffused with three millennia of historical and theological memories that some writers have felt they had to struggle actively against it in order to make it speak personally for them. One must imagine the peculiar interplay of dissonance and resonance when a language echoing Genesis, Jeremiah, the Psalms, the Talmud, the Midrash, and the liturgy, in its idioms, vocabulary, syntax, tonalities, is called on to respond to a pogrom, a revolution, a world war, genocide. Of course I don't mean to imply that there is anything particularly miraculous about the mere writing of a modern poem or story in Hebrew, but rather that it often creates imaginative difficulties for the writer, at the same time giving him an intermittent perspective of historical distance from the contemporary world he is rendering. In the case of the greatest modern Hebrew poet, H. N. Bialik, the perception of an unbridgeable gap between his grand biblical language and a modern spiritual decadence eventually led him to abandon poetry: nothing unreal could be allowed to survive, and the inner emptiness of the age finally made his language seem to him infected with unreality.

Stephen Spender has recently proposed that the Jewish poet, in contrast to poets deriving from the Christian and Greco-Roman traditions, sees himself above all as the voice of his people, and so writes with "purposes . . . didactic and mystical, not aesthetic." This seems to me decidedly an outside view of the matter. It is true that on occasion some modern Jewish poets have assumed the mask of the poet-prophet, but the very act of choosing to work through the European world of literary forms has generally meant a deep identification with European conceptions of art as individual expression and aesthetic value as an end in itself. Even Bialik, who speaks as an alienated, despairing prophet in *The City of Slaughter*, is more thoroughly characteristic of his own major phase when in *The Pond* and *Splendor* he conceives the poetic imagination as the creative center of existence. Especially in the case of poets writing in Hebrew, one can sometimes detect a dialectic tension between the prophetic and the aesthetic impulse, but for this very reason Hebrew, so long employed chiefly to record the course of God and His people through history, provides striking evidence of the self-affirming impetus of art in modern literature. Probably the most notable instance in Hebrew of such self-affirmation is the poetry of Bialik's great contemporary, Saul Tcherni-chovsky. This poet of the Crimea-Ukraine border region, an eyewitness to the mayhem of world war, revolution, and civil strife, often responded in his work with cries of outrage and anger, occasionally even with the fulminations of a militant Jewish nationalism. It is noteworthy, however, that Tcherni-chovsky's supreme assertions of the power of poetry occur in the midst of two historical cataclysms—his two sonnet-cycles, *To the Sun* and *On the Blood*, conceived in Odessa during the Russian civil war, and *The Golden People*, his long narrative poem on bees (and through the bees, on nature and art, po-etry, history, and the future of man), written in Tel Aviv during World War II, near the end of his life.

Of the two sonnet-cycles, *On the Blood* is the more cen-trally concerned with art and politics, unabashedly affirming art as the sole redemptive force in a history where the loftiest ideals, once politicized, are translated into the most cynical and ruthless ideologies. *On the Blood* is flawed in comparison with its companion cycle, at times unnecessarily crabbed in expression, occasionally lapsing into oratorical rhetoric, but the effect of the ensemble is stunning. The cycle, or "corona," is an intricate interlocking of fifteen Petrarchan sonnets, the last line of each poem constituting the first line of the poem after it, and the fourteenth sonnet ending with the first line of the cycle, followed by a final sonnet made up of all the preceding first lines, in sequence. Tchernichovsky's adoption of this extraordinarily difficult Renaissance form to face the historical chaos around him is suggestive: in a world of universal havoc, the poet insists on an elaborate traditional form that requires fine control and conciseness, a ramified syntax of words and images and ideas, thus confirming the power of poetry to make order even out of the dark night of the Western soul. The historical landscape here is what one might expect. As the end of the fourteenth sonnet renders it, man is drowning in rivers of blood, "A twilight of culture . . . confusion of realms. . . ./ Is darkness descending or dawn breaking?/ Stunned, we peer into the thick of the twilight,/ Tired of mankind and the legacy of the past." Every political ruler, every priest of a world-redemptive faith, finally becomes an inquisitor, announcing a doctrine of truth and love but creating a world where "falsehood reigns" and "Love goes sour like yeast in dough,/ Stinking over the heretics' pyres."

Against this grim historical reality, the poet can at least aver that his "mastery"—and Tchernichovsky uses a Hebrew root usually associated with tyrannical rule—of the realm of beauty is a form of power that does not involve the shedding of blood. But what good can it do? Tchernichovsky's answer, in the thirteenth sonnet, has been attacked by commentators as an instance of towering naiveté: "Masters of song and her lovely mysteries,/ Only you unite pasts and futures./ In the hymn of Akhneton, sung among pyramids,/ And the psalms of the son of Jesse poured forth in supplication." It is the quiet beauty of song, in the next quatrain, that strengthens the heart of slave and worker, stirring them to hope; and at the end of the sonnet: "If God has decreed a redemption to come,/ The world will be redeemed through poetry and song." Tchernichovsky, in the view of Baruch Kurzweil, one of his major critics, foolishly posits here an autonomous realm of poetry while unwittingly contradicting himself by choosing as examples two poet-kings very much implicated in the brutal processes of history, one of them the ruler of an empire built on the exploitation of slaves, the other responsible for both individual murder and the deaths of thousands in battle.

The contradiction between politics and poetry in Akhneton and David is in fact so glaring that it is hard to believe Tchernichovsky's reference to them could have been inadvertent.

Contents

Preface

These essays present an argument which is the complementary opposite of the one proposed in *After the Tradition,* my previous book on modern Jewish writing. That earlier collection of essays, as its punning title was meant to suggest, was an attempt to explore the ambiguous relationship—often more supposed than real—between Jewish writers and the variegated background of Jewish historical experience. In the present volume, by contrast, I am much more centrally concerned with Jewish writers as a symptomatic, if extreme, instance of the predicaments of twentieth-century literature, and so I repeatedly direct attention not so much to the writers' sense of their cultural past as to their feeling for their imaginative medium and how it bears on the urgencies of the historical moment. From one point of view, then, this is a book about the troubled encounter between the literary imagination and modern history as seen through the strong focusing prism of a dozen or more Jewish literary figures.

The destructive course of public events since 1914 has sometimes inspired doubts in both writers and readers about the validity of an activity so seemingly fragile and futile as literary creation. A good many modern writers, from Mann and Lawrence to Pynchon and García Márquez, have responded to these inner questionings by using literature as a means of conjuring up a vision of history as impending doom. There is also, however, an antiapocalyptic tendency in modern writing which has not, I think, been given all the attention it deserves. Some of the most original writers of our century, though keenly aware of the looming apocalyptic shadow cast by their historical situation, have chosen to affirm through their work the prerogatives of the imagination, using it inventively and courageously to demonstrate the very possibilities of human wholeness that the realm of politics has often seemed determined to destroy.

This antiapocalyptic stance is of course by no means distinctively Jewish, though, as I shall argue in one of the essays, there may be some inherited Jewish mental predispositions that make one version of it easier to adopt. What seems to me instructive in regard to the power of the affirmation of the imagination against terror in modern literature is that it should occur at all among Jews. To begin with, Jews before modern times had no real tradition of an autonomous aesthetic realm—though perhaps that may be precisely why some modern Jewish writers have clung to aesthetic values so fervidly. More crucially, no people has been more nakedly exposed to the terrible shocks of modern history than have the Jews. This has not meant, as far as I can see, that Jewish writers have heard a different message from history than writers from other backgrounds, only that in many signal instances they have heard it at a higher decibel level, and sometimes perhaps sooner. The Jew, his fate virtually defined by his wandering from one crossroads of historical disaster to the next, has often been an acutely sensitive index of Western culture's disturbances and confusions, and it is the literary application of that general cultural fact which is the real subject of this book.

In order to define, then, the general context in which I seek to place modern Jewish writing here, I begin with an introductory essay that deals with Nabokov, writing out of the Russian émigré experience; with Hermann Broch, an Austrian-born Jew converted to Catholicism; and finally with Saul Tchernichovsky, a Russian-born Hebrew poet driven by the Revolution to Germany, then to Palestine. The works I consider by these three preeminently refugee writers, deriving from three radically different cultural spheres, represent three strikingly different lines of defense of the imagination, each conceived during the dark years of Nazi ascendancy. The affinities among such manifest differences will, I hope, suggest something of the broad presence of the whole antiapocalyptic mode.

The remainder of the book is devoted to a variety of novelists and poets, one major critic, and one major historian, who have variously written in English, Hebrew, Yiddish, German, and Russian. This is meant to be a suggestive selection rather than a comprehensive picture. My own interests in Hebrew literature have led to a very substantial representation here of Hebrew writers, though I would hope that the unfamiliarity of some of these authors to American readers will be compensated for by the freshness of perspective they can offer, paradoxically grappling in a tradition-steeped language with the unprecedented forces of modern history.

I have chosen to write about most of these figures because their careers have moved me, because they have found ways to be witnesses for the humanistic values of literature in the most ghastly historical circumstances. The best of these writers and books seem to me exemplary lives and works, and that is finally the quality which, however analytic the approach, I have tried to convey in these essays.

Berkeley
January 1977

1 The Modern Context

The choice of these two ancient rulers as exemplary bearers of the redemptive word of poetry is surely meant to point up a paradox. Poetry is not an autonomous realm but it has a power to work through history, transcending the political actions and intentions even of its own creators. The fact that David was a warrior king, that he murdered Uriah the Hittite, that, implacable even on his deathbed, he commanded Solomon to pay off old scores with his enemies, may affect the generations of man far less than do his psalms. The consequences of a deed done in history are of a limited magnitude, or at least eventually are no longer clearly traceable in the endless crisscrossings of subsequent historical events. The words of the poet-king, on the other hand, live on through an unending progression of literal and figurative "translations," kindling the imagination of an Augustine, a Judah Halevi, a George Herbert, opening up the feelings of countless men and women to a sharing of anguish and longing as facts of their humanity, to a trust in the coming of light after darkness. Poetry thus becomes the medium for an ongoing "affiliation with the human community"; in Tchernichovsky's words, it "unite[s] pasts and futures," thus sustaining the vision of a possible human community. This is not, I think, a naive faith in poetry. The assertion that the world will be redeemed through poetry and song is preceded by a conditional clause —if there is to be any redemption at all. Poetry here, as in Nabokov, is defined in terms of what politics cannot be. The opposition is formulated in the sonnet-cycle through a central metaphor of cult: the priests of worldly power are the perpetrators of a mendacious, murderous idolatry; the priests of poetry may in the end perhaps not avail, but at least they keep faith with making and remaking life instead of death in the name of life.

Tchernichovsky's affirmation of poetry attains still greater resonance in *The Golden People,* less by direct assertion than by demonstration through the wonderful moments of serene imaginative amplitude that occur in the long poem. Written, like *The Death of Virgil,* in the dark Hitler years, it, too, is from one point of view a taking stock of the resources of poetry; but it also brings into play in a single poetic edifice all the identities that were Tchernichovsky—naturalist, classicist, pantheist, nationalist, wondering child on the Russian steppes, bemused old man in Zion, a Jew speaking to Jews and reaching out for the wisdom and understanding of all men. The structure of the poem, then, itself illustrates the unique unifying power of poetry. The beehive to which the narrator constantly returns, surrounding it with a cloud of personal and literary recollections, is variously an image of the kibbutz, of the dreaded new collective order of mankind, of a perfectly adjusted harmony between individual and group, creature and nature. Correspondingly, the song of the hive— the same Hebrew word means "song" and "poetry"—is a "dirge of slaves . . . bemoaning strangled feelings," or a beautifully attuned answering voice to nature's timeless song. On the one hand, the poet worries analytically at the meaning of the hive and its song in expository hexameters; on the other hand, he evokes the song itself in stanzaic forms (like that of "The Ballad of the Hive") which attain an exquisite lyric purity scarcely equaled in modern Hebrew poetry. War, revolution, and the prospect of the end of mankind flicker darkly in the background of the poem's sun-drenched perspectives, but in the foreground poetry delights in the beauty that it produces, demonstrating the mind's firm hold on a unity that is not mechanical and repressive, keeping the incipient apocalypse of the present in touch with past visions of order and peace after violence.

Exemplary in this regard are the three short poems grouped together by Tchernichovsky under the rubric of "Honey Songs." The subject of the first is biblical, the second Greek, and the third Roman, so that a community of civilization among the three source-cultures of the Western world is implied in the very sequence of the poems. The second and third poems are in fact adaptations of poetic epigrams preserved in *The Greek Anthology*, while the initial poem is an original invention. The first poem ponders the riddle of Samson and the lion, eliciting from the paradox of sweetness out of strength some suggestion of poetry's alchemic working on the violent stuff of experience. (One might recall that Yeats in "Vacillation" settles on just this enigma of the lion and the honeycomb as the emblem of poetry transfiguring history and death.)

The road to Timna lies bare from Zorah on down to the
  valley.
On both sides are vineyards. By the dip, gleaming white,
A leonine skeleton, bone-sinews still clinging to it:
Beautiful bone by a marvelous bone of sheer power.
A swarm of bees buzzing casts sacred song in its
Labor over each flower, each bush and each tree.
In the carcass, at its midmost, honeycomb wealth to be taken
By the man who smote the lion: for from the strong will
  come forth sweet.
A young lion he met, a young lion did he smite:
Young lion, young beast, young lion and human young . . .
Man, why fear desert-lion's wrath—you will rend him!
Wild beast has never stood ground before man.[1]

I fear that my crude approximation of the original can give
only the dimmest notion of the quiet poise of the Hebrew,
which combines classical hexameters with Biblical diction and
a hint of Biblical cadences. The serene control with which lion,
beesong, and young Samson's triumph are evoked betokens
a faith in man and his imagination, uncannily makes the fantastic assertion of the last line a plausible conclusion to the
poem. The middle piece of the group of three poems, recasting
lines by Apollonidas, is, after the implicit violence of the Samson verses, a hushed entreaty to let no harm befall the bees
as they fill their chambered home with golden nectar. Finally,
the third poem balances the first by conjuring up a matching
image, after Philippus, of song and sweetness issuing from
the relics of violence. Realizing for the Hebrew reader of 1941
a still moment of peace after war drawn from the ancient
Roman world, the poem nicely illustrates the necessity of
poetry and the literary heritage for the modern imagination.
Any statement about killing yielding to beauty extracted
from the poem and asserted discursively would have to seem
only wishful thinking. Embodied concretely in the poem,
which is itself meticulously placed in a larger poetic context,
such an implication has the conviction of experienced truth.
The poem, conceived at the nadir of historical horror as a
"translation" of ancient poetry, creates a moment of grace in
words, becoming thus a guarantor of spiritual sanity by intimating through a wholeness in language that there is a

possible wholeness outside of language which man may yet attain:

> Prow sheathed in iron, war-galley's weapon, remains of
> The battle of Actium—rests on the shore of a quiet sea.
> Become now a beehive and honey-filled hollows of wax.
> All around it the buzzing swarm bustles.—This,
> The sacred boon bestowed by Caesar: he decreed,
> And the enemy's armament sends forth the blessing of
>   peace.

—1971

2 Portraits

*"I am easy in my mind now," Akhmatova
said to me in the sixties. "We have seen how
durable poetry is."*

—Nadezhda Mandelstam
Hope Against Hope

*The people need poetry that will be
    their own secret
to keep them awake forever,
and bathe them in the bright-haired wave
of its breathing.*

—Osip Mandelstam
Voronezh Notebooks

Osip Mandelstam:
The Poet as Witness

*In memory of Yosef Haefrati, the gifted literary scholar,
killed on the Golan Heights, April 17, 1974.*

There is something oddly legendary about the life and posthumous career of Osip Mandelstam, as though he had died not in a Soviet concentration camp in 1938, with a death certificate issued in due form by the totalitarian bureaucracy, but in some shadowy recess of medieval mystery. He is just now beginning to be recognized in the West as one of the major twentieth-century poets; many of those who can read him in the original regard him as one of the three or four greatest Russian poets since Pushkin; but he has achieved this prominence only through an uncanny resurrection after Stalin's attempt to bury his poetic legacy together with him. His poetry has survived largely through the efforts of his extraordinary wife, Nadezhda, much of it actually in an "oral tradition," held fast, line by unpublishable line, in her tenacious memory and in that of a few loyal friends. There is a much more varied oral tradition about Mandelstam's life and death,

25

a good deal of it contradictory, and one of Mme. Mandelstam's functions as a memoirist has been to sift these sundry accounts, trying to separate fact from fabrication.

Toward the end of the first of her two large volumes of memoirs, *Hope Against Hope* (translated by Max Howard, Atheneum, 1970)—it is a book that will surely remain one of the great texts on the nature of totalitarianism—she attempts to penetrate the curtain that fell between her and her husband when he was taken off for the second and last time, on the night of May 1, 1938, by agents of the NKVD. Over the years she spent exiled in the easternmost part of European Russia and in Central Asia, and later when she was permitted to reside again in Moscow after 1964, various survivors of the Great Terror came to see her with what they presented as eyewitness testimonies of her husband's last days in the transports and the camps. These she checks against one another and against what she herself knew of her husband's condition and habits with the shrewd skepticism of an experienced criminal lawyer. Among the stories to which she seems to grant full credence is one told her by a certain physicist, who chooses to remain anonymous, and who claims to have been in the Vladivostok transit camp at the same time as Mandelstam. One night in the camp, the physicist—Mme. Mandelstam designates him "L."—was invited by a non-political, that is, criminal, prisoner to climb up to a loft with him where, with a whole gang of criminals, L. might listen to some poetry. In the candlelit loft L. made out a barrel on top of which were laid out an open can of food and white bread, unimaginable delicacies in the prison world where no meal was more than a cup of watery soup. "Sitting with the criminals was a man with a gray stubble of beard, wearing a yellow leather coat. He was reciting verse which L. recognized. It was Mandelstam. The criminals offered him bread and the canned stuff, and he calmly helped himself and ate. . . . He was listened to in complete silence and sometimes asked to repeat a poem."

Whether or not the incident actually occurred as reported, the very existence of the story and its acceptance by the poet's widow should suggest that poetry retains an intensity of meaning and value in Russian culture far surpassing any role it now plays in the West. (Could one imagine a story told about Yeats, Valéry, or Wallace Stevens fascinating a rough audience of criminal compatriots, enjoying their protection?) Even should it prove quite faithful to fact, the anecdote has the quality of legend in projecting into a vividly dramatized form a sensed inner truth of the poet's character and the aspirations of his work—like the old story about Judah Halevi, the great medieval Hebrew poet, who was imagined to have been trampled to death by an Arab horseman after finally arriving at the gates of Jerusalem and reciting his "Ode to Zion." The stubble-bearded bard performing to convicts for sustenance in the candlelit loft is the same Mandelstam who from his youth cherished the idea that people would always be good to him because of his gift for poetry. He was not, however, by any means a naive man, and this seemingly childish belief was, as we shall see, rooted in a deeply meditated set of ideas on the nature of poetry and its ontological, spiritual, and political implications.

Osip Mandelstam was born in Warsaw in 1891, the son of a prosperous Jewish leather merchant. When he was still quite small, the family moved to Petersburg, a fact worth noting in its historical context, since Jews were not then permitted to reside in the city, which means that Emil Mandelstam had managed to obtain for himself the status of "privileged Jew." In 1904 Osip was sent to the prestigious Tenishev Commercial School in Petersburg—a decade later one of its students would be Vladimir Nabokov—where he received a thorough classical education (classical antiquity was to pervade his verse) and, extracurricularly, a good dose of Social-Revolutionary Marxism (this he would outgrow). After graduating from the Tenishev School in 1907, Mandelstam traveled in Western Europe, spending some time in Paris and Heidelberg, studying Old French literature, and quite consciously preparing himself for the vocation of poetry he already felt he was destined to fulfill. In 1911, for a while he undertook studies in Romance and Germanic philology at Petersburg University, and in order to escape the university's anti-Jewish *numerus clausus,* he converted to Lutheranism. The conversion, according to his widow, was strictly *pro forma,* but the uncertain evolution of Mandelstam's relation to Christianity is a question to which I shall return.

In 1912, Mandelstam became associated with an important group of younger poets who called themselves Acmeists, and who were rebelling against the Symbolist school which had provided the leading emphasis in Russian poetry for more than a decade. The Acmeists, as Clarence Brown characterizes them in his admirable critical study of Mandelstam, were remarkably close in aims and sensibility to the Anglo-American Imagists of the same period—with even a common literary genealogy by way of Théophile Gautier and the French Parnassians.[1] Against the Symbolists' mystical pursuit through poetic language of a hazy beckoning Beyond, the Acmeists cultivated qualities of clarity and hardness in their verse, sought to create out of the tactile and visual concreteness of things here and now a new chaste poetry of classical precision. Mandelstam's first volume of verse appeared in 1913 with the appropriately Acmeist title, *Stone*. Even in translation, one can see that Mandelstam, scarcely out of adolescence, was an astonishingly poised poet. Here, for example, is a poem in his early Acmeist manner, sharply visual, polished to a smooth hardness in its tactile and kinesthetic unity, and explicitly affirming the serene control of the artist. Mandelstam was eighteen when he wrote it:

On the pale blue enamel
conceivable in April
the birches raised their branches
and vespered imperceptibly.

The fragile netting froze
the pattern fine and small
like the design on porcelain
plates—precisely drawn
when the courteous artist limns it
on the firmament of glass,
conscious of his passing power,
unmindful of sad death.[2]

[1] *Mandelstam* (Cambridge University Press, 1973). English readers owe a large debt of gratitude to Brown, who has done so much to uncover Mandelstam, and has himself translated most of Mandelstam's prose with grace and clarity.

[2] The translation is one of those done by Clarence Brown for the purposes of his critical book, and of these, one can say that they are at least quite usable by a contemporary reader of English. Brown has collaborated with W.

Stone would be followed by only two other volumes of verse in Mandelstam's lifetime, *Tristia,* published in 1922, and, in 1928, *Poems,* which incorporated both the previous volumes and added to them twenty new poems, written between 1921 and 1925. Mandelstam had rapidly moved beyond the Acmeist manner to a more difficult, personal, meditative, and complicated associational style. At the same time, by 1922, after directly witnessing the horrors of the Civil War and the first improvised stages of the Bolshevik terror, he had come to see the full dire implications of the Revolution for everything he truly valued. His sense of estrangement from the new totalitarian Russia led to a five-year period of silence as a poet in the later twenties. By 1929, when it was clear that Mandelstam would not and could not march to party directives in his poetry, he became *persona non grata,* and his verse was no longer publishable, not really because it was counterrevolutionary but because it insisted on a realm of imagination utterly beyond revolutionary jurisdiction. After achieving a sense of inner release in 1929 by lashing back in

---

S. Merwin on *Selected Poems of Osip Mandelstam* (Atheneum, 1974) and many of these renderings are wonderfully elegant, moving English poems. The most striking ones are surely finer than even the best of Merwin's own fairly impressive poetic production, if that is any indication of the power of the originals. Nevertheless, my colleague Simon Karlinsky, the eminent Slavicist, has suggested to me that Merwin's poised versions of Mandelstam are like monochromatic representations of richly colored paintings, and Brown's generally accurate construal of the original sometimes falters. By all critical accounts, Mandelstam's Russian verse is a continuous pyrotechnic performance of word-play, sound-play, and layered allusiveness, typically using traditional metrical schemes and rhyming forms to generate a vibrantly expressive musicality. But what happens when anyone but a poet of towering genius tries to cast Mandelstam in English rhyme or to reproduce his word-play is painfully illustrated by Bernard Meares's attempts in *Modern Poetry in Translation 17.* The rhymes clink and tinkle absurdly, the diction is dolloped with little bits of poesy like "beauteous plight" and "divine abyss," and Stalin, in a devastating poetic assault on totalitarianism, is rendered in cute Disney fashion as "the gremlin in the Kremlin." A disaster in the opposite direction is *The Complete Poetry of Osip Emilevich Mandelstam,* done in collaboration by Burton Raffel and Alla Burago (State University of New York Press, 1973). The best one can say of this is that it gives some rough idea of the contents of all the extant poems, but it is very difficult to experience these translations as poetry. Raffel has a tin ear; his renditions are arhythmic and often unidiomatic, and in stumbling after the guidance of his native informant he very frequently succeeds in making gibberish out of whatever the original may mean. For the time being, then, our best English approximation of Mandelstam is clearly Brown and Merwin, and it is their versions that I will be citing here unless I indicate otherwise.

an essay, "Fourth Prose," at the Soviet literary hacks who had subjected him to a campaign of vilification, Mandelstam began again to write poetry freely, dictating, as always, to his wife, who hid the precious notebooks from the secret police as the couple moved back and forth across Russia. He was arrested for the first time in Moscow in 1934, after an informer had conveyed to the Cheka the text of his withering poetic lampoon of Stalin. Though his interrogation in the Lubianka, the dreaded Moscow central prison, induced a psychotic episode after his release, he got off "easily" with a sentence of exile to the Urals, and the extraordinary flow of creative activity that had begun in 1930 continued more or less unbroken until his final arrest. The death certificate given to his brother in 1940 lists the date of death as December 27, 1938, the cause: "heart failure."

A good part of the subsequent Mandelstam story has taken place on the other side of the world. In 1955, a carefully annotated edition of Mandelstam's collected works in Russian was published in New York by two distinguished émigré scholars, Gleb Struve and Boris Filippov; between 1964 and 1971 this was to be reissued in an expanded three-volume edition. Once the collected works appeared in New York, Nadezhda Mandelstam tells us, she felt she could breathe easy for the first time in seventeen years, knowing that the great trust that had been her principal reason for going on alone through such bleakness was now fulfilled: her husband's surviving poetry would be passed on to posterity. By the later sixties, as cultural policy in the USSR again became more repressive after the brief illusory interlude of the Thaw, a new underground literature, or *samizdat,* of forbidden works circulated in typescript, began to flourish, and Mandelstam was soon a cult figure in this world of clandestine Russian letters. His widow's first volume of memoirs was also intently read in *samizdat,* while its publication abroad in 1970, followed by the appearance here of a second volume, *Hope Abandoned* (translated by Max Hayward, Atheneum, 1973), makes the poet's exemplary stance against the despotism of the revolutionary regime a matter of unforgettable public record for Western readers. A qualified, ambiguous, "rehabilitation" of Mandelstam was granted after Khrushchev's anti-Stalin speech at the Twentieth Party Congress in 1956, but the publication of a volume of his selected poems, first announced in 1959, was somehow delayed until 1974.

It is a miracle of fortunate coincidence that so extraordinary a poet should have had as a wife so extraordinary a witness. *Hope Against Hope* focuses on the four years from the moment when the knock on the door in the night introduced the Mandelstams directly into the realities of the *univers concentrationnaire*. *Hope Abandoned* works backward to the early years of the couple's relationship, beginning in 1919, and forward to Nadezhda Mandelstam's exile in Central Asia and her efforts after 1956 to effect a full rehabilitation of her husband. The later volume could have benefited from some extensive pruning: part of the argument is repetitious of *Hope Against Hope* or internally repetitious; the abundant disquisitions on poetry and criticism rarely justify their length; and there is perhaps a greater element of paying off old scores against Russian literary figures than one would like. Nevertheless, *Hope Abandoned* gives us a great deal of fascinating biographical material and contextual information on the poems, and it contains many passages remarkable for their insight into how people behave in the most harrowing historical circumstances.

What makes Mme. Mandelstam so valuable a memoirist is above all the unsentimental clarity with which she views experiences that might invite pathos, self-pity, or a swollen rhetoric of outrage. It is this that enables her in *Hope Against Hope* to reveal in such convincing concreteness the tenor of life under a maniacally arbitrary regime of terror; in this one respect, Stalinism was worse than Hitlerism, for even loyal party membership and pure Christian ancestry provided no guarantee against the anonymous denunciation and its terrible consequences (the secret police had its quotas to fill, just like the factories, and the human material was finally a matter of indifference). This same steely clarity of vision is present in Mme. Mandelstam's second volume, perhaps most strikingly in her indignant response to a remark by Anna Akhmatova—an intimate friend of both the Mandelstams and herself one of the major Russian poets of the last two generations—that people abroad envied the Soviet victims their suffering. To Mme. Mandelstam's tough-minded way of thinking, such a remark could only be sheer posturing. "There was nothing to envy. There was absolutely nothing at all uplifting about our suffering. It is pointless to look for some redeeming feature; there was nothing to it except animal fear and pain." And with this she goes on for three memorable pages to describe the actual experience of animal fear under a reign of terror, how time itself clots into endless heavy moments in the consciousness of the potential victim waiting day and night for the hidden agents to come.

There is one aspect of Nadezhda Mandelstam as witness that poses special problems in getting a proper bearing on the contradictory figure of her husband, and that is the evident seriousness of her Christian belief, made particularly explicit in the second of her two volumes. Like him, she was born a Jew; during the intensity of their years together, they seem to have shared some sort of private exploration of Christian faith; but I think there are grounds for inferring that she has gone quite beyond where he was in this respect during the years of his mature achievement. Their relationship, as she makes clear in *Hope Abandoned,* had been an unusual mixture of exuberance and deep intimacy marked with certain lines of stress. Mandelstam in many ways was quite tyrannical toward his wife, insisted on refashioning her in his own image. She was generally submissive, thinking of herself as a foolish slip of a girl who needed instruction, but there were also hot sparks of rebelliousness in her which occasionally flared up, and I am led to suspect in her present Christian posture something of the loyal disciple who goes beyond the master, or diverges from him, in seeming to follow his path. This does not, let me emphasize, lead the memoirist to any explicit misrepresentation of Mandelstam's allegiances, for she is completely candid even about those of his Jewish loyalties which she cannot quite fathom, but it strikes me that the general tenor of the two volumes may be a little misleading in regard to the role of Christianity in the poet's work.

Mme. Mandelstam's sharp lucidity in discussing the events of the past half-century is so immediately impressive that one has to read through most of her thousand pages to realize that her ultimate view of reality is rather eerily other-worldly.

Toward the end, she begins to talk of a reunion in the hereafter with the soul of the departed Osip, and of the supreme joy of dying with the name of Christ on one's lips. I have no way of ascertaining whether Mandelstam himself ever expressed interest in these consoling beliefs, but in the moments of his utmost seriousness—which is to say, when he was making poetry—the vision of human existence he articulated was very different from this, even in those poems where he made use of Christian symbols. He is much closer to Wallace Stevens's sense of man living "unsponsored, free" in "an old chaos of the sun" than to any outlook of traditional Christianity. There is no affinity for martyrdom, no yearning for celestial refuges anywhere in his verse. These lines from a 1922 poem are perfectly continuous with whatever he wrote, early and late, though this particular emphasis becomes stronger and more resonant as he begins to enter more and more into the perceived shadow of his own death:

> The warm droppings of a few hens
> and a tepid muddle of sheep.
> For life, for life and care, I'll give up everything.
> A kitchen match would keep me warm.
>
> Look, all I have with me is a clay pot
> And the twittering of the stars in my thin ears.
> I can't help loving through unfledged bird skin
> the yellow of grass, warmth of the black earth.

It is quite in keeping with this sense of things that Mandelstam never thought of himself as a martyr after he had been made the object of persecution, never imagined his fate as an imitation of Christ. His widow, whatever her own commitments of belief, is too keen an observer not to recollect this firmly, and she states the matter with epigrammatic succinctness: "M. had no taste for martyrdom, but the price one had to pay to live was much too high."

Did Mandelstam's Jewish origins have anything to do with the nature of his imaginative work, with the stance toward reality that he ultimately assumed? Was he a vestigial Jew, merely an ex-Jew, or a Jew somehow productively conscious of his Jewishness? The second possibility was never open to him, and I think one can say, with only a little schematic simplification, that in the course of his maturation he moved perceptibly from the first position to the third, from a vestigial Jewish identity to one that was integrated into his imaginative life.

To begin with, as the gifted son with literary aspirations of Russified bourgeois parents, being a Jew must have seemed more a hindrance than anything else, an obstacle to entering into the fullness of Russian culture. Mandelstam's lack of compunction about going through the forms of conversion in order to be admitted into Petersburg University is not really surprising. In the autobiographical chapters he composed in 1925 under the title, *The Noise of Time*, the Jewish aspects of his parents' home constitute a moribund realm of obsolescent rituals and traditional objects in tatters and shreds.[3] On the bookshelves of his "enlightened" father, unread Hebrew volumes lay gathering dust a shelf below Goethe and Schiller, and two shelves below his mother's Pushkin and Lermontov. His father, like many comfortable Jewish burghers of the period, hired a Hebrew tutor for the boy, but the language with its "spiky script" remained alien, impenetrable, and the child vividly sensed that this, too, was an empty charade when he saw his young Hebrew nationalist tutor hide his Jewish pride upon going out into the street.

On a visit to his grandparents in Riga, Mandelstam recalls his grandfather placing a black and yellow cloth over his shoulders and making him mumble some uncomprehended Hebrew words. The memory looks suspiciously like a compound of actual recollection and projected fantasy, since there is no traditional practice of placing a *talit* over a child in this way except in synagogue on the festival of Simchat Torah; but the distortion is revealing, for it betrays a sense of being swathed, entangled, in the musty vestitures of a moribund Judaism. The slightly puzzling yellow of the cloth must be that dull brownish-yellow hue that the wool of an old prayer shawl characteristically assumes. In the private symbology of his poetry and prose, Mandelstam would repeatedly use yel-

[3]See *The Prose of Osip Mandelstam*, translated by Clarence Brown (Princeton University Press, 1965).

low and black as the emblematic colors of Judaism, often reinforcing through them a sense of Judaism as belonging to an inverted netherworld, apart from the multicolored pageantry of Russian reality. In a poem written in 1916, he thinks of himself born into that ancestral world illumined by a black sun: "At Jerusalem's gate/ a black sun has risen./ The yellow one frightens me more."

The paradoxical complement to the images of Jewishness as decay and perhaps interment is his reiterated vision of it, again in *The Noise of Time,* as a realm of formless origins: "All the elegant mirage of Petersburg [evoked in the preceding paragraphs] was merely a dream, a brilliant covering thrown over the abyss, while round about there sprawled the chaos of Judaism—not a motherland, not a house, not a hearth, but precisely a chaos, the unknown womb world whence I had issued, which I feared, about which I made vague conjectures and fled, always fled." The flight from the unknown womb world invites psychological conjecture, especially since Mandelstam oddly fancied his marriage to a Jewish woman as an ultimately incestuous union, an idea he stressed in a 1920 poem where Nadezhda figures as the biblical Leah who in turn—the refraction of sources is typical of Mandelstam—blends with Lot's daughters.

For the younger Mandelstam, in other words, to become preeminently Russian, and beyond that, European, was to define oneself by joining with what was patently other, and so to escape the threat of a primal merging with one's origins. Clarence Brown aptly observes that the implicit opposite to "Judaic chaos" was Christian order, and it is Christianity not as a corpus of belief but primarily as an aesthetic idea, the embodiment of an elaborated order, that attracts this poet devoted to the creation of architectural coherence in language. The allure of order was compounded by a sense of Christianity as a sphere of serious spirituality that stood in contrast to the jejune worldly rationalism of his parents' post-traditional Jewish home. For a while he entertained the notion of the church as the necessary foundation for society, but, his widow informs us, by the 1920s he had completely dropped this idea.

What is behind the younger Mandelstam's theorizing about

the need for Christianity is a distinctive Russian version of a familiar modern pattern: the writer of Jewish origins who is impelled at least in part to deny or denigrate his Jewishness in order to participate fully in the literary culture of his country. On the crudest level, but also the one most universally shared, the phenomenon is perceptible in the feeling of so many literary people in this predicament that there is something *unseemly* about being a Jew, something that goes against the very nature of cultivated letters; and the young Mandelstam in fact appears to be troubled by feelings of this sort. Such a sense of malaise, or inferiority, may be no different for a writer than for anyone else suffering from the anxieties of belonging to a cultural minority, but what complicates the situation of the imaginative writer is the profound way in which any national literature constitutes an enormously nuanced, self-allusive system intimately linked with a particular history and a particular set of traditions. For someone from a minority, in other words, to enter into the system and create from within it involves a difficult process of assimilation in depth, what becomes in many a hyper-acculturation.

The Christian character of so much European literature of course poses special problems for the Jewish writer embarked on the adventure of assimilation. In the West, where the Christian aspect of literary culture has tended to be somewhat diffuse or merely residual over the last two centuries, it was usually sufficient for a writer of Jewish origins to make himself into a reasonable facsimile of his counterparts in the majority culture in regard to matters of style, taste, intellectual reference, but not of creed: in America, for example, one could compose a substantial list of such self-consciously acculturated poets, critics, novelists. In Russia, as far as an outsider can judge, the case seems to have been somewhat different, at least until quite recently. The two giants of the nineteenth-century Russian novel were of course deeply serious Christians. The turn-of-the-century Russian intellectual scene was marked by a reawakened interest in Christian mysticism; and the Symbolists, who were Mandelstam's first models as poets even though he was to break with their poetic procedures, were profoundly involved in Christian religious ideas—in pointed contrast to most of the French Symbolists, from whom they were supposed to have derived.

Russia, then, becomes an instructive extreme instance of the problematics of literary assimilation, offering in our century a literature with strong bonds to Christianity and at the same time a literature where, as nowhere else, Jews achieve the highest artistic eminence. The identification of Russian things with Christian belief is, I suspect, more potent for someone who is primarily a writer of poetry than it is for a writer of prose. Pasternak, who was also born a Jew and with whom Mandelstam maintained a guarded friendship, enthusiastically embraced Christianity, and his conversion surely had some connection with his highly conscious aspiration to attain a place of honor in Russian poetry. Babel, on the other hand, the great short-story writer whom Mandelstam also knew and admired, was not tempted by Christianity as such, though in dealing in his fiction with moral character operating in the medium of history, his tendency to hyperacculturation took the form of an oscillating fascination with the alien Cossack ethos of virility and violence.

Perhaps the apogee of Mandelstam's romance with Christianity is a 1915 essay, "Pushkin and Scriabin," of which only fragments have survived. From the passages Clarence Brown incorporates in his critical study, one can readily observe the strained intermarriage between Mandelstam's personal conception of art and his tendency at that early point in his career to identify art with Christianity. Since redemption and sacrifice have already been effected by Christ, Mandelstam argues, these qualities have no place in art, which is thus left to be absolutely free, to constitute its own sphere of joyous playfulness. It is uniquely through Christianity, then, that art becomes a realm of spontaneous freedom. The rather abstract ingenuity of the argument, of course, has nothing whatever to do with the historical facts of Christianity and the nature of art under the Christian dispensation. The notion of art as play and freedom is something Mandelstam would cling to always, for which he would eventually die, but by the twenties he disavowed "Pushkin and Scriabin" as his aesthetic credo—at least partly, one can assume, because of its programmatic insistence on the Christian component of art.

It is revealing that Mandelstam's fullest, most original statement on the nature of poetry, "Talking About Dante" (1933; translated by Clarence Brown and Robert Hughes, *Delos 6*, 1971). manages to discuss the author of *The Divine Comedy* for some 16,000 words without once considering him as a Christian poet. Dante's poem is described as a vast "stereometric body," a many-hued wonder of "crystallographic" form, the supreme realized example of the infinite transformability of poetic material, but it is never spoken of as a statement of Christian faith, a poetic unity made possible through the systematic coherence of classical Christian theology. By this point in his life Mandelstam was sure of the idea of lucid order as a product of humanistic culture, and he no longer needed to associate that idea with Christianity. He had a deeply abiding sense of being heir to a Judeo-Christian tradition, but, as Mme. Mandelstam observes in *Hope Abandoned,* he linked that tradition with the Hellenic one as part of a general Mediterranean heritage of civilizing values; and I think the inference is clear that he came to see Christianity and Judaism alike as bodies of humanistic achievement, not of theological imperatives. Having shifted to that perspective, he was able to adopt a more affirmative attitude toward his own Jewishness, which could now be seen with less ambivalence not as a hindrance but as a valuable, historically authenticated point of departure for profound participation in an overarching European culture.

"As a little bit of musk fills an entire house," Mandelstam noted memorably in *The Noise of Time*, "so the least influence of Judaism overflows all of one's life." In context, the implications of the statement are more ambiguous than might appear, for what immediately follows is that description of the Judaism of his childhood as a moribund world, so the clinging pungency might, by inference, be an odor of decay. The younger Mandelstam indeed exhibits an element of uneasiness about his Jewish origins: in the pre-Revolutionary days in Petersburg, he never invited anyone to his family home, rarely mentioned his parents in conversation, and impatiently disclaimed kinship with another Mandelstam whose path he had crossed. He also, however, resisted the suggestion that he adopt a Russian last name, as many Jewish writers had done, so even at the beginning his vague embarrassment was balanced in part by some residual Jewish pride. The simile of the little bit of musk tends to have greater validity, with more positive implications, for the later Mandelstam, though one must be very careful not to pounce on the aphorism and use its authority to insist on a "Jewish key" to Mandelstam's achievement. Perhaps the essential point to stress here is not the debatable issue of the assertion's objective validity but simply that it had a certain psychological validity for Mandelstam. That is, he came to associate some of his most basic values and imaginative allegiances with his Jewishness, whatever may have been the actual channels through which he came to them. If Judaism had threatened the poet as an unknown womb world, it could also on occasion provide him an organizing myth for his own experience.

Ineluctably, Mandelstam was almost everywhere perceived as a Jew in the world of Russian poetry which his achievement rapidly dominated. At the very outset, after having been taken briefly under the protection of the older Symbolist poet, Zinaida Gippius, he was tagged "Zinaida's Jew-boy," perhaps with a degree of playfulness but certainly not without an element of wry hostility. The attacks on him that began in the later twenties were often laced with anti-Semitism, and that has been true even posthumously, with certain Russian nativists recently referring to him as a "Jewish cancer" on the body of Russian poetry. The mature Mandelstam, especially in the last decade of his life, tended more and more to respond to this repeated imputation of his being a Jewish outsider by insisting on his Jewishness as a major source of his poetic vision, as his distinctive avenue of entrance into the higher European civilization. He took an avid interest in whatever he encountered of Jewish culture, his widow comments in connection with his friendship and enthusiasm for the prominent Yiddish actor and director, Mikhoels (later murdered by Stalin). As the Stalinist barbarism deepened, he appears to have identified imaginatively with historical Jewish suffering as an inspiring model for confronting his own dire situation. Particularly revealing in this respect is the story with which he turned aside the inquiry of a GPU commandant in Voronezh in 1935 when he was challenged about his current occupation. Deprived of regular employment, he replied, he was devoting himself to the study in Spanish of the work of a certain Jewish poet who had spent years in the dungeons of the Inquisition, every day mentally composing a sonnet, released only to be imprisoned again and put in chains—whereupon he continued to compose sonnets.

Altogether, the idea of historical continuity assumed progressively greater central importance for Mandelstam, and his belonging to the preeminently history-harried, history-laden people became in this connection a dynamic element of consciousness. "His conviction," we are told in *Hope Against Hope*, "that culture, like grace, is bestowed by a process of continuity led M. to see the Mediterranean as the 'holy land.'" The Mediterranean sacred soil included for him Greece and Italy as well as Palestine, and, by an association of climate and the actual geographical contiguity of the Black Sea, site of a Hellenic culture, the Crimea and the Caucasus, where he traveled with his wife and wrote some of his most glowing poetry. Mme. Mandelstam herself puzzles over this professed affinity for Mediterranean culture, suggesting that it makes no particular sense for a Russian boy raised in Petersburg to imagine he had a biological bond with the Mediterranean world simply because of his Jewish parentage. The point, of course, is not that such an identification with Mediterranean values need be actually grounded in facts of heredity, only that it establish itself as a potent fact of consciousness for the poet. Though Mandelstam was an intensely Russian poet—some of his poems are so dense with allusions to earlier Russian poetry and history as to be impenetrable in any translation—he urgently needed an imaginative bridge out of his time and place, and his awareness of himself as a Jew gave him a sense of inner distance, a feeling of privileged at-homeness in the broad continuum of cultural values that went back three millennia and that was now threatened by the revolutionary reign of bureaucratized brutality. The yearning after the Mediterranean is a theme that has ample precedent in nineteenth-century Russian poetry, but it is given a special poignancy and urgency by Mandelstam's consciousness of his

Jewish origins. His widow's comment in *Hope Abandoned* on the presence of Jewish themes in his poetry makes perfect sense in the light of this general orientation: such poems were "not numerous—but always deeply significant."

By the end of the 1920s, the "Judaic chaos" always to be fled had given way to a sense of Jewishness as an ancient aristocratic lineage. At the beginning of "Fourth Prose" (translated by Clarence Brown, *Hudson Review*, Spring 1970), Mandelstam reflects with satirical tartness on the assimilated bourgeois Jews of Petersburg, "descended from rabbis of patrician blood," who ended up seeking the waters of salvation at Turgenevian and Lermontovian spas. Later in "Fourth Prose," he makes a special point of assuming the stance of a Jew against the ravening pack of party-prodded hacks (Soviet "writerdom") that wanted to destroy him: "I insist that writerdom, as it has developed in Europe and above all in Russia, is incompatible with the honorable title of Jew, of which I am proud. My blood, burdened with its inheritance from sheep breeders, patriarchs, and kings, rebels against the shifty gypsyishness of the writing tribe."

Two years later, in 1931, he would explore the identification with an ancient Jewish king as a key symbol of his own poetic power in "Canzone," one of the remarkable poems in his mature style of permutated allusions. "Canzone" offers a view out across the Armenian landscape as an optical emblem of poetic vision. Armenia, the land of Ararat, and, as Mandelstam called it elsewhere, a "younger sister of Judea," merges with biblical Zion, and the sharp-eyed poet, enriched with "the Psalmist's legacy to a seer," imagines himself peering through "exquisite Zeiss/ binoculars, King David's precious gift" (translation by Max Hayward in *Hope Abandoned*). These visionary lenses give a precise definition to details of the landscape, a primary intensity to color in a world where everything has ominously faded. Thus the "Mediterranean" poet, recollecting a recently visited Armenia as he writes in Moscow, dreams of fulfilling his ancient vocation by leaving the northern regions "to steep in vision destiny's finale/ and say *selah* to the Chief of the Jews/ for his crimson caress."

Mme. Mandelstam devotes several intriguing paragraphs to that peculiar crimson caress, connecting it with Rembrandt's painting, *The Prodigal Son,* that hangs in the Hermitage in Leningrad, in which the figure of the forgiving father is bathed in a reddish aura from his mantle. The Russian color-word, *malinovy,* we are informed in a note by Max Hayward, derived from *malina,* raspberry, and carries connotations of richness, mellowness, warmth. For our purposes, what is most important is the association of crimson with royalty in the figure of the poet-king of ancient Israel, and the fact that by identifying a rich intensity of color with the Jewish heritage Mandelstam was precisely reversing his earlier version of Judaism as faded yellow and stark black over against the polychromatic splendor of the Russian world. Instead of a chaos of origins, the Jewish past had become a vividly imagined myth of origins.

Let us keep ultimate distinctions clear. Osip Mandelstam did not believe either in Judaism or Christianity: he believed in poetry. For a time, he was inclined to associate poetry with Christianity because of his notions of Christian order and of the apparent spiritual seriousness of Christianity. Eventually, he emphasized instead the crucial historical consciousness made available to him as a poet by the fact of his being a Jew, and perhaps the Jewish stress was a more congenial one now precisely because it involved not belief but a sense of participation in a long cultural tradition. In a 1912 manifesto, "The Morning of Acmeism" (a full translation appears in Brown's critical study), Mandelstam talks about the way "a poet raises a phenomenon to its tenth power," producing a "monstrously condensed reality." And that reality, he goes on to say, "is the word as such."

As time went on, Mandelstam would enrich and complicate his conception of the reality generated by the word as such, but two decades later, in his remarkable essay on Dante, it is a conception to which he still remains faithful. Poetry, he announces at the beginning of the essay, is neither part of nature nor, in any ordinary sense of the term, an imitation of nature; "but it is something that, with astonishing independence, settles down in a new extra-spatial field of action, not so much narrating nature as acting it out by means of its instruments, which are called images." These images, of course, are cast in language, and so dynamically interact with one another in a poem in regard to their linguistic and phonetic properties as well as their visual ones. In this way Mandelstam arrives at the view that within the independent, extra-spatial field of its operation, poetic material is not referential but generated by the poem's restless exploration of its own patterns, image begetting image through the complicating reinforcements of multiple association and sound. Poetry is of course made out of human experience in this world, but it achieves its "monstrously condensed reality" through its freedom to follow its own uncannily non-discursive, asyntactical logic of images and sounds.

This doctrine of language and reality has little to do either with Judaism or Christianity, or, for that matter, with any "Judeo-Christian tradition," though the Jewish notion of inexhaustible revelation through words and their exegesis may be more congenial to such an aesthetic than the Christian idea of the Logos, the single incarnate Word. What the doctrine does reflect is Mandelstam's personal relation to the Old Testament and the New, to the corpus of Homer, Ovid, Dante, Villon, Pushkin, as luminous patterns of language. Once he could imagine for himself a connection with Judaism not through the remembered mustiness of his grandfather's house but through words—those of a Spanish poet or of the Psalmist, those of the biblical narrator telling the story of his namesake Joseph—he was free to conceive himself as a Jewish poet, custodian of Mediterranean crimsons and blues and golds in the bleakness of a northern landscape and a harsh time. Homer could as easily have been the imagined source of his legacy as David, and, indeed, there are rich and abundant allusions to Homer in his verse, but it was more natural for him to fashion his personal myth of the poetic vocation out of Psalmist and Levite because of his pressing consciousness of himself as a Jew.

The inner freedom of poetry to "condense" reality was in Mandelstam's view absolutely indispensable to civilized existence—the people needed it as they needed air, bread, and light, he would write in a late poem, "to keep them awake forever"—and it was just this freedom that a totalitarian regime could not tolerate in the least degree. Mandelstam's decision to write the "Stalin Epigram" in 1934 and to read it to a group of friends was a necessary one for him, even with the knowledge that it would probably mean his death. As his wife justly notes in *Hope Abandoned,* he needed an act of defiance like that, and like "Fourth Prose" before it, "to smash the glass cage in which he was imprisoned and regain his freedom" in order to preserve his own life-sustaining poetic voice. "You cannot write poetry in a glass cage,"[4] Mme. Mandelstam concludes, "—there is no air." There is compelling logic in his representation of Stalin in the fatal poem as a kind of mythic antitype to poetry, the implacable issuer of "words like measures of weight" which kill, who arrogates all language to his own homicidal purposes and surrounds himself with fawning retainers that can only grunt and squeal like beasts.

One senses in the magnificent poetry of the so-called *Voronezh Notebooks,* the poems Mandelstam wrote in his exile in the Don region, 1935–37, a paradoxical quality in the midst of terror that Walter Benjamin once associated with Kafka—a radiant serenity. It is a quality, I think, that derives in great part from the ultimate faith Mandelstam placed in the abiding validity, the indispensability, of the poetic enterprise, which he was now living out, writing out, to its utmost consequences. To be sure, he was not entirely free of chill premonitions about his own imminent fate and, equally, that of mankind. There are poems, therefore, that touch an ominous note of intimated apocalypse, like the one in which he watches lines of prisoners crossing "the plains' beaten weight" and wonders whether crawling across these expanses is "the one whose name we shriek in our sleep—/ the Judas of nations unborn." What is remarkable is that the apocalyptic vision should be given such a secondary emphasis in the *Voronezh Notebooks.* Mandelstam's poetic celebration of the here and now was never more intense, more sensuously alive, than in these poems. His private Mediterranean myth provides one imaginative source for this celebration, surfacing here and there in the explicit imagery of Cretan pottery, Greek flutes, the Italy of Dante, the yea-saying sea, and, repeatedly, the

[4]My colleague Robert Hughes has suggested to me that the Russian phrase would be more accurately rendered as "bell jar."

display of Mediterranean blue. More immediately, the actual Voronezh landscape is present in all its multiplex, poignant particularity—green trees "exploding" out of the muddy spring earth wreathed in milky fog, the ice-clogged canals of a jagged winter scene, a master colorist's version of Deep Saddle-Bow Mountain in yellows and reds, "raspberry and pure gold." It is easy enough to accept on the evidence of the poems alone Nadezhda Mandelstam's assertion that during the Voronezh period the couple were happy as puppies, draining every lived moment to the fullest.

The joyous intensity with which Mandelstam effects these condensations of reality as a *Dichter der irdischen Welt*—a phrase coined by Erich Auerbach to characterize Dante's acute poetic focus on the earthly realm—is perfectly complemented by the utter conviction and dignity of the poems in which the poet quietly, unaffectedly defies his persecutors.

> You took away all the oceans and all the room.
> You gave me my shoe-size in earth with bars around it.
> Where did it get you? Nowhere.
> You left me my lips, and they shape words,
>   even in silence.

In the supreme imaginative clarity of these last poems, Mandelstam stands beyond ethnic origin or credal affiliations as a luminous witness for poetry itself—not its martyr but its exemplary practitioner, demonstrating the vivifying freshness of the poet's transformational play with language even under the impending darkness of the final terror. History and the literary tradition kept running through his head as he crystallized the present moment in his verse, and he may well have thought of his bond with the people that through two millennia had been left only its words, its moving lips, by its oppressors, yet with that had achieved much, and had persisted. In the engulfing cataclysm of his own era, Mandelstam could reflect on the stubborn durability of the whole broad multilingual literary tradition that had come down to him somehow unbroken through all its historical vicissitudes; and so, with the confidence of a master in his perfected craft, he could hope at the end that his poetry, too, would survive the murderous new order determined to extirpate it and all it stood for.

> Mounds of human heads are wandering into the distance.
> I dwindle among them. Nobody sees me. But in books
> much loved, and in children's games I shall rise
> from the dead to say the sun is shining.

—1974

Walter Benjamin:
The Aura of the Past

"For the critic," Walter Benjamin once wrote, "the highest court of appeal is his own colleagues. Not the public. Even less posterity." The statement reflects the stance of intellectual rigor and self-skeptical inner distance that Benjamin maintained toward everything he cared about seriously—literary criticism, literary experience itself and its future in an age of technology and mass societies, Marxism (though perhaps here there were lapses in the rigor), Zionism, European culture, Jewish tradition and its theological categories of vision. The statement also suggests something of the retrospective irony that historical circumstances have cast on Benjamin's life and career, for it is only posterity that is now realizing, prominently in Germany, rather dimly elsewhere, his stature as a critic.

When Benjamin took his own life in September 1940, after having been turned back at the Spanish border in his flight from Nazi-occupied France, he was already, at the age of forty-eight, what would be generally recognized only posthumously, the major German literary critic of his time. His friend Bertolt Brecht is reported to have called his death the first real loss to German literature caused by Hitler. At the time, however, his importance was sensed only in a few limited circles of German intellectuals, some of them Marxists, most of them Jewish. Benjamin had begun publishing his criticism in periodicals less than a decade before Hitler's rise to power; after 1933, of course, he had no outlet in Germany, and the Swiss publisher that had undertaken to print a volume of his selected essays went bankrupt, leaving almost the entire edition stored in a basement where it would be discovered more than twenty years after the author's death. An additional irony, one that might have been felt keenly by Benjamin himself, was the fact that he was also for the most part neglected in France, where he lived after 1933, though he had devoted a substantial part of his intellectual effort to French literature, had made Baudelaire and Proust defining figures in his critical conception of modern experience, and Paris the focal point for his vision of nineteenth-century culture.

The emergence of Benjamin from the honorable underground of unrecognized genius began signally in 1955 with the publication in Frankfurt of a two-volume edition of his writings. Since then he has been the subject of numerous articles in German periodicals, sections of not yet collected works have appeared in periodicals, and German literary intellectuals, especially the younger ones, have come to see him as possessing the same stature in German criticism between the two wars that Brecht has in the German theater of that period. Outside Germany, his reputation has advanced much more slowly, to say the least. A selection of his essays published in France in 1959 received so little attention that the publisher abandoned the plan to bring out a second volume. Now, a generous sampling of Benjamin's literary criticism has been translated into English for the first time[1]; the essays included give ample evidence of one of the most original criti-

[1] *Illuminations*, translated by Harry Zohn, edited with an introduction by Hannah Arendt (Harcourt, Brace & World, 1968).

cal minds of recent decades, and the book ought to have the impact of a revelation in literary circles here, but so far it seems to have been greeted mainly with silence.

All this suggests that Hannah Arendt is right in attributing Benjamin's failure to receive adequate recognition during his lifetime more to the radical peculiarity of his literary enterprise, the anomalousness of what he sought to achieve, than to the historical circumstances of his career. The problem is not Benjamin's "difficulty," though he is at times alternatingly—even simultaneously—difficult and lucid because he combines the poet's sense of dramatic verbal gesture with a metaphysician's love of abstractions; the real problem, as Hannah Arendt argues, lies in Benjamin's incommensurability. Because he does not fit readily into any familiar category or recognizable tradition—a German-trained mind enamored of French modes of literary discourse, moving from theological concerns to literary texts with a professed allegiance to dialectical materialism!—one naturally gropes for rubrics that will cover him. Hannah Arendt proposes that we consider Benjamin above all as a man who *thought poetically* (her italics), that is, thought primarily through metaphor; and while this may be at least partly true, I wonder how helpful a classification it is, how it enables us to distinguish Benjamin from critics as different as Coleridge and Valéry, for whom there is also no profound disjuncture between critical and poetical thinking.

Gershom Scholem, the distinguished historian of Jewish mysticism, in an important essay on Benjamin, his intimate friend from student days on, is not moved to exercise the same ingenuity of analysis one finds in Arendt, but his more obvious generalization seems closer to the mark: Benjamin, Scholem contends, was fundamentally a metaphysician, in fact a rare instance of the "metaphysician pure and simple."[2] What I assume Scholem means is that although Benjamin's mind was continually and passionately engaged in literary texts, he never explicated them, only intermittently commented on or evaluated them, but instead used them as points of departure (and of return) for larger speculations. What

[2]"Walter Benjamin," *Yearbook of the Leo Baeck Institute*, 1965.

interested him about literary modes, about literature itself and language itself, was above all their ontology. I should hasten to add that this makes Benjamin sound more abstract than he is in fact; rhetorically, his argument is often articulated through the most vividly concrete particulars, and conceptually, he has an acute sense of the complex historical moment and its bearing on the arts, so that an ontology of literature for him is always deeply implicated in a sociology and anthropology of literature, and never separated from the imaginative feel of the particular literary experience.

The disparity between Arendt's Benjamin and Scholem's Benjamin is worth pursuing. Arendt's introductory essay inevitably draws on Scholem since, as Benjamin's confidant and closest correspondent over the years, he is an invaluable source of biographical and bibliographical information; but Arendt speaks of Scholem with a peculiar mixture of overt respect and muted suspicion. Clearly, much of her suspicion is of Scholem as representing the Jewish and Zionist pole in Benjamin's life. It is on the question of the relevance of Benjamin's Jewishness to his intellectual endeavor that the two stand farthest apart, and that issue is bound to be one of the most elusive yet crucial considerations in any attempt to place Benjamin.

This metaphysical critic of German and French letters wrote virtually nothing on explicitly Jewish matters, yet, by all testimonies, he was continually concerned with questions of Jewish tradition, Jewish identity, and Zionism as both a national and personal alternative. Scholem attests to his repeated, animated involvement with these subjects in conversation, and even reports one discussion in Paris in 1927 with Judah Magnes, the first president of the Hebrew University, in which Benjamin asserted that if he came to Palestine, he envisaged his eventual role as a commentator of traditional Jewish texts. Though Arendt undertakes a rather ample biographical sketch of Benjamin in her introduction, she scarcely mentions any of this, nor does her survey of Benjamin's intellectual sources intimate what we know from Scholem, that Benjamin read seriously in the history of the Kabbalah, that he was deeply impressed with the theology of Franz Rosenzweig (whom he quotes a number of times in his essays), and that he could even evince great enthusiasm, at least at an early age, for Ahad Ha-Am, whom he read in German translation.

These omissions are significant, for Arendt sees Benjamin's Jewishness primarily as a sociological fact, and a negative one, while in Scholem's view strands of Judaism as a philosophical vision are woven into the fabric of Benjamin's thought through its underlying concern with revelation, redemption, tradition, and the role of language in the interplay of these three categories. Scholem describes the Judaism of messianic expectation as a goal Benjamin "approached asymptomatically throughout his life, without ever attaining it." Arendt's view, on the other hand, would seem to follow closely that of the French critic, Pierre Missac, who in an intelligent general essay on Benjamin, turns Scholem's image around and suggests that Benjamin was carried away from Judaism by the inexorable winds of history though he never entirely freed himself from it.[3]

For Hannah Arendt, at any rate, what Benjamin's Jewishness chiefly gives him is an energy of disengagement. Like other German Jewish writers of the earlier twentieth century, Benjamin emerged from the asphyxiating milieu—ably described by Arendt—of the Central-European Jewish *haute bourgeoisie*, knowing himself to be neither fully a German nor, in his parents' sense, a Jew; he therefore was able to sharpen his social and moral perceptions through the very denial of the smugness, the hypocrisies, and the appalling self-deceptions that surrounded him. Zionism, then, according to Arendt, was for Benjamin primarily a means of affirming the essential rottenness and wrongness of Jewish existence in Europe, just as Marxism served to affirm for him much the same thing about the entire bourgeois order; but he could never go all the way either to Jerusalem or to Moscow because all he could honestly take from the two ideologies was a perspective of radical critique, never a solution to the insoluble.

This is a shrewdly argued view that carries with it some

[3]"L'Eclat et le secret: Walter Benjamin," *Critique*, August-September 1966.

weight of justice, but I suspect that it fails to account adequately for an impulse other than the negative one in Benjamin, and finally makes out of him more of a prophet of doom than he actually was. And one must add that Hannah Arendt is not above distorting biographical facts in the interest of her thesis. Thus, she claims that Benjamin, improvident about financial matters, was prepared, or at least thought he was, to hire himself out to "the Marxists" for a thousand French francs a month, or alternately, "to study Hebrew for three hundred marks a month if the Zionists thought it could do them some good." The most generous assumption one can make about this story is that it is a gross misrepresentation: Scholem and others had been interested in bringing Benjamin to teach at the Hebrew University, but from the language used here we are led to infer an equation between becoming an intellectual prostitute for a vicious Stalinist propaganda machine (something utterly inconceivable for Benjamin), and serving as a tool for a different ideological clique of unsavory manipulators known as "the Zionists." Such moments make one wonder how reliable a guide to Benjamin Hannah Arendt can be, at least in regard to his Jewishness and his relationship with Zionism.

Perhaps we can better focus the whole perplexed image of Benjamin by devoting some attention to the actual nature and direction of his critical writing. If Benjamin's achievement is somehow incommensurable, it is certainly not incomparable, and here I believe a comparison may offer a useful perspective on him. Of the critics who rose to prominence in America and England in the earlier twentieth century, during that great age of letters which preceded our own, I can think of only two who equal Benjamin in subtlety of analytic imagination, in intellectual independence and venturesomeness, and in the vigor of their interest in the interinvolvement of society and literature, of moral and aesthetic values; those two are Edmund Wilson and Lionel Trilling. Trilling will serve the purpose of comparison better because he happens to be a Jew, and a Jew whose cultural experience and allegiances are antithetical to Benjamin's in virtually every significant respect.

Now Trilling has throughout his career taken an honorable course toward his Jewish origins, whatever ambivalence he may have felt and sometimes expressed, by openly affirming them, hardly enthusiastically but with a certain sense of self-respect. (It is worth recalling that his earliest criticism and fiction, in the later twenties, appeared in a Jewish periodical, the *Menorah Journal.*) Nevertheless, what is remarkable about Trilling in this regard is that his career is such an achieved process of hyper-acculturation. It is a process that was never possible for Jews in Europe either socially or psychologically, that has not been generally felt to be necessary in this country since the thirties, and that could only have been achieved then by a gifted spirit. Trilling at twenty-one, writing, paradoxically, for the *Menorah Journal,* could on occasion sound offensively like a mock-Englishman—as, indeed, some of his disciples, unconsciously parodying him, sometimes still sound today—but by the time he comes to his mature work in the late thirties and forties, the "mock" component has quite disappeared: the son of East-European Jewish immigrants has accomplished what would hardly occur to an American intellectual of Protestant background to attempt, has implicated his thought and feeling so deeply and finely in the British cultural tradition that in the quality of his imagination and the nature of its assumptions, in the poise and cadences of his prose, in all the minute calibrations of his intellectual life, he is thoroughly a spiritual compatriot of Coleridge, Wordsworth, Newman, Matthew Arnold.

One could hardly imagine a more striking contrast to Benjamin, that scarcely German critic of German and French literature, inventing his own peculiar variety of masterfully aphoristic German prose, working toward a definition of modern European culture at least partly through his distance from it as a Jew, all the while wondering whether he ought not to learn Hebrew, follow his friend Scholem to Jerusalem, and there become a latter-day Rashi or Ibn Ezra. In order to show how this contrast enters into the specific nature of the criticism itself, I would like to set side by side some parallel observations by each of the writers. Here, to begin with, is an instance where both critics have arrived independently at what looks like much the same insight. The Trilling quotation is from his justly famous essay, "Manners, Morals, and the Novel":

Snobbery is pride in status without pride in function. And it is an uneasy pride of status. It always asks, "Do I belong—do I really belong? And does he belong? And if I am observed talking to him, will it make me seem to belong or not to belong?" It is the peculiar vice not of aristocratic societies which have their own appropriate vices, but of bourgeois democratic societies.

And here is Benjamin, commenting on the central importance of the analysis of snobbery in Proust's critique of society:

For the attitude of the snob is nothing but the consistent, organized, steely view of life from the chemically pure standpoint of the consumer. . . . But the pure consumer is the pure exploiter—logically and theoretically—and in Proust he is that in the full concreteness of his actual historical existence. He is concrete because he is impenetrable and elusive. Proust describes a class which is everywhere pledged to camouflage its material basis and for this very reason is attached to a feudalism which has no intrinsic economic significance but is all the more serviceable as a mask of the upper middle class.

The most obvious differences in formulation are the differences between the idiom of British empiricism and a self-critical liberalism on the one hand, and of an imaginative Marxism, on the other hand, with its characteristically Central European interest in theory. What preoccupies Trilling is a question of moral psychology, and so his exposition flows quite naturally into hypothetical speech: "How would I feel, what would I tell myself, if I were in such and such a position?" What concerns Benjamin here is a matter of social philosophy, and in keeping with that perspective he brings to bear a more emphatically analytical power of generalization. Marxism, of course, helps him establish swift, precise connections among social attitudes, class structures, and their economic bases, though one senses in the legislative generalizations a controlled note of personally perceived moral outrage that is worlds away from the self-righteousness of parlor-and-campus radicals or the mouthing of formulas by party hacks. Marxist theory is clearly useful to Benjamin, but his sensibility and the nature of his interests continually push him beyond it, and even here his language reflects a profound dissatisfaction not merely with the particular structures of bourgeois society but with the very imagination of human life upon a material base. (In general, the question of whether Marxism was finally a constructive element in Benjamin's intellectual enterprise remains to be resolved. Hannah Arendt, for example, is skeptical about Scholem's assertion that Brecht and his radicalism were a "baleful influence" in Benjamin's life, but what else is one to conclude when Brecht was capable of objecting to as brilliant a piece of criticism as Benjamin's essay on Kafka because it "gave aid and comfort to Jewish fascism"?)

In any case, the characteristic that sets apart Benjamin's formulation most decisively from Trilling's is its emphasis on paradox, and paradox typically expressed with an aggressive, gnomic compression—the pure consumer is the pure exploiter, and he is concrete because he is impenetrable and elusive. Paradox in general is a rhetorical form that originates in a tension of ideas in the mind of the speaker and is usually meant to elicit some state of tension in the audience; for Benjamin that tension carries with it some of the threatening quality with which his subject presents itself to his imagination. Trilling, one feels, can write about the phenomenon of snobbery with reasonable detachment, as though from a relatively protected position: he is finely aware of both the destructiveness and the inner emptiness implicit in what he is talking about, at the same time that he regards it coolly as one of the besetting ills of a highly imperfect though obviously livable form of social organization.

There is, by contrast, something more uncompromising in Benjamin's sharper formulation of the contradictions of the phenomenon; one might say that he writes about his subject from a condition of naked exposure to it. The more enigmatic of his paradoxes here—that concreteness flows from impenetrability and elusiveness—would seem to be very much the shrewd and pained insight of an outsider, who senses the elaborate overlay of forms, styles, mores, of a self-protecting class as a cover for its lack of inner coherence and definition. Trilling makes virtually the same observation when, at the end of the paragraph from which I have quoted, he describes the dominant emotion of snobbery as a "sense that one is not quite real but can in some way acquire reality"; Benjamin's decision, however, to cast this idea in the paradoxical form he gives it has the effect of implicating the reader, too, in the experience of bafflement and exclusion of someone trying to penetrate a resistant snobbish milieu. It is a way of seeing things, I would venture, that makes special sense for a Jew always consciously Jewish in a Central European cultural situation.

This contrast between the psychologically protected, acculturated critic and the exposed, unassimilable one has to do not merely with their identity as Jews but with the kind of literary tradition to which each relates. Here a comparison of comments on a literary genre rather than a social phenomenon may be helpful in locating the difference between the two. At the end of "Manners, Morals, and the Novel," Trilling offers this summarizing generalization about the distinctive nature of the novel:

Its greatness and its practical usefulness lay in its unremitting work of involving the reader himself in the moral life, inviting him to put his own motives under examination, suggesting that reality is not as his conventional education has led him to see it. It taught us, as no other genre ever did, the extent of human variety and the value of this variety. It was the literary form to which the emotions of understanding and forgiveness were indigenous, as if by the definition of the form itself.

And Benjamin, in a finely suggestive essay called "The Storyteller," which argues that the art of storytelling is dying out because of the demise of "the epic side of truth, wisdom," contrasts the characteristically modern narrative genre, the novel, with the traditional story:

The birthplace of the novel is the solitary individual, who is no longer able to express himself by giving examples of his most important concerns, is himself uncounseled, and cannot counsel others. To write a novel means to carry the incommensurable to extremes in the representation of human life. In the midst of life's fullness, and through the representation of this fullness, the novel gives evidence of the profound perplexity of the living.

Trilling's notion of human variety is not unrelated to Benjamin's sense of mankind's "perplexity" (*Ratlosigkeit* in the original is a shade stronger—the state of being at a loss, even helpless), but the general orientation of the two is radically different. In context, both critics, quite properly, make *Don Quixote* the ultimate point of reference in their conception of the novel, but Trilling is closer to the rationalist eighteenth-century view of *Quixote*, seeing it almost as an embryonic novel of education in which the reader becomes a discriminating observer of the interplay between appearance and reality, while Benjamin, in this respect resembling rather the Romantic interpreters of Cervantes's novel, seems to locate its center more in the striking and dangerous implications of the Don's madness. Trilling, with a secure base of orientation in the rich profusion of English culture since the Renaissance, regards the novel from his viewpoint of social critic and moral psychologist as an extraordinary instrument of self-knowledge. Benjamin the metaphysician, always with a strong sense of pre-modern culture and its theological anchorage, sees the novel more as what the late R. P. Blackmur called a "technique of trouble," a means of ruthlessly exposing the most deep-seated insoluble predicaments of modern existence. (It is worth noting, incidentally, how characteristically Benjamin's mind operates quite outside the prefabricated structures of Marxist theory. His idea here that the distinctive mimetic purpose of the novel is "to carry the incommensurable to extremes in the representation of human life" has an originality and breadth of suggestiveness that cannot be matched in Marxist theorists of the novel like Georg Lukács and Lucien Goldmann.)

Trilling's conception of the novel leads us from Cervantes to Fielding to Jane Austen, George Eliot, Henry James, E. M. Forster, while with Benjamin's uncounseled, solitary individual we move from Cervantes to Stendhal, Flaubert, Melville, Dostoevsky, Kafka. One would look in vain for the pushing of the incommensurable to extremes in the moral education of Emma Woodhouse, as one would look in vain for understanding and forgiveness in the harshly unrelenting moral exposure of Emma Bovary. The difference, of course, is in part a simple difference between Continental and British literary experience, between a literature created against a background of despotism, changing regimes, violent revolution, and one created in a parliamentary democracy under conditions of slow, often drastically inadequate, but nevertheless peaceful reform. Trilling, so much at home in the British tradition, seems in some ways emotionally cushioned against the vast shock-waves of modernity that have been running through Western culture since the seventeenth century; Benjamin, partly because of his intense self-awareness as a Jew though obviously not only for that reason, feels the earth quaking beneath his feet, beneath all of us, and makes his criticism into a seismographic reading of the quake, while never totally abandoning faith in the instruments of reason and the redemptive possibilities of human culture.

The ultimate importance of Benjamin's critical enterprise may well be that it gives us one of the most far-reaching, abidingly relevant definitions of modernity that any critic has articulated, and the emphasis placed in his definition on the decline of wisdom is noteworthy. We are all wearily familiar with notions of modern experience as a failure of faith, a breakdown of values, a loss of community, but to put all those negative processes in terms of a loss of wisdom introduces rather new implications. In this view, what man needs to sustain himself above all else is not belief or a particular kind of social organization but *learning*. Human communities depend ultimately on being the bearers of living traditions, where there is something of growing substance that master imparts to disciple, one generation to the next, and so for Benjamin one of the most crucial symptoms of modernity is the erosion of tradition. Wisdom, learning, and tradition hardly seem Marxist categories, and they are of course not uniquely Jewish ones, but they must have presented themselves with peculiar force to the imagination of a writer keenly aware of the Jewish past, who had closely read Rosenzweig, Buber's versions of the Hasidic masters, and the history of the Kabbalah.

In order to make still clearer the distinctive perspective Benjamin brings to bear on the modern condition as a self-aware European Jew, I would like to offer one last comparison —of an extended observation of his with one of Trilling's on the paradigmatic modern writer, Kafka. Admittedly, the comparison is bound to be a little unfair to Trilling because Kafka does not sit very comfortably within the compass of his sensibility, while there are profound affinities between Kafka and Benjamin—cultural, intellectual, and above all spiritual affinities. Precisely for that reason, however, one can see the startling difference between the two critics in their relationship to modern experience and its historical antecedents. Trilling, contrasting Kafka with Hawthorne in the course of an essay on Hawthorne, has this to say about the German writer:

Of Kafka's power an impressive index is the fact that his version of man's dark odyssey proceeds without touching upon cases of conscience. In such relations between man and man as are represented in Kafka's work, it is never a possibility that one man can help or injure another. . . . What an intransigence of imagination is needed to conceive man's spiritual life as having no discernible connection with morality! . . . An imagination so boldly autonomous, once it has brought itself into being, conceives of nothing that can throw it off its stride. Like the dream, it confronts subjective fact only, and there are no aesthetically unsuccessful dreams, no failed nightmares.

Before going on to Benjamin, I might observe how peculiar a statement this is, peculiar especially in its uncharacteristic lack of accuracy. It is simply contrary to the facts of Kafka's books to say that no one in them can help or injure his fellow, and as for cases of conscience, some very intelligent Kafka specialists—Bluma Goldstein, for example—would claim that he scarcely writes about anything else. Trilling, of course, imagines the case of conscience as it would occur in a novel by Henry James, without seeming to allow that there are other, more terribly imperative or darkly submerged ways in which moral alternatives can present themselves to a character conceived by his creator as a morally responsible agent. The notion of a boldly autonomous imagination is more convincing, though even here Trilling moves a little too easily into invoking the model of the dream because he stands so completely outside Kafka's own cultural and literary context. By contrast, Benjamin's characterization of Kafka's imagination in a letter to Scholem is packed with ideas that seem utterly persuasive:

Kafka's real genius was that he tried something entirely new: he sacrificed truth for the sake of clinging to its transmissibility, its aggadic element. Kafka's writings are by their nature parables. But it is their misery and their beauty that they had to become *more* than parables. They do not modestly lie at the feet of the doctrine, as the Aggadah lies at the feet of the Halakhah. Though apparently reduced to submission, they unexpectedly raised a mighty paw against it.

This is why, in regard to Kafka, we can no longer speak of wisdom. Only the products of its decay remain. There are two: one is the rumor about the true things (a sort of theological whispered intelligence dealing with matters discredited and obsolete); the other product of this diathesis is folly—which, to be sure, has utterly squandered the substance of wisdom, but preserves its attractiveness and assurance, which rumor invariably lacks.

This analysis brilliantly illustrates why talk about Kafka's fiction as dream and nightmare is finally loose talk. Dreamlike elements, to be sure, are abundant enough (but are they so rare in older kinds of fiction?); the close-worked structure of the parable, however, is the antithesis to the associative flow of the dream, even when the expected didactic content of the parable is obscure, or elusive, or ironically negated by the parable's narrative form. What Benjamin perceives is that Kafka, far from imagining spiritual life as having no connection with morality, writes out of a sense of desperation that the legitimating source of morality may have disappeared, and the "intransigence" of his imagination is precisely an expression of this desperation. He is a writer committed by his cultural tradition and the nature of his imagination to be, in Benjamin's sense, a storyteller, trapped in the era of the novel; language remains for him the medium of wisdom, learning, and tradition at a point in time when the chain of tradition has broken, with no certain wisdom left to impart. Because Benjamin is in some significant respects the same kind of Jew as Kafka, he is able to understand completely the strange beauty and terror of this response to modernity in Kafka as Trilling cannot. Kafka's parabolic fictions, in Benjamin's profound view of them, are not, most essentially, dreams or theological allegories or enigmatic psychograms or prophetic myths, but a body of Aggadah in search of a Halakhah, lore in quest of Law, yet so painfully estranged from what it seeks that the pursuit can end in a pounce of destruction, the fictional rending the doctrinal.

I am led to wonder whether Benjamin's analysis of Kafka has not touched on the most basic point of substantive contact between Kafka and Agnon, who has been compared so frequently to the German writer. (Benjamin, interestingly, was personally acquainted with Agnon, and in his correspondence he speaks in the highest terms of praise about the Agnon stories he read in German translation.) Agnon is much more of a ventriloquist of age-old tradition than Kafka, and so his own Aggadah has often seemed to speak for the eternally revealed Halakhah, but many of his boldest, most compelling fictions assume in their own way the masks and gestures of wisdom, learning, and tradition in a world where, manifestly, tradition has become a musty smell, wisdom a madman's guess or a bad joke, and learning a futile reflex. According to a Hasidic tale that Agnon himself, among others, has transmitted, the Baal Shem Tov used to go to a certain spot in the forest when he had something difficult to perform, where he would light a fire, then accomplish the task through prayer. His disciple, the Maggid of Meseritz, could no longer light the fire, but at least he knew the appointed place and the prayer to recite. A generation later, Rabbi Moshe Leib of Sassov had lost the secret of the prayer as well, but he still knew his way to the place in the forest. At the end of the line, Rabbi Israel of Rizhyn, the great-grandson of the Maggid, could neither light the fire nor say the prayer nor find his way into the forest, but at least he could tell the story. This is very much the condition of Kafka, and of Agnon, left to tell stories when what is urgently needed is the secret path, the holy fire, the divine words. Benjamin was preeminently a critic who knew what such storytelling meant, and understood in all its ramifications the condition of being bereft of fire in the trackless dark of this world.

In order to define that condition against the historical background of modern experience, Benjamin repeatedly invokes a process which he calls the decline of aura. The concept is worth commenting on because it is central to his critical orientation, indeed, to what could justifiably be called his critical vision. Benjamin has a fine comprehension of the ways in which urbanization, industrialization, and the development of new communications media profoundly affect man's modes of perception, his relationship to objects, to people, and to his own consciousness. These changing relationships are alluded to frequently in his discussion of literary figures and confronted directly in a major essay, "The Work of Art in the Age of Mechanical Reproduction." The root implications of an era of global television and space telemetry are already firmly grasped in this response to the early period of the sound movie; whatever of Marshall McLuhan is worth keeping is contained in two or three sentences here of Benjamin's, though of course with a clarity of historical perspective one would not look for in McLuhan.

What is intriguing about Benjamin's view of this whole process is the peculiar ambivalence he maintains toward it. He is obviously fascinated, perhaps even excited, by the movement of modernization, from its early impact on Baudelaire with his new aesthetic of shock, to its ultimate issue in the modern art of the cinema. At times he appears to see redemptive possibilities in the processes of modernization, as when he imagines the film as the means of making the critical experience of art for the first time available to the masses. More often, and perhaps despite himself, he describes those processes as a progressive erosion of what is most preciously human in human experience.

Thus, in his essay on Baudelaire, Benjamin conveys a sequence of negative change with succinct finality: "The replacement of the older narration by information, of information by sensation, reflects the increasing atrophy of experience." And even in the essay on art and mechanical reproduction, there is a curious ambiguity of judgment. The growing impulse "to get hold of an object at very close range by way of its likeness, its reproduction," is interpreted as an "adjustment of reality to the masses and of the masses to reality," which, for a good Marxist, should surely be an encouraging development. But Benjamin chooses to describe the process in language like this: "To pry an object from its shell, to destroy its aura, is the mark of a perception whose 'sense of the universal equality of things' has increased to such a degree that it extracts it even from a unique object by means of reproduction." Despite the calm tone of theoretical analysis, one gets a sense of a kind of rape perpetrated, uniqueness and separateness violated, a tyrannic perception of the universal equality of things imposing itself on a world once suffused with aura.[4]

Roughly, the distance between Benjamin's hopefulness and his dismay about the modern world is the distance between his Marxism and his Judaism. Some words of explanation about his concept of aura may make this connection clearer. He seems to have conceived aura alternately, and complementarily, in psychological and anthropological terms. Psychologically, to sense the aura of things is to experience them as objects of the imagination, inexhaustibly desirable and inexhaustibly delighting; it is to see things as Wordsworth evoked them in the *Immortality Ode*, "Apparelled in celestial light,/ The glory and the freshness of a dream" (the precise meaning of "glory" in Wordsworth's English is "aura"). Or, to suggest a more explicitly theological parallel, Benjamin talking about aura in the natural world sounds very much like Buber describing a displacement of the I-it by the I-thou: "Experience of the aura . . . rests on the transposition of a response common in human relationships to the relationship between the inanimate or natural object and man. The person we look at, or who feels he is being looked at, looks at us in turn." Paradoxically, when Benjamin describes the same experience elsewhere more from a viewpoint of historical anthropology, he emphasizes not rapport or intimacy but distance and unapproachability, defining aura as "the unique phenomenon of a distance, however close it may be." The paradox is a characteristic piece of brilliant shrewdness in working with the kind of idea that would tempt many thinkers into soft-minded effusion. Aura means access to the kind of intimate closeness possible only when what we relate to relates at the same time to us, but aura also means inviolability, the awareness of a perfect uniqueness utterly beyond the realm of utility or manipulation, and so the object possessing aura has built-in distance, however close we come to it.

Benjamin thus relates aura to what he calls the "cult

[4]As a fascinating gloss on Benjamin's essay, I would recommend Nabokov's *Invitation to a Beheading*, (G.P. Putnam's Sons, 1959), written in Berlin just a year earlier (1935), in which photography is used as the most perfectly appropriate art form in an ideal model of the totalitarian state.

image" of objects, which, in direct contrast to the mechanically reproduced image, can never be separated from the object's presence, can never be distributed, broadcast, enlarged, cut up, pasted over, absorbed into the helpless world of merely used things. The existence of aura, then, presupposes a sacral, perhaps ultimately theological, view of reality. Benjamin was, it should be stressed, intensely alive to the new possibilities of art after the decay of aura, astutely observing the substitution of shock for aura and the willful destruction of empathy in Baudelaire and modern poetry after him, in Brecht's Epic Theater, and in films. But when he talks about the "atrophy of experience" he means the atrophy of aura, which thus becomes not a neutral process but an ultimate disaster of modern culture: Benjamin is perhaps closest to his spiritual kinsman Kafka in being unable, or unwilling, to accept a reality stripped of its sacral dimension.

This underlying commitment to a vision of life rooted in theological values helped Benjamin to comprehend modern processes of cultural breakdown more vividly than he might otherwise have done; at the same time it is a chief source of a quality in his own work that he once attributed to Kafka, a strange "radiant serenity" that informs his writing even in its chillingly apocalyptic passages. This is a surprising enough quality to find in any writer with such a raw nerve of response to the disturbing nature of modern experience, even more surprising in someone at his time and place. For the entire span of Benjamin's literary activity is less than two decades, and his most productive, original period was from 1933 to the last months before his death. One marvels at the man's dedication to his calling, the way he could in grim exile patiently pursue the definition of European culture, of art and language, at a time when a new mobilized barbarism threatened to engulf everything he cared about and sought to understand. Scholem has suggested that the reason Benjamin could not bring himself to leave Europe for Palestine, even at the eleventh hour, was that he could not abandon his work at the Bibliothèque Nationale on the book he would never complete, *Paris, Capital of the 19th Century.*[5]

[5]"Erinnerungen an Walter Benjamin," *Der Monat*, September 1966.

As a Jew, Benjamin was never fully part of an indigenous stream of European culture—thus the logic of his Zionism—but for the same reason he was of European culture as a whole, committed, one might say, to the idea of European culture. "Even in the hour of death," according to a Talmudic dictum, "you should devote yourself to the study of the Law," and the statement could serve as an apt image of Benjamin in his last years. His writing, that is, implicitly affirms the ultimate importance of the kind of "study" he had set as his lifework, and its radiant serenity derives in part from that affirmation, made as it is by an extraordinarily supple and original mind confidently aware of its own powers even when delineating the dimensions of chaos.

Benjamin is acutely conscious of the forms assumed by chaos in our political, moral, and spiritual lives, but, unlike so many modern writers, he is not secretly enamored of chaos in any way, and that is the other source, to which I referred first, of his paradoxical serenity. As a thoroughly modern imagination, he devoted most of his critical attention to those writers and those cultural phenemona through which he could trace the decline of aura, through which, that is, he could honestly confront the world around him. Yet what attracts him most profoundly is the possibility of life imbued with aura; it is a possibility that the literature of the past and the exercise of the imagination keep alive for him. And what fascinates him most about modern writers is the ability of a few of them to devise strategems for recapturing at least an oblique glint of aura, or for creating the simulacrum of it. Thus, he is drawn to Valéry both for the critical statement and the poetic application of the idea that "artistic observation can attain an almost mystical depth"; to Kafka, who surrenders truth to retain its transmissibility, in whom storytelling assumes its old Scheherazadean purpose of postponing the future, fending off death; to Nikolai Leskov, whose fiction preserves something from the immemorial wisdom of the traditional teller of tales.

Benjamin's quest in literature for even the bittersweet residue of bliss is clearest of all in his involvement with the work of Proust. He is, to be sure, aware of Proust as a critic of society and a poet of decay, but his own persuasively stated emphasis is on what he describes as the "elegiac form" of a "will to happiness" in Proust. The intricately elaborated, sensuously realized image in Proust is the French novelist's way of rescuing fragments from a remembered world bathed in aura: "He lay on his bed racked with homesickness, homesick for the world distorted in the state of resemblance, a world in which the true surrealist face of existence breaks through. To this world belongs what happens in Proust, and the deliberate and fastidious way in which it happens." As elsewhere, Benjamin perceives so well because he himself feels much the same thing. His sense of homesickness, cultural and, ultimately, theological, makes more intelligible his attachment to Marxist messianism, to Zionism, to the Jewish past, and to the nineteenth century. Homesickness, however, is the etymological equivalent of nostalgia and all too easily leads to nostalgic excesses. Benjamin's greatness as a critic is, finally, his ability to preserve an absolutely unsentimental lucidity in his existential homesickness, and thus to perceive through it both the precise configurations of modern experience and the shape and substance of a vital coherence to which the human spirit, even as it plots its own subversion, still stubbornly aspires.

—1969

Gershom Scholem: History and the Abyss

"The desire to destroy," wrote Bakunin, "is also a creative desire," and he managed to inflame—indeed, his ideas still inflame—tens of thousands of minds through his incandescent vision of "the whole of Europe, with St. Petersburg, Paris, and London, transformed into an enormous rubbish-heap." A century before Bakunin, precisely the same ecstatic lust for destruction joined with the same messianic fervor had flared up in the teachings of an obscure Polish Jew named Jacob Frank, though Frank's initial field of reference was theological, not political: "Wherever Adam trod a city was built, but wherever I set foot all will be destroyed, for I came into this world only to destroy and to annihilate. But what I build, will last forever." Bakunin's impact, of course, has been, quite literally, terrific: the Russian anarchist's doctrine has haunted the modern literary imagination and has provided political fanaticism an unfailing source, down to the

Bomber Left of our own days, for the dream of redemption through a purifying rite of cataclysmic destruction. Frank, on the other hand, is not likely to have come to the attention of anyone but a serious student of Jewish history, yet this self-chosen messiah of an antinomian sect, both in his psychology and his program of action, offers us, no less than Bakunin, a disturbingly instructive instance of the paradoxes of modernity. Both show us modern man, deformed by his personal and cultural past, in the awful desperation and contradictions of his efforts to smash the old molds at whatever cost and create a shining new order.

The juxtaposition of Bakunin and Frank may suggest something of the peculiarity of Gershom Scholem's enterprise as a historian. His work on Jewish mysticism, messianism, and sectarianism, spanning now half a century, constitutes, I should think, one of the major achievements of the historical imagination in our time. I would contend that it is of vital interest not only to anyone concerned with the history of religion but to anyone struggling to understand the underlying problematics of the modern predicament. Yet all along Scholem has been laboring in a forgotten vineyard choked with thorns, a field whose very existence was scarcely recognized before he began his researches in Germany after World War I. The figures he has illuminated—Frank, Sabbatai Zevi, Eleazar of Worms, Abraham Abulafia, Moses de Leon, Isaac Luria—are names virtually unknown outside the orbit of Hebrew culture, and many of the myriad texts he has edited, analyzed, used to reconstruct a vanished past, had been buried in oblivion even within that orbit. Yet Scholem has never exhibited the slightest trace of nervousness about "parochialism" in his chosen specialization. On the contrary, his books and articles are informed by a serene confidence that these are eminently worthy objects of study for anyone curious about man and his culture, and in fact one can think of few more impressive demonstrations that human experience has been more various and devious, more intriguingly complex, than our stubborn stereotypes of it.

Gershom Scholem was born in Berlin in 1897, the son of an assimilated bourgeois Jewish family. In his adolescence he became a convinced Zionist, began learning Hebrew, and for this egregious failure in his duties as a patriotic German was peremptorily banished from his father's house. He studied mathematics and physics, then Semitic philology, in Berlin, Jena, and Berne, completing a doctorate at the University of Munich in 1922. A year later he emigrated to Palestine, and from the founding of the Hebrew University of Jerusalem in 1925 until his retirement in 1965 he lectured there on Jewish mysticism, creating a new department as he had virtually created a new field of study, over the years making a deep impact on generations of Israeli students while his reputation among historians of religion steadily grew through his publications in German and English and his frequent visits to American and European institutions of higher learning.

It is symptomatic of the neglect Jewish mysticism had suffered that the first two decades of Scholem's career had to be devoted chiefly to the editing and explication of the basic mystical texts and to compiling bibliographies for the field. His first substantial work of synthesis and historical overview is *Major Trends in Jewish Mysticism* (1941), (3rd rev. ed., Schocken, 1961) initially published in English (from a German manuscript version) and based on a series of lectures given in New York in 1938. This "first work," however, is the mature fruit of twenty years of scholarship—an introductory survey that is, in fact, the definitive book on the subject, and gives every prospect of remaining so. Scholem's subsequent books have, then, necessarily been explorations in depth of subjects already covered in single packed chapters in *Major Trends*. In 1948 he published in Hebrew *Reshit Ha-Kabbalah* ("The Origins of the Kabbalah," not available in English), a study of the mystical movement in Provence and Spain in the twelfth and thirteenth centuries that led to the creation of the *Zohar*. In 1957, again in Hebrew, he published his major two-volume biography of the seventeenth-century pseudo-messiah of Smyrna, Sabbatai Zevi, with extensive consideration of the mass movement inspired by Sabbatai and of Sabbatianism's larger historical reverberations. American readers now have an opportunity to examine this work, the most sustained example of Scholem's formidable thoroughness as a historian, with the publication in English of *Sabbatai Ṣevi: The Mystical Messiah* (Princeton University Press, 1973).

Both *Major Trends* and *Sabbatai Ṣevi* have become land-marks of modern Jewish scholarship, the one a comprehensive summary and synthesis, the other, at the opposite pole, a study in detail of a particular crucial phenomenon. *On the Kabbalah and Its Symbolism* (Schocken, 1965), originally published in German in 1960, offers a general description of the phenomenology of Jewish mysticism, explaining the psychological and institutional categories with which it works, the dynamics and tensions peculiar to it as well as those shared with other mystical systems. In 1960 there also appeared his technical study, *Jewish Gnosticism, Merkabah Mysticism, and Talmudic Tradition* (2nd ed., Bloch, 1965). Finally, *The Messianic Idea in Judaism* (Schocken, 1971) is a generous selection of Scholem's major papers, chiefly from the late fifties and the sixties, again exploring the phenomenology of Jewish mysticism and of Jewish messianism, with particular attention given to Hasidism, to Sabbatianism and its exotic heirs, and to the problematics of tradition in all these currents of Jewish experience.

What, briefly, are the nature and scope of the mystical heritage that Scholem's pioneering work has brought to light? The nine chapters of *Major Trends* firmly delineate the field. I shall return later to Scholem's general definition of mysticism, but for the moment let me suggest that the common tendency of Kabbalism as he sees it is to work feverishly —and unwittingly—against the grain of classical Judaism while adhering passionately to the classical Jewish system of belief. That is, Judaism, as an institutionalized religion, establishes an abyss between man and God, while Jewish mysticism devises strategies for spanning the chasm; classical Judaism is anti-mythological, Kabbalistic theology "attempts to construct and to describe a world in which something of the mythical has again come to life, in terms of thoughts [those of Jewish tradition] which exclude the mythical element"; conversely, the biblical faith conceives of revelation as the direct utterance of a personal God, while Kabbalism is heavily influenced by gnostic conceptions of an impersonal divine reality of which God the Creator who addresses man is merely an intermediary manifestation. Many of these tendencies are common to other mysticisms, but the Kabbalists put a very special stress on the eschatalogical impulse implicit in much mystical thought, and they are distinctive in their central notion of language as a profound reflection of ultimate spiritual reality, in their concomitant devotion to exegesis as a mystical activity, in their extravagant claims for the authority of the very tradition they radically reshape, and in the special status of their teaching among mystical legacies as "a masculine doctrine, made for men and by men."

The historical phenomenon of Jewish mysticism as Scholem traces it in *Major Trends* stretches from esoteric doctrine taught in Pharisaic circles in the days of the Second Temple down to the Hasidic movement that flourished in Eastern Europe during the later eighteenth and nineteenth centuries. The earliest recoverable phase is Merkabah (Divine Chariot or Throne) mysticism, a gnostic tradition rooted in Hellenistic thought. Its literary remains, scattered over most of the first millennium C.E., are peculiarly not speculative but descriptive —of the glittering reality imaged in the Divine Throne or the Divine Palaces *(Hekhalot)*. Accordingly, the Merkabah mystics are pervasively conscious of God's otherness, even in mystical ecstasy; their vision fixed on the radiance of the Godhead, they exhibit little interest in man or in the moral dimension of spiritual life. The next major mystical movement, the Hasidism of twelfth- and thirteenth-century Germany, in some ways moves to the opposite pole, being less concerned with the mysteries of the Godhead than with man's acts, and assuming a deeply pietistic, penitential, ascetic, and often thaumaturgic character.

The most brilliant development of Jewish mysticism comes with the emergence of the Kabbalah proper in southern France and in Spain around the year 1200. Scholem distinguishes two strands of Kabbalah, ecstatic and theosophical. The former, dominated by the figure of Abraham Abulafia (b. 1240), involves an elaborate system of meditation (especially on the letters of the Hebrew alphabet) and even breathing exercises which are reminiscent of yoga and which may ultimately derive from the same Indian source as yoga. It was the theosophical strand, however, which was to be the more influential, receiving its supreme expression in the *Zohar*, or Book of Splendor, composed, as Scholem has conclusively demonstrated, by a Spanish Jew named Moses de Leon toward the end of the thirteenth century. The intricacies of its doctrine of the Godhead defy brief summary,[1] but the haunting imaginative power of Moses de Leon's literary mélange—"a mixture of theosophic theology, mythical cosmogony, and mystical psychology and anthropology"—proved to be of vital historical importance. Through this remarkable power, the book quickly attained immense popularity, indeed, became the only text after the Talmud to achieve the rough Jewish equivalent of canonical status. It was the basis for the last major theoretical development of Jewish mysticism, the Lurianic Kabbalah that arose in Safed in the early sixteenth century. Isaac Luria and his disciples placed a new central emphasis on cosmogony, conceived creation as a breaking of divine vessels, an emanation of divine light, sparks of divine essence entrammeled in husks of evil from which they must be redeemed. In short, the Lurianic doctrine elevated Exile to a powerfully dramatic principle of cosmic process; it represented a boldly original mystical theology that was also ideally suited to the propaganda of mass movements of spiritual revival. Like the *Zohar* itself, Lurianic teaching was taken up enthusiastically by most segments of the Jewish people, all over the Diaspora. Finally, Lurianism provided the ideological apparatus for two successive movements which shook the structure of traditional Jewish society—the mystical heresy of Sabbatianism that enveloped most of the Jewish world around the year 1666, and Hasidism, the popular mystical movement stirred by charismatic leaders that sprang up in Podolia and Volhynia nearly a century later and profoundly affected East European Jewry at the dawn of the modern period.

Now, Scholem's work is clearly of far more than antiquarian interest, but it is important first to recognize his enormous value as a sheer archeologist of culture, digging tirelessly through vast moldering mounds of literary remains neglected for the most part by others. He has, ultimately, a definite interpretative view and a clear commitment to certain

[1]The interested reader may peruse the suggestive sampling put together by Scholem in *Zohar: The Book of Splendor* (Schocken, 1963).

values, but his work cannot be faulted for tendentiousness because it is based on such painstaking research, always intent on determining the precise and particular facts no matter how much they may upset anyone's established views, including his own. His biography of Sabbatai Zevi is surely a model for the patient reconstruction of a life and a movement (three centuries distant) from all the available sources, and at the same time an instance of revisionist historiography at its most acute. Scholem has rare gifts for synthesis and generalization, as several of his more recent essays on Jewish messianism and tradition demonstrate,[2] but his mind is equally remarkable for the way it adheres to the smallest particles of particular historical experience.

One sees this faculty operating on a small scale with dazzling effect in the essay "The Curious History of the Six-Pointed Star," on the history of the Star of David as a symbol, included in *The Messianic Idea in Judaism*. Scholem discards a series of old chestnuts, follows the forerunners and occasional occurrences of the device through some twenty-five-hundred years of iconography, necromancy, and occult symbolism, distinguishing its shifting and overlapping uses until its final adoption in nineteenth-century Germany as a "Jewish" symbol that could be for German citizens of the Mosaic persuasion completely analogous to the cross for Christians. The sifting of texts and facts concludes with a wryly pointed observation: "Just at the time of its greatest dissemination in the nineteenth century the Shield of David served as the empty symbol of a Judaism which itself was more and more falling into meaninglessness." This sort of essay, one assumes, is a relatively easy spin-off project for a scholar like Scholem, but precisely because it seems so unlike labored scholarship I find the experience of reading it a little dizzying, for the mind that has made it is able to contain in lucid simultaneity such a welter of disparate, far-flung fragments of the lived past. Islamic amulets and Christian manuals of sorcery, alchemical handbooks from the early Middle Ages to the late Renaissance, Kabbalistic tracts from every-

[2] See *The Messianic Idea in Judaism,* especially the first three essays and the brilliant "Revelation and Tradition as Religious Categories in Judaism."

where; the politics, ritual practices, art, and folkways of Christians and Jews in thirteenth-century Anagni, fifteenth-century Prague, sixteenth-century Budapest, seventeenth-century Vienna—all these give the impression of having been not merely surveyed but somehow securely *possessed* in all their concrete particularity. Reading such a historical essay, one is forced to revise one's limited notions of what knowledge can be.

To contain so many materials is a capacity of mind; to possess them is a quality of imagination, and it is this that makes a serious technical scholar like Scholem also a writer of compelling general interest. He writes always with respect for the integrity of his subjects, even those that previously have been considered marginal or "pathological," and so he can enter into them empathetically at the same time that he views them analytically in historical context. One vivid case in point is his commentary on the hymns of the *Hekhalot* mystics in *Major Trends in Jewish Mysticism:* "The immense solemnity of their style, the bombast of their magnificent phrases, reflect the fundamental paradox of these hymns: the climax of sublimity and solemnity to which the mystic can attain in his attempt to express the magnificence of his vision is also the *ne plus ultra* of vacuousness." One might note that "paradox" is one of Scholem's favorite words, and few scholars have had such a deep understanding of how sickness and health, destruction and creation, nonsense and profundity, have intermingled in the same spiritual phenomena. "Vacuousness," in context, is not so damning as it may sound here since it has a precise theosophic referent and hence a definite psychological function. In any case, Jews familiar from the liturgy with repetitious acrostic hymns like *Ha-Aderet v'Ha-Emunah* will be startled to learn that these poems were composed to serve a hallucinogenic function for their original users in the early centuries of the Christian era. Scholem makes this clear without resorting to clinical vocabulary, illuminating the experience he describes as if from within while analyzing it from without:

Almost all the hymns from the *Hekhalot* tracts . . . reveal a mechanism comparable to the motion of an enormous fly-wheel. In cyclical

rhythm the hymns succeed each other, and within them the adjura-
tions of God follow in a crescendo of glittering and majestic attributes, each stressing and reinforcing the sonorous power of the word.
The monotony of their rhythm—almost all consist of verses of four
words—and the progressively sonorous incantations induce in those
who are praying a state of mind bordering on ecstasy.

Scholem's endowments as a historian can hardly be in question, but that is not to say that he has not had his detractors
in the world of Jewish scholarship, who have generally ac-
knowledged his gifts while arguing that he has used them for
dubious, if not nefarious, ends. It is the general orientation of
his enterprise that has laid him open to attack, and that needs
some setting in perspective. Modern academic historiography
was invented as a serious discipline in early nineteenth-century Germany, and modern Jewish historical scholarship developed very soon thereafter in the same cultural sphere,
using the same intellectual tools. There was, however, an
important ideological disparity between the two scholarly
movements, as Scholem pointed out in a 1959 lecture at the
Leo Baeck Institute on the *Wissenschaft des Judentums*, or
Science of Judaism. The early generations of German historians, inspired by the ideals of German Romanticism, were
nationalists, and what they sought was an "active comprehension of the organism of their own history in the sense of a
positive, nationally oriented perspective and future." The
proponents of the *Wissenschaft des Judentums*, on the other
hand, were at bottom cosmopolitan in outlook, perhaps, indeed, the most dogged heirs of the already fading cosmopolitan vision of the Enlightenment. Though their subject was the
national experience of one people, their standpoint was as
men of a larger European culture in which an experience so
fiercely particular, so redolent of other times and places, could
only be an anachronism; and so they often tended to study
Judaism as the dead remains of a completed past, not as a
living body pregnant with the future. Gerson D. Cohen has
proposed that Scholem be viewed as a neo-Romantic historian,[3] and in fact the brief notation I have quoted on the
Romantic quest for an organism of national history and a

[3] Annual Roland Lecture in Jewish Studies, Stanford University, May 1972.

perspective on a national future could well be taken as the thumbnail program of Scholem's own enterprise. If, however, that enterprise can in one aspect be described as Romantic, it is a hard-headed, shrewdly skeptical Romanticism, and a Romanticism, as we shall see, steeped in the bitter juices of modern experience, impelled by the concerns of a characteristically modern imagination.

The founders of Jewish historical scholarship, I would add, were motivated not only by the ideology of an intellectual movement but at least as much by the vulnerable sensibility of a new social class. Only a generation or two beyond the ghetto, in an era when assimilation was a beckoning horizon, they sought to confirm in their study of Judaism the values of propriety, prudence, practical reasonableness, and rational faith on which their newly acquired German *Bürgerlichkeit* rested. When Scholem observes that "their bias represents a form of censorship of the Jewish past," thinking chiefly of a post-Enlightenment ideological bias, one could also note that this bias is equally composed of a bourgeois recoil from all that might offend a sense of decency in "good" society. Thus, the *Wissenschaft* scholars developed a peculiar notion of what came to be known as normative Judaism. What was central to Jewish experience tended to be thought of as legalistic, rationalist, prudential, this-worldly, and fundamentally conservative; spiritual phenomena sharply diverging from this general norm had to be viewed as suspect aberrations. In this manner, Jewish mysticism, Jewish enthusiastic and antinomian movements, the profound involvement of Jews through the ages in magic and the occult, all were studied grudgingly as manifestations of the sickly medieval spirit that temporarily beclouded the clarity of Jewish devotion to eternal verities and rational ideals.[4]

[4]In a personal reminiscence published in Hebrew, Scholem tells a revealing anecdote of his own early confrontation with the Science of Judaism. As a very young man in Germany, he was introduced to an elderly Reform rabbi who was a student of Heinrich Graetz, the major synoptic historian of the *Wissenschaft des Judentums*. This rabbi was reputed to be the only *Wissenschaft* scholar interested in the Kabbalah. It turned out that in fact he had a splendid private collection of Kabbalistic manuscripts and rare editions. "How marvelous, sir," cried the enthusiastic young Scholem, "that you have been able to read and study these sources." To which the old man replied: *"Was? Den Quatsch soll ich auch noch lesen?* (What? Am I expected to

Scholem's work, then, might helpfully be viewed as a sustained act of social rebellion, somewhat like the rebellion of the Nietzschean movement of early twentieth-century Hebrew poets and writers to which it is closely allied. One might almost say that he has uncovered for moderns the heritage of a historical Jewish counter-culture, except for the fact that, as his investigations have proven, it was very often the dominant culture. In any case, he has managed to rescue from the murk of the past a rich body of vitally Jewish experience that challenges many of the comfortable values of German middle-class respectability in which the Science of Judaism developed and in which he himself grew up. His writing, in other words, has been not only a decisive revocation of that censorship of the Jewish past which he mentions but also a deftly wielded weapon, for all its heavy apparatus of scholarly footnotes, used to *épater les bourgeois*.

Although Scholem's influence in the world of Jewish scholarship has been enormous, the inertia of established views he has had to overcome has also been considerable. The fact that he is not merely fencing with nineteenth-century ghosts in his historical revisionism was made strikingly clear in a review-essay of *The Messianic Idea* by Jacob Agus in *Judaism* (Summer 1972). Agus is a man of serious Jewish knowledge, a prolific writer on theological matters, and, preeminently, a figure of the American rabbinical establishment—which, as it turns out, is in some matters not so unlike the old German-Jewish bourgeois establishment as one would like to think. Agus has, to be sure, the highest praise for the scope and intelligence of Scholem's undertaking, but the ease with which in the very act of praise he closes his mind to the major conclusions of Scholem's researches is quite breathtaking. Thus, Scholem's studies of Sabbatai Zevi, both in the two-volume biography and in a series of scholarly articles early and late, have forcefully demonstrated that, contrary to nineteenth-century views, the Sabbatian messianic movement of the 1660s had immense reverberations, at its peak enveloping

---

read this nonsense also?)" Scholem concludes: "At that moment my eyes were opened and I realized what the Science of Judaism was all about." *Molad*, no. 164–165, 1962, p. 135.

most of the Jewish people in all the far reaches of the Diaspora, and continuing as a highly ramified and active underground for nearly a century and a half. Scholem in effect sets
Sabbatianism at the beginning of modern Jewish history, as
the first concretely realized historical moment when the whole
Jewish people experienced its own incipient emergence from
the ghetto world into a radically transformed existence. A
world thrown so violently askew would for many never re-
sume its old balance. Though the exact role of Sabbatianism
as a causal factor in the various movements that followed it
is still open to debate, Scholem has unearthed a current of
Sabbatianism (there were good reasons why the participants
themselves should have kept it hidden) running through the
rabbinical leadership for a century after the death of the
apostate messiah, feeding into Hasidism, the Hebrew Enlightenment, the Reform movement, even the French Revolution.

With all this, Agus, after reading, we can assume, Scholem's thousand pages of carefully documented argument, can
still blandly assert—revealingly, in a "word of caution" to the
reader unversed in Jewish sources—that "one must see the
Sabbatian eruption in perspective, as a marginal aberration."
It is true, he concedes, that the movement briefly swept the
whole people and that the energies of its aftermath were not
quickly spent, "But the intellectual leaders of the people, in
spite of their anguished situation, quickly regained their equilibrium." No evidence at all is offered for this flat assertion.
Apparently, it is sufficient simply to see things "in perspective," and a rabbi's commitment to reasonable faith is taken
to be a self-validating measure of what really happened in
Jewish history.

As a historian, Scholem is a modernist in much the same
sense that Conrad, Kafka, Mann, and Faulkner are modernists. Like these imaginative writers, his insights are often
deeply troubling, and it is the business of an establishment
figure like Agus to blunt or deflect such an argument wherever it is most probing. But it may be helpful to consider in
detail how Scholem is a modernist both in his choice of subject
and in the qualities of imagination he brings to bear on it.
What, to begin with, is the peculiar appeal of mysticism to a

writer whose work begins in the very peak years of European literary modernism, whose mature life has witnessed two world wars, the Holocaust, and the bloody rebirth after two millennia of a Jewish commonwealth? Mysticism, Scholem states at the outset of *Major Trends in Jewish Mysticism,* approvingly quoting Rufus Jones, "is religion in its most acute, intense, and living stage." Clearly, acuteness, intensity, and vitality have been among the great desiderata of the modern spirit in its quest for personal authenticity against what has often seemed the dead and empty formalism of the cultural heritage. The specific meaning of these three qualities as they are associated with mysticism is worth pursuing. I think that implicit in all of Scholem's work is an assumption that mysticism is, finally, the most authentic variety of religious experience because it is the most daring, aspiring to a naked directness of confrontation with divinity, seeking to break through the intervening barriers of institutionalization and received tradition.

Along with the definition of Rufus Jones, Scholem cites Aquinas's characterization of mysticism as *cognitio dei experimentalis,* the experiential knowledge of God. Elsewhere, in his masterful essay on revelation and tradition, he emphasizes the mediated nature for rabbinic Judaism of every experience after the initial revelation. As a result, exegesis becomes the characteristically Jewish means to knowledge and perhaps even the characteristically Jewish mode of religious experience. What the Kabbalists, with their letter-and-word mysticism, sought was to get back through exegesis to a species of revelation, to work or contemplate their way through the mediating words of the sacred text to the unmediated Word out of whose infinite declensions and permutations all language and all being come into existence. The Kabbalah is fundamentally a linguistic mysticism, at least in method, and this is surely part of its fascination for Scholem, who shares with his friend Walter Benjamin an abiding interest in the paradoxical ways language, as civilization's endlessly refined and conventionalized instrument, can put man in touch with the potent wellsprings of ultimacy that underlie and antedate all civilization.

Scholem is, of course, equally concerned with how mysticism fits into, or obtrudes from, particular historical contexts, and in this regard his generalization on the relation between mysticism and history in *On the Kabbalah and Its Symbolism* throws a good deal of light on his interest in the subject as a modern: "Mysticism as a historical phenomenon is a product of crises." His inquiries have shown how Jewish mysticism responded to the most terrible historical traumas with apocalyptic systems that renewed the hope of redemption and sustained the life of tradition. To cite the major instance of recent centuries: the Kabbalah, crystallized in late thirteenth-century Spain, provided the vocabulary of spiritual explanation for the banishment of 1492, was then articulated as a general doctrine of cosmic redemption by the Lurianic school in sixteenth-century Palestine, and in its subsequent dissemination decisively shaped minds and offered the ideological tools for the great messianic upheaval of the seventeenth century. It will be apparent even from this hasty sketch that Scholem conceives mysticism not only as the product of historical crisis but as an active force generating further crisis. The Lurianic doctrine of cosmic exile, developed among the refugees from Spain in the decades after the expulsion, did not encourage the exiles to accommodate themselves to their harsh circumstances. On the contrary, "The emotions aroused by these sufferings were not soothed and tranquilized, but stimulated and whipped up."

Though he is not merely a historian of ideas, Scholem writes with a profound respect for the autonomy of the spiritual realm in historical experience, and though he exercises a fine awareness of contexts, he emphatically rejects the "modern naiveté" of sociological or psychological determinism, with its roots in the simplistic positivism of nineteenth-century science. Thus, the actual social composition of the Sabbatian movement makes it quite impossible to reduce it to a rebellion of disadvantaged classes; the movement's special appeal to the most prosperous and legally liberated centers of seventeenth-century Jewry preclude explaining it simply as a response to the persecutions of the period; and even Sabbatai Zevi's manic-depressive psychosis, discussed at great length, does not diminish the power and complexity of the theology built around his personality. "If there was one general factor underlying the patent unity of the Sabbatian movement everywhere, then this factor was essentially religious and as such obeyed its own autonomous laws."

What is it about mysticism that makes it the most appropriate religious response to historical crisis? To begin with, as Scholem points out in a variety of ways, there is a constant tension in mysticism, precisely because it is a *cognitio dei experimentalis,* between imperative personal experience and the religion of fixed norms outside the experiencing self. When a historical crisis occurs, the contradictions within the body of tradition are made manifest, and the new discoveries of a daring self avid for intensities come into the foreground of theological explanation, helping to reconcile the promises of tradition with the sharp disappointments of history. Mysticism, to invoke another of Scholem's favorite words, is by its very nature dialectical, continuously mediating between the absoluteness of the self and the inviolability of tradition, and as such it is ideally suited to coping with a historical reality that vacillates between opposite poles, violently overturning preconceptions and expectations. The Sabbatians after the apostasy of their messiah constitute an extreme case in which "all reality became dialectically unreal and contradictory," but such radical confusions have in one way or another challenged most mystical movements, just as again and again they seem to have engulfed historical experience in our own century.

The fitting response to this kind of traumatic and contradictory historical reality was a religion of extremes, and here again Scholem's explorations of Jewish mysticism jibe with a deep-seated conviction of modernism, that the truth is to be sought in extremes, the historical Judaism revealed in his work being distinctly a Judaism for the readers of Dostoevsky, Kafka, and Rimbaud. Looking back over Scholem's *oeuvre,* one sees a crowd of sharp visual images that forever unsettle one's complacent assumptions about what Jews may have done or been: the early Hasidic ascetics of thirteenth-century Germany, plunging themselves into snow and ice, exposing their bodies in summer to ants and bees; the Jewish women and children of Safed, Aleppo, Smyrna, writhing in prophetic paroxysms, reciting verses in automatic speech, flung to the ground in a self-induced hypnotic trance at the advent of Sabbatai Zevi; the bizarre psychosexuality of Sabbatai himself, who devised weirdly erotic rites, such as a marriage ceremony between himself and the Torah, while his first two flesh-and-blood marriages were unconsummated and the third was to a woman whose promiscuity was notorious in the Jewish world from Amsterdam to Cairo; the orgiastic cult of the Frankists in Poland, or of their Turkish counterpart, the crypto-Jewish Dönmeh sect, which celebrated a spring festival of ritual fornication unwittingly drawing on the old worship of the Magna Mater indigenous to Asia Minor.

Scholem treats all this with the utmost seriousness, fitting it into a large imaginative perspective of interpretation. Here, there is a third key term, in addition to "paradox" and "dialectic," which he invokes again and again. If the two already mentioned terms describe both historical process and the nature of deity, the third term, "abyss," does that and more, representing in an image a kind of ultimate principle of ontology in Scholem's vision of the world. Thus, Jewish mysticism in general attempts "to make visible that abyss in which the symbolic nature of all that exists reveals itself." Sabbatianism and its sundry offshoots are repeatedly described as opening an abyss at the very heart of Judaism. The implicit logic of messianism itself, once it becomes a real operative force in history, is to thrust toward a hitherto sealed abyss of chaotic possibilities: "Every acute and radical messianism that is taken seriously tears open an abyss in which by inner necessity antinomian tendencies and libertine moral conceptions gain strength." Franz Rosenzweig, as the most probing of modern Jewish theologians, is said to have "ripped open the abyss in which the substance of Judaism lies hidden." (True knowledge for Scholem often turns out to be forbidden knowledge.) The apocalyptic element in Rosenzweig's thought "provided a recognition of the catastrophic potential of all historical order in an unredeemed world." Even the legend of the Thirty-Six Hidden Just Men is characterized, perhaps a bit gratuitously, as being sustained by a "somewhat anarchic morality" because it confronts us with the idea that "we can never fathom" the nature of our neighbors. The mystic, Scholem tells us at the beginning of *On the Kabbalah and Its*

Symbolism, wants to encounter "Life" (the quotation marks are his); but this primordial Life, ceaselessly engendering and annihilating form, "is the anarchic promiscuity of all living things. Into this bubbling cauldron, this continuum of destruction, the mystic plunges."

Scholem generally avoids psychoanalytic vocabulary—because, I think, it might seem clinically reductive in its application to phenomena that above all need rescuing from the contempt of the learned—but it is hard to escape the parallel between his notion of an abyss upon which the lid of civilization sits precariously and Freud's view of culture in *Civilization and Its Discontents*. In any case, the abyss for Scholem seems to be not just the function of pent-up psychological forces but also the substantive nature of reality outside the human psyche, and here a more apposite source for his vision could well be the Nietzsche of *The Birth of Tragedy*. Nietzsche's notion of a Dionysian truth in excess, of contradiction at the heart of nature; his guiding concept of a dangerous dialectical tension between the Apollonian love of form and order and the Dionysian impulse to orgiastic release, to fusion with the inhuman chaotic potency that underlies existing things—all these have their parallels in Scholem. Even Nietzsche's contempt for the self-deceiving optimism of Socratic culture (essentially, nineteenth-century German academic culture) with its antimystical bias has its analogue in Scholem's rebellion, less visionary, more grounded in an exacting intellectual discipline than Nietzsche's, against the bias and tacit censorship of the *Wissenschaft des Judentums*. Finally, that abyss of formlessness from which culture arises implies the necessity of myth for Nietzsche: only through myth can man remain in touch with the realm of the irrational that is the matrix of reality and also give it an imaged order, a sequence of dramatic actions, which can be grasped by a finite human consciousness. "Without myth," Nietzsche asserts, "every culture loses the healthy natural power of its creativity: only a horizon defined by myths completes and unifies a whole cultural movement."

Now, myth has always been a problematic phenomenon for Judaism. One might well say, as the late Yehezkel Kaufmann repeatedly argued, that the whole tendency of biblical monotheism was to conduct a systematic purge of myth, leaving only a few vestigial literary allusions whose original meanings were no longer even understood. The need for myth, however, might be driven underground but could not be entirely extinguished. Scholem quite candidly describes the Kabbalah in the opening chapter of *Major Trends* as a "revival of myth" from the innermost recesses of historical Judaism, and it is clear that he shares the modern fascination with myth that begins signally in *The Birth of Tragedy* and flowers in some of the major imaginative works of the earlier twentieth century. His exemplary exposition of the theosophic doctrine of the *Zohar* excites the imagination as it does largely because he perceives so surely the resurgence of old mythological images in the new mystical lore, male and female gods coupling in cosmic exultation, confirming the unity of the world and the eternal meaning of transient human life through the power of their divine sexuality.

Scholem, let me stress, is a student of mysticism, not a mystagogue, and he has none of that peculiar nostalgia for primal mud that has characterized many latter-day myth-mongers. He lucidly recognizes that the Celestial Bridegroom and the Celestial Bride of the *Zohar* are only a step and a half away from the pagan excesses of the Dönmeh sect adoring a mother goddess in orgies. For all his interest in antinomian extremes, Scholem is committed to civilized restraints and to the values and ordered achievements that can be realized within those restraints. Nevertheless, his entire study of Jewish mysticism implicitly argues that a spiritual tradition entirely cut off from myth is cut off from living connection with ultimate reality and so doomed to wither.

I hope the foregoing will suggest something of the range of implication in the qualities of acuteness and intensity that Scholem associates with mysticism. The third of Rufus Jones's intertwined categories, vitality ("religion in its most . . . living stage"), calls for further commentary because it bears a rather special relationship to Scholem's Zionist commitment. He is perfectly open about the nature of that commitment in the brief foreword to *The Messianic Idea*. The essays are addressed, he tells us, not to dilettantes but to people with a passionate interest in Judaism and its past;

moreover, "This book is written by a man who believes Judaism to be a living phenomenon which . . . has not yet exhausted its possibilities" and whose future forms one cannot presume to predict.

Scholem's primary period of research is precisely the era of Jewish history considered in many older views to be a period of decadence after the peak achievements of the Bible, the Talmud, the Spanish philosophers and poets. In this era, running from the later Middle Ages to the threshold of modernity, he discovers a mysticism richly developing until it becomes the dominant force in the Jewish people, manifesting great spiritual boldness, intellectual subtlety, and an unflagging sense of national vigor in the most dire historical circumstances. At the core of the Kabbalah, especially as it received its definitive formulation in the school of Isaac Luria, "lay a great image of rebirth," and what is especially remarkable about this image of rebirth is that it remained strongly particularist in its Jewishness while at the same time achieving an embracing universalism of outlook, erecting a splendid cosmogony out of the historical experience of the Jews. "Kabbalistic myth had 'meaning,' because it sprang from a fully conscious relation to a reality which, experienced symbolically even in its horror, was able to project mighty symbols of Jewish life as an extreme case of human life pure and simple."

This understanding of the Kabbalah offers a new perspective on the rise of modern Jewish nationalism. Zionism may be seen not as an act of historical desperation, the implicit admission of what Georges Friedmann has called "the end of the Jewish people," but, on the contrary, the last of the great visions of rebirth that began driving the Jews toward new horizons some six centuries before Herzl, a movement not only stimulated from without but animated from within by a deep source of national vitality. (It might be noted that the organic conception of national history mentioned by Scholem in connection with the German Romantics is in fact his own implicit view of Jewish history.) In the model of the Lurianic Kabbalah, moreover, one glimpses the possibility that the reborn Jewish state may somehow amplify its nationalism with the universalist vision of Jewish tradition and not subside into being a Bulgaria of the Middle East. These historical precedents of national renascence are all the more convincing because they are not presented tendentiously: Scholem is careful not to interpret the messianic or mystical movements as "proto-Zionist" in any simplistic sense; he in fact argues at length that Hasidism through its stress on the goal of ecstatic communion *(d'vekut)* aimed at a "neutralization" of messianism after the great Sabbatian outburst; and in his studies of the antinomian movements he is sharply conscious of the fact that the other face of the coin of redemption is destruction.

The dialectical play, however, between redemption and destruction is intimately associated with the vitality Scholem attributes to the Kabbalah. Seeing in the regnant rabbinic tradition during this period an acquiescence in the passivity and abjectness of Exile, an increasingly arid—perhaps one might say, bourgeois—religion estranged from the sources of living religious experience, he writes out of the ultimate conviction that rebellion was a historical necessity, though he knows that the aftermath of any rebellion may be chaos. This is one reason why he is so deeply fascinated by the Sabbatian movement, for the Sabbatians destroyed the world of rabbinic Judaism from within while remaining thoroughly Jewish in their consciousness. They were, as Scholem puts it in his classic essay, "Redemption through Sin,"[5] "revolutionaries who regarded themselves as loyal Jews while at the same time completely overturning the traditional religious categories of Judaism." There is surely a good deal of enthusiastic empathy with the Sabbatian rebellion in Scholem's studies of it—one is struck, for example, by his vivid description of a contemporary portrait of Jacob Sasportas, the arch-opponent of the Sabbatians, showing "the face of a Jewish Grand Inquisitor," dour, stern, harsh, irascible, arrogant. One should add, however, that this imaginative identification with the rebels does not dim Scholem's perception of the pathological elements among them, the reign of terror (the phrase is his)

[5]See *The Messianic Idea in Judaism.*

they imposed during the months of their total ascendancy, and the ultimate futility of their rebellion.

In any case, what emerges from the multifarious mystical matters discussed by Scholem is a powerful sense of the protean nature of Jewish experience. Where we might have been inclined to view the various modern ideologies of Jewish survival as a splintering of classical Jewish unity, a fateful breaking away from the grand continuity of the Jewish past, Scholem shows us a historical Judaism itself fissured with sharp divisions and marked by the most extreme variety. Halfway through the first volume of *Sabbatai Şevi*, he makes explicit this large implication of his work: "There is no way of telling *a priori* what beliefs are possible or impossible within the framework of Judaism. . . . The 'Jewishness' in the religiosity of any particular period is not measured by dogmatic criteria that are unrelated to actual historical circumstances, but solely by what sincere Jews do, in fact, believe, or—at least—consider to be legitimate possibilities." This will obviously not sit well with contemporary Jewish dogmatists, spokesmen for the various rabbinical, communal, and Zionist establishments or for ideologized notions of the Jew as enlightened internationalist, but the mass of historical evidence Scholem marshals to support his assertion is formidable. His stress on the vital Jewish consciousness of the pseudomessianic movements has been attacked as a spurious partisan attempt to validate secular Zionism in terms of Jewish history, but the real point about Scholem's work is that it is postideological. Though he is personally committed to the Zionist renascence, what his researches actually do is to open the doors of the mind to a genuine Jewish pluralism, grounded in the spectacular plurality of Jewish historical experience.

Scholem has the kind of ironic intelligence that delights in contradictions, that can hold the multiple attributes of the subjects it scrutinizes in clear simultaneous view, and that is even capable on occasion of a certain teasing archness, for all its scholarly gravity. (The whimsical tone of Borges's poetic allusion to Scholem is not really inappropriate.) As a result, his account of the Jewish past can accommodate the full power of its most seemingly alien manifestations while seeing in overview the distinct limitations of their historical field of operation. Similarly, he can affirm the revolutionary significance in Jewish history of the Zionist fulfillment with an acute awareness of its looming ambiguities. This rare amplitude of perception is beautifully evidenced in the lead essay of *The Messianic Idea in Judaism.* I would like to conclude by quoting an extended passage from this essay because it illustrates so finely Scholem's incisive critical perspective on the very past whose pulsating life stirs his imagination, and shows how his involvement in the past is intellectually linked with a deep concern for the complexities of history unfolding in the present. Celebrations of the noble impulse of Jewish messianism past and present are the great cliché of modern Jewish intellectuals, no matter how distant they may be from any connection with historical Judaism. Scholem, who knows the messianic phenomenon and has appreciated its distinctive power from the most intimate familiarity with all its manifestations, is able to penetrate beyond the banalities of the apologists to the profound historical contradictions at the root of the messianic idea:

The magnitude of the messianic idea corresponds to the endless powerlessness in Jewish history during all the centuries of exile, when it was unprepared to come forward onto the plane of world history. There's something preliminary, something provisional about Jewish history, hence its inability to give of itself entirely. For the messianic idea is not only consolation and hope. Every attempt to realize it tears open the abysses [again, the key phrase] which lead each of its manifestations *ad absurdum.* There is something grand about living in hope, but at the same time there is something profoundly unreal about it. . . . Thus in Judaism the messianic idea has compelled a *life lived in deferment,* in which nothing can be done definitively, nothing can be irrevocably accomplished. One may say, perhaps, the messianic idea is the real anti-existentialist idea. Precisely understood, there is nothing concrete which can be accomplished by the unredeemed. . . . The blazing landscape of redemption (as if it were a point of focus) has concentrated in itself the historical outlook of Judaism. Little wonder that overtones of messianism have accompanied the modern Jewish readiness for irrevocable action in the concrete realm, when it set out on the utopian return to Zion. It is a readiness which no longer allows itself to be fed on hopes. Born out of the horror and destruction that was Jewish history in our generation, it is bound to history itself and not to meta-history; it has not given itself up totally to messianism. Whether or not Jewish history will be able to endure this entry into the concrete realm without perishing in the crisis of the messianic claim which has virtually been conjured up—that is the question which out of his great and dangerous past the Jew of this age poses to his present and to his future.

—1973

Lea Goldberg:
Poetry in Dark Times

For nearly a century now, serious readers and writers of poetry have been repeatedly subject to inner questioning about whether poetry still matters. The often-described breakdown of community in this period between the poet and his audience of course reflects central facts of modern social and cultural history, and it inevitably leads the poet to doubts about the validity of his enterprise, though in some cases those doubts seem to have preceded the breakdown, acting as a contributing cause to it. In any event, the various turnings of poetry to violent and disjunct forms of expression, on the one hand, or to hermetic realms of self-regarding artifice, on the other, are ways in which poets have coped with their own impelling anxiety as to whether something as quiet and as purely verbal as a poem could carry any weight of significance in the growing din of industrialized, urban societies and modern historical upheaval.

Such anxiety is bound to have a special edge in the smaller language-groups, surrounded as they are by major language blocs in a period of international mass media and mass culture. A writer like the Israeli poet Lea Goldberg lived her life and wrote her poems troubled by the same doubts that pursue poets everywhere, to which was added the awareness that her work could only be known and perhaps mean something to a scant few thousand in a tiny corner of the world. Yet her career succeeded in becoming within its limited compass an exemplary career, attesting to the sustaining value of literary endeavor even in an age that calls into question the social and ontological bases of literature.

The death of Lea Goldberg now leaves a still space of felt absence in Israel because in her life she was so much a cultural presence there, and because her life marked a moment in culture that now seems irrevocably past, both in Israel and everywhere else. She was not what one would call a commanding figure, but she managed to become a necessary one. She translated from half a dozen languages with grace and precision, everything from Petrarch and Shakespeare to Tolstoy and Brecht; she wrote children's poetry and stories with a warmth and lively inventiveness that have delighted a generation of young Hebrew readers; she initiated the study of comparative literature as an academic discipline in Israel; and, surely most important, one can say with some confidence of her what one would venture to say of very few contemporary poets anywhere—that she has written a good dozen poems, perhaps twice that many, which will continue to give pleasure in another hundred years.

Born in Kovno three years before the outbreak of World War I, educated there in one of the Hebrew *gymnasia* that were the last great institutional flowering of the Hebraist movement in Eastern Europe between the two wars, Lea Goldberg went on to study in Berlin and then in Bonn, where she received a doctorate in Semitics just as the reign of barbarism descended in 1933. Two years later she arrived in Tel Aviv, beginning adult life again in the unfamiliar white glare of an utterly new physical and cultural landscape—"it seems if you just turned your head," she would write later in a poem on Tel Aviv, 1935, "your hometown church would be floating out in the sea." At once she entered into the bustle of Tel Aviv literary activity, bringing with her a deep sense of at-homeness in European culture rare among the typically autodidact Hebrew writers of her generation and beyond the reach of the native generation that followed.

The movement of modern Hebrew literature, beginning in Enlightenment Germany and moving in stages eastward across Europe, had been conceived initially as part of a cosmopolitan vision of European culture: Hebrew was to emulate, but not slavishly imitate, the exemplary achievements of the various modern literatures and thus take its place in the creation of a new reasonable world of mutually respecting, civilized peoples. The vision, to be sure, was historically naive, and in any case the performance of Hebrew writers generally reduced the grand ideal to a pathetic slogan, but the ideal was not entirely a contemptible one for all that. Lea Goldberg, through her location in history, her personal peregrinations, her literary gifts, was one of the last people in a really advantaged position to translate into credible fact this vision of a Hebrew renaissance intimately and intricately associated with the whole varied range of European high culture.

In her memoir of the remarkable Viennese Hebrew poet, Avraham Ben Yitzhak Sonne (the friend of Hermann Broch, Arthur Schnitzler, Robert Musil, and others), Lea Goldberg wryly observes, "Listening to him, I would sometimes think, that's the way our intelligentsia ought to talk, if we had a Hebrew-speaking intelligentsia." This is just what she herself was—not exactly a literary intellectual in the American sense, not really an academician, and certainly not a "lady poet," but an authentic member of a Hebrew-speaking intelligentsia that existed more as an ideal than as a cultural fact. "Intelligentsia" may suggest, among other things, a self-conscious class of intellectuals impelled by a sense of social commitment or explicitly political identity, and of these qualities there was no lack among the European-born Hebrew literati. In Lea Goldberg's usage, however, the term also implies urbanity— in fact, she later invokes the English word to characterize Sonne—and few Hebrew writers have possessed that faculty of cultivated, discriminating discourse as she did.

The virtues of her literary criticism, and its limitations, are precisely those of good conversation. The beginning of her essay on Chekhov is exemplary: "It is hard to talk about Chekhov. Perhaps harder than about any other writer. He was so careful with the use of words, hated every superfluous word; and in speaking or writing about him there is a sense of uneasiness: one can hardly stint words, but in their profusion, many will seem superfluous." As an unaffected admission of critical humility before the mastery of the artist, this is perfect, and the ease of clear statement itself illustrates the interchangeability of writing and speaking that the writer assumes in her passing reference to them here. The essay that follows, like most of Lea Goldberg's criticism is in keeping with this beginning—sensible, informed, persuasive, but finally less than illuminating. For all her literary intelligence and her minute knowledge of criticism and scholarship in the various Western languages, she seemed to shrink with a kind of aesthetic reticence from the spinning of theories, the erecting of systems of interpretation, the deployment of elaborate apparatuses of technical analysis, all those studied strategies and devices through which critics achieve, or aspire to, "brilliance." If as a result her criticism often merely restates aptly what an intelligent reader could more or less see for himself, it has the compensating virtue of continuously preserving the notion of both literature and criticism as modes of humanistic discourse. The frequent, thoroughly natural use of the first person plural in her criticism is a clue to its distinctive quality: her "we" is not of the authoritative editorial variety, nor is it a rhetorical ploy to implicate the reader in the attitudes and conclusions of the writer, but, quite simply, it is spoken on behalf of all us human beings for whom and about whom another human being—Chekhov, Tolstoy, Boccaccio, or whoever the case may be—wrote a work of art to make some abiding sense of our shared human condition.

The commitment to civilized discourse may also explain something about the nature of Lea Goldberg's poetry, which, written with the fullest awareness of the labyrinthine obliquities and bold discontinuities dominating modern poetic idiom, remained always direct, lucid, almost deceptively simple in form. She was a devoted student of the French, German, and Russian Symbolists, but the only poet close to the Symbolist movement she noticeably resembles is Verlaine, with his melodic orchestration of assonance, alliteration, and rhyme, his attachment to stanzaic forms, and the general attitude toward style he announced in his famous *Art Poétique:* "Take eloquence and wring its neck." Modern Hebrew poetry, freighted with allusion, rising against a vast background of biblical high style, had characteristically cultivated grand effects, pathos, passion, and prophetic rage, while Lea Goldberg brought to Hebrew verse a subtle sense of beauty in small words and small things, a gracefulness and even playfulness of style. Here, for example, is a little poem called "The Alley," one of a series of evocative vignettes of Lithuanian provincial life grouped together under the general title, *From My Old Home.* I have tried to offer in my translation some equivalent for the witty interplay of rhythm and rhyme in the original:

> The alley is narrow.
> Pail bumps pail.
> A girl's laughter.
> Scarlet ribbon-tail.
>
> Flitted past,
> Barefoot best.
> Gray stone
> Caressed.

I do not mean to imply that poetry for Lea Goldberg was in any way a flight from the horrors of history or the pain of adult life into a world of pretty little things. On the contrary, one senses in the quietly stated beauty of her brief lyric poems a certain tough strength precisely because that ordered beauty stands in tense relation with a dark background of chaos, ugliness, suffering. If she shows great fondness, at times to an excess, for the legacy of imagery of Romantic poetry and traditional folksong—setting suns, lonely birds in the sky, blossoming cherry trees, the murmur of strummed instruments—these traditional properties often seem freshly perceived and surprisingly persuasive because the poet has rediscovered them, somehow through inner struggle has won back from the chaos of modern experience the recurrent objects of eternal beauty. Blood-madness and death wait in the shadow of the flowering cherry tree, which is why we are ready to believe that the tree—"a white storm of florescence" —is really there for the poet, not simply an easy invocation of literary tradition.

In this regard, Lea Goldberg's single ventures into drama and fiction, her play, *The Mistress of the Castle*, and her novel, *That Is the Light*, make explicit a pattern that is implicit, or has already been worked through psychologically, in the best of her poems. The fictional settings and imaginative modes of the two works are very different. The play deals with a young survivor of the Holocaust during the immediate postwar period in a manner that tends toward melodrama and quasi-allegorical schematization. The novel, incorporating more obviously autobiographical elements, is a subdued realistic account, rendered from the protagonist's point of view, of a 1931 summer spent at home in a Lithuanian town by a troubled young girl who has been off studying in Berlin. Yet the underlying movement of plot in the play and the novel is essentially the same. In each case, a sensitive girl, not yet come of age, has been confronted by the adult world with personal and historical facts of terror that tempt her to choose madness—seen as a virtual suicide—rather than adult life. In each case, the protagonist finally resolves, in the words of the novel, that "our lives will be life . . . in utter defiance of all the makers of history who torture children and murder their parents." Interestingly, in each case it is a piece of poetry—in the play, a children's song, in the novel, a remembered line from the medieval Hebrew poet, Moses Ibn Ezra—that the protagonist clings to as a talisman to help her out of the nightmare of violated childhood into a hoped-for world of light.

The simplicity, then, of Lea Goldberg's language represents in part an almost ascetic avoidance of any stylistic intimations of sublimity or profundity or exaltation that have not been fully earned by the poet through her experience. Her own *art poétique* is spelled out in this passage from a late poem, "On Myself," where musings on the nature of the poetic act—a recurrent concern in her verse—merge with self-revelation:

I have no hard words—
Valves of hallucination.
My images are
Transparent like church windows
Through which
One can see
The changing of light in the sky
And the falling
Like dead birds
Of my loves.

The apparent incongruity of the metaphor in the second line
here is purposeful, ironically expressing a suspicion that
poems with grand visionary qualities use language as an ingenious mechanical apparatus to produce what may finally be
trick effects. The poet's own imagery, by contrast, has the
simple function of stained glass, to let in the plain light of day,
only coloring and patterning what is "out there" with the
significant forms of a traditional art. (One thinks of George
Herbert's "Church Windows.") The controlled statement of
personal loss in these lines is typical of Lea Goldberg at her
best: avoiding the sentimentalism of self-pity and the extravagance of self-dramatization, she expresses pain in a way that
is at once chastened and almost blunt, depending for its
strong effect only on its final placing and on the plummeting
rhythm of the last words.

If there is an element of starkness in her late work that
does not entirely typify the earlier poems, her poetic style on
the whole is nevertheless spare, understated, at its weaker
moments perhaps too given to easy musicality and obvious
conventional imagery, but for the most part orchestrating
avowedly traditional materials with exquisite tact. Thus, at
the beginning of one of her reminiscent poems about the
Lithuania of her childhood: "Servant girls singing like gui-
tars,/ Barefoot, with the setting sun." There is no effort to
surprise here, nothing of the typically modern tendency to
give individual images and words a quality of violent autonomy, no element in this line and a half that is not drawn from
the repertory of familiar poetic tradition. Yet the elements are
adjusted together to achieve a finely luminous effect, produc-

ing the kind of total poetic phrase that lingers in the ear of the imagination.

There are whole poems wrought entirely from such traditional images and conventions. The more successful of these are not imitative but rather become quietly resonant renewals of a familiar poetic heritage. At times it seems almost as though Lea Goldberg were harking back to some medieval conception of the poetic act, in which "originality" is not sought after at all, where the poet aims rather to achieve a delicately attuned, graceful variation on received patterns, the "truth" of the poem being a product of the interaction between assured individual craftsmanship and the expressive possibilities of the tradition. Thus, a poem called "Last Brightness" is in effect a fine distillation of untold poems about autumn, parting, and bereavement, making a personal statement through the imagistic clarity and strategically managed musicality with which it reworks the known conventions:

> The gleaming of gold deceives—
> This is the last brightness.
> A glassy blue now crowns
> The heads of the mountains.
>
> Another few days, before long,
> Stripped trees will be standing
> Like ancient, mute instruments
> Beautifully strung.
>
> A pale and trembling morning
> Will touch chill stone.
> And a bird on its way to exile will call
> From cold heavens.

What makes this poetry, however, more than a judicious synthesis of traditional materials is the faculty of immediate vision it clearly exhibits. It is a quality easier to see in the poetry itself than to describe, so I will offer two final examples to illustrate how the imagination seems to perceive poetic objects directly rather than labor to contrive them into poetry. The first poem is called "Night":

The sky sways in the wind,
Like a tree shaking its leaves
Stars shake,
Green and damp
And their scent—wild grass.

The sky sways in the wind—
And we below
Behold the flowering:
Now, now . . .
Did you hear?
In the skytop
The rustling of stars is distraught.

Most poems which, like this one, pursue a single metaphorical comparison from beginning to end have the effect of turning the comparison into a conceit, or, at any rate, clearly represent the "elaboration," as we say, of a central metaphor. Here, the perception of stars as leaves—with its double suggestion that the vault of the sky is within hand's reach and, disturbingly, is shaken by the same winds that sweep the unstable earth—seems rather an immediate experience, not consciously elaborated but followed from moment to moment; so that "Did you hear?" near the end is not a rhetorical affectation but a cry that springs from the immediacy of what is seen.

My last example is somewhat more complicated. One of a group of poems with the Rimbaudesque title, "Illuminations," its two stanzas would appear to stand in a relation of parable and meaning, but that relation is not made explicit, and each remains an independent moment of revelation, overlapping the other, extending its possibilities of implication:

Across one of the hills
Flies an orange bird
Whose name I do not know.
But the olive trees know her,
The wind, pursuing her, sings:
Your home is here.

In the eyes of a small Arab girl
At the edge of the village in ruins

An orange bird flutters
Whose name I do not know.

This is one of those rare instances in which ultimately political facts have been transmuted into the fuller and more subtle mode of meaning of poetic statement. The lines linger over the ambiguities of estrangement and belonging; express the speaker's troubled sense of unnavigable distance between herself and the bird, the landscape, the Arab girl; encompass suffering in an almost painterly image of beauty—the bright bird against the somber gray-green of the olive trees—that does not prettify the suffering but, on the contrary, reveals it more sharply, leads us to ponder its enigmatic intimations.

Lea Goldberg was herself heavily burdened with the awareness of how difficult it is to go on with poetry in a world that brutally violates every object of poetic desire and every image of poetic order. Many of her late poems are meditations on silence ("All my psalms were slaughtered./ All my words/ Were killed./ Even the name of this stone on my mouth/ I cannot pronounce"); and in fact during the last four or five years of her life she virtually stopped writing poetry. This is another facet of the affinity she felt for Avraham Ben Yitzhak Sonne, whose minuscule production is the purest example in Hebrew literature of a movement toward *écriture blanche*, actually ending in a beautiful hymn to wordlessness. In this connection, there is one especially unsettling passage in Lea Goldberg's book on him. Commenting on Nietzsche's poem, "On the Bridge in Venice," which ends with the words, *"Hörte mir jemand zu?"* Sonne observed to Lea Goldberg: "Poetry seeks an echo but no longer finds it. That question-mark after the cry remains unanswered. From this point, the debacle begins. Language has had its day, behind it there is nothing more." The debacle has indeed begun. It is hard to imagine a serious poet now who does not feel compelled in one way or another to ask himself Nietzsche's question, whether there is anyone to listen to him, and the fear that it is all over with language itself cannot be very far from any of us.

Language, however, no matter how we blunt it, maim it, degrade it, prostitute it, remains the uniquely human invention, and therefore poetry, as the most complex expressive ordering of language, remains an indispensable human activity. It is suggestive that the major poet of the Israeli war generation, Yehuda Amichai, recalls in a poem on Lea Goldberg's death that during the Negev campaign of 1948, he carried with him everywhere in his battle-pack a pamphlet edition—battered, held together with scotch tape—of *From My Old Home.* What Lea Goldberg's poetry has meant to many Hebrew writers and readers is itself testimony to the abiding strength of this most fragile form of human discourse.

—1970

May it never befall you,
All you who pass along the road!
Look about and see:
Is there any agony like mine,
Which was dealt out to me,
When the Lord afflicted me
On His day of wrath?

—Lamentations 1:12

Uri Zvi Greenberg:
A Poet of the Holocaust

The relation of Hebrew poetry to the Holocaust is a peculiar
one, largely because many readers and some writers of Hebrew poetry tend to have rather special expectations of it as
an instrument of response to national calamity. The old tradition of Hebrew poetry as a vehicle of prophetic burden has not
entirely been dissipated, despite the aesthetic preference of
most younger Israelis and the practice of most Hebrew poets
below the age of fifty. In regard to historical disaster, the
paradigm of the biblical Book of Lamentations remains especially potent. Composed, one may still assume, in the immediate aftermath of the conquest of Jerusalem in 587 B.C.E., it
records the horrors of bloody defeat in a heavily cadenced
accumulation of grim, concrete images, setting history in the
deepening perspective of divine purpose; and the book has
become with the passage of time the focus of a national rite,
solemnly chanted in a minor key every year on the Fast of the

103

Ninth of Ab. After the model of Lamentations, each major persecution from the massacres of the First Crusade onward elicited its own *kinah*, or dirge—usually drawing heavily on the language and symbols of Lamentations, Jeremiah, and the Midrashim about the destruction of the Second Temple—and these in turn often became part of the official liturgy for the day of national mourning.

It is, I think, this long chain of historical precedents which particularly fostered in Hebrew circles a dim sense that poetry should be able to yield some sort of definitive account of the Holocaust, a reverberant evocation of its terrible meaning under the aspect of eternity. Now, this expectation was based on two obviously anachronistic assumptions. To begin with, it presupposed the possibility of meaning in the face of such events, assuming by constraint what the author of Lamentations could assume quite naturally, that a higher plan was unfolding through history, however ghastly some stages of its implementation might be. The second assumption was that it was still possible for a poet to submerge his individuality in a collective identity, as Hebrew poets for three millennia had done, and thus to speak for the whole people in its historical anguish. In point of fact, the overwhelming direction of Hebrew poetry in recent decades has been toward a concentration on private and quotidian experience, toward the cultivation of a nuanced personal voice, and, as in other modern literatures, toward the affirmation of selfhood, not peoplehood, as the proper sphere of literary expression. Given this fundamental tension between classic Hebrew precedent and contemporary poetic practice, it is a serious question whether there can still be any convincing alternative to the prevalent modern stance of the poet as the explorer of his own experience.

Among Hebrew poets in our time, the one great exception that proves—in the proper sense, tests—the rule is Uri Zvi Greenberg. Greenberg, born in a Galician village in 1894 and a resident of Israel since 1924, is such a thorough maverick, such an uncompromising extremist in all his aesthetic and ideological positions, that there is a strange sort of integrity in the very purity of his oppositionalism. His politics are on the far fringe of the messianic Right: he worked as an organizer and publicist for the Revisionist movement in the thirties; during the forties he was active in the terrorist Irgun; he seems to entertain the notion of a restoration of the Davidic dynasty as something more than a poetic conceit; and he has denounced as backsliders and traitors all who lack his single-handed dedication to fulfilling the manifest destiny of the Jewish people, which is to triumph by might over its historical enemies, Christianity and Islam. There is hardly any point in debating Greenberg's political views; what concerns me is how these views have determined his posture as a poet, how far they are compatible with what readers not sharing his outlook might perceive as good poetry. Let me say at the outset that I think there is real poetic genius in Uri Zvi Greenberg. It is precisely the presence of genius that makes it worth considering how, given his commitments, he has used or abused his gifts.

Though much of Greenberg's earliest Hebrew poetry (he had written first in Yiddish) was intensely personal and showed conscious affinities with European expressionism, he began to insist as far back as 1924 on the obligation of the poet to serve as the voice of national destiny in the making and to eschew at all costs the arid aestheticism of the Gentiles. By 1928, he was calling for the emergence of a Hebrew Walt Whitman (with himself clearly in mind), Whitman being conceived as someone grander than a mere individual poet, the bardic singer of a nation's soul. Special dispensation could be made for a poet like Whitman as having been "molded from the clay of a Hebrew prophet," but in the same manifesto Greenberg declared an absolute difference between Jewish and Gentile creativity: "The foreign peoples have nine muses, but ours is the tenth, the hidden muse: Judaism with all its aspects in the light of messianism." As the political crisis in Palestine and in Europe grew graver through the thirties, Greenberg pursued his own declared program more and more vehemently in his poetry. He was in Poland on a mission for the Revisionists when the war broke out in 1939, and was barely able to escape and make his way back to Palestine. Then, as the tide of mass murder rapidly engulfed what had been for centuries the teeming centers of European Jewry, destroying, among millions of others, Greenberg's parents and sister, he began to produce the enormous poetic outpouring of wrath and anguish that would become *Streets of the River: The Book of Dirges and Power* (1951).

Streets of the River is at its best a strong book, indeed, a deeply disturbing book, and one that is strenuously intended to resemble nothing so much as itself, or the earlier poems of its author. Not surprisingly, it was seized on in the years following its initial publication—the Hebrew original has been reissued several times, though an English edition has not yet appeared—by a good many Hebrew critics as the awaited inspired text on the Holocaust, the authoritative utterance for our traumatic times of the prophetic voice in the language of the classical prophets. Now, over twenty years after the appearance of the volume, a more sober appraisal seems warranted. The scale of the book, its originality, and what must be called the grandeur of its conception, clearly still set it apart as the most substantial poetic response in Hebrew, perhaps in any language, to the destruction of European Jewry. In these 385 pages of verse—lyric, dramatic, narrative, balladic, and hortatory—there is poetry that one can guess many generations of Jews will continue to live with, compelled by the mesmeric force of Greenberg's vision of genocide and regeneration. Nevertheless, what is likely to strike a reader at this distance from the events and the composition of the poems is the yawning gap between achievement and failure in the same poetic structure. On the one hand, many of the poems have a delicate, hauntingly poignant lyricism or dazzling moments of hallucinatory power; on the other hand, there is page after repetitious page of doggerel and rant, conveyed through hollow rhetorical flourishes in mechanical rhythms and rhymes, or, alternately, in sprawling free verse. This startling discrepancy seems to me worth exploring because I think it may reveal something about the intrinsic problematic of making poetry respond to an ultimate historical horror.

Greenberg means not only to record the immediate pain of a people's bereavement but to bring to bear on it a transhistorical perspective, which is to say, to fit the historical suffering of the Jews into a large structure of myth. The

people of Israel is seen as a great irreversible river-tide flowing out of Abraham—his name, *Av Ram*, is etymologized as "High Father"—across the centuries, past the green banks of the alien Gentile world. Its fate is to be hated and persecuted, its divinely appointed destiny is to prevail triumphant. Abraham is "the lord of law, vision, and yearning," qualities which are presumed to be the unique legacy of Israel. Greenberg repeatedly emphasizes blood as the medium for the transmission of this heritage, and his view of history is frankly, defiantly, racist. Humankind is divided into two irreconcilable groups: the seed of Israel, which bears within it the gifts of true belief, compassion, lawfulness, and the Gentiles, who are by the necessity of their inner nature ravening forest beasts, showing at best only the deceptive veneer of civilization in a Beethoven, a Goethe, or a Kant.

It hardly needs to be said that this drastic polarization of humanity does considerable violence to historical fact, however much Jews have suffered at the hands of Gentiles, but, again, the question I would like to pursue is not the tenability of Greenberg's beliefs but what kind of poetry he makes out of them. In any case, *Streets of the River* is shot through with contradictions within its own mythic version of the Jews as the unique people of mercy and refined spirituality because the militant poet lays great stress on the most primitive, vengeful layers of the Bible as the basis for renewed Jewish existence. Even rabbinic Judaism tends to be translated back into the fierce ethos of the most archaic passages of the Bible, as in the chilling moment when the poet, in the presence of his murdered father, recites the following benediction, taking off from the rabbinic formula for a blessing said before the performance of a divinely enjoined act: "Blessed are you, O Lord our God, King of the World, who sanctified us through Your commandments and commanded us to take blood for blood, life for life."

To be fair to the quality of Greenberg's achievement, one must say that the visionary strength of his imagination is such that within this skewed framework of myth he is able to create images of the Holocaust as a cosmic event that are utterly compelling. Let me cite just one example from many possible ones, an apocalyptic moment that occurs in the opening poem of *Streets of the River:*[1]

> It is not the morning star ascending in the east.
> Look, brother,
> It is a skull, a Jew's skull, whose skin has been stripped,
> Still in its fresh redness burning brightly
> As in the Creator's thought before the creation of man.

It is the last line here that provides the special Greenberg twist, wrenching horror into a perspective of theological grandeur, joining death with birth, annihilation with creation. For the most part, however, it is in those poems which emphasize most directly the grand myth of Jewish history that one feels Greenberg's greatest lapses as a poet. Not to belabor the point, I will offer just a half-dozen characteristic lines from a long poem called "Song of the Great March." Prosodically, the lines have a Whitmanesque rambling quality for which Greenberg shows excessive fondness, and which itself has the effect of encouraging in him a tendency to prosy expository statement:

> Here we are now, the Jews in the world, with all that land of
>   killing going 'round in our hearts.
> An army ancient of days, but weaponless, its flags torn,
>   wound-dark, pain-heavy,
> And without commanders to go before it, experts of distance,
>   adept in maneuvers. . . .
> We are all an army that persisted in battle though battered,
>   our souls like our flesh stricken with stillness,
> But our will to live, to come back to reign as we reigned,
>   from field to sea, fortress, and wall,
> Has not been battered in battle, not subdued by the sword,
>   nor yielded to the teeth of despair and pain.

Poetry places far greater demands on the imagination than ideology in regard to the perception of complexity and variety, and what one senses here, as in many extended passages of *Streets of the River,* is that the verse medium has been reduced to a rumbling vehicle for an ideological message.

[1]The translations throughout are my own.–R. A.

Part of the trouble is that we know too much about Jewish history through its various and ambiguous course for this to carry much conviction, and one suspects that even an extremist like Greenberg, in some corner of his consciousness, knows too much about Jewish history really to be able to imagine it adequately, concretely, in this melodramatic image of an embattled army. There is something at once hackneyed and vague about the handling of the whole military symbolism, and Greenberg, as though finding himself deprived of his better poetic resources, resorts to facile word play (which I have tried to imitate at a couple of points in my translation) and to stringing together political slogans ("our will to live, to come back to reign . . .").

The underlying problem of confronting the Holocaust by means of a myth might be stated in another way. The essence of historical experience, as Philip Rahv has persuasively argued, is constant change and innovation, while myth by its nature implies cyclicality, timeless repetition. To render history as myth, then, is to violate the essentially multifarious character of history. This is precisely what Greenberg does. Again and again he insists that Jewish history, from Abraham to Auschwitz, is a single repeated tale of persecution and persistence. In all times and places he sees the same enemy in a thousand different masks, "The same implements of torture, the same cellars of terror." Amalek, Assyria, Babylonia, Rome, Spain, and Portugal, the medieval Germanic states and modern Germany, are equally "the terror itself without trope or simile: there is nothing else, it's all of them." It is putting it mildly to say that there is a flattening and simplification of the facts of Jewish history in this vision of them. One, of course, must grant lines of continuity in this body of history, but the awful uniqueness of the Holocaust itself is diminished by its being set at a dead level with all previous tribulations —as, for example, when the furnaces at Auschwitz are equated with the furnace of Ur of the Chaldees, the latter being strictly an invention of rabbinic legend in which Abraham was tried and found steadfast, and surely belonging to a drastically different world from that of the Final Solution. What it is possible for a poet to imagine credibly about history depends in part on his own location in history. For the Psalmist or for the author of Lamentations, the coordinates of knowledge of a whole culture made it natural to see historical events falling into a neatly traceable pattern of recurrence, or of ebb and flow. In the middle of the twentieth century, to insist on such a pattern means willfully to impose a cloudy generality on the commonly perceived multiplicity of historical experience; and, on the level of poetic style, this leads to exhortation instead of evocation, to vagueness, contrived allegorical tableaux, stylistic clichés, and mere ideological catchwords.

A final problematic aspect of this attempt by a modern poet to create a national myth in his work is the kind of *persona* that addresses us through the poems. In fact, as we shall see, there are two very different *personae* in *Streets of the River*, roughly correlated with its successes and failures, but the one Greenberg consciously wants to be prominent is precisely the sort of speaker that a national myth would seem to require— an authoritative voice of the genius of the people through the ages, thundering dire warnings, trumpeting affirmations. The poet of *Streets of the River* presents himself as a prophet and castigator, as a consuming fire of truth, a lonely, sharp-toothed panther among the complacent fools of his generation. At moments, he has flashes of real poetic megalomania, as when, at the climax of one vision, he announces, "And the wall/ Of mighty existence collapsed before the sun of song."

To point to the extravagance of all this is not to question its sincerity; nothing is sincerer than fanaticism, and Greenberg often seems close to that condition. The more crucial consideration is not sincerity but authenticity, which is a matter not only of the speaker's expressive intention but also of how that intention can be received and construed by others in the specific cultural and historical context for which the poem was created. When the prophet Amos walked into the central square of Bethel and began denouncing the ruling elite of the Israelite kingdom, he was acting in a concrete context in which it was thoroughly credible, though also rather dangerous, for a man to speak poetry as the direct message of God. When a modern poet like Greenberg assumes an analogous posture, most of his contemporaries, not sharing the assumptions of his poetical faith, are likely to perceive such writing

as an extreme act of grandiosity. The subtle, profound operation of rhetorical credibility upon which all literary authenticity depends then breaks down, the prophet in his own eyes having become a pompous preacher in the eyes of others. Though we may read in general by a willing suspension of disbelief, the writer has to make it at least feasible for us to effect the suspension.

I would suggest that in most cases the only workable way to use biblical materials for the expression of contemporary experience is somehow to stand the sources on their heads, borrowing images, symbols, and situations for the expressive needs of a very different kind of poetic voice. Let me propose for a moment a contrasting example to everything I have been considering so far in Greenberg, both because it is instructive in its own right and because it may provide a useful perspective on the other *persona* of *Streets of the River*. Amir Gilboa, a generation younger than Greenberg, is also European-born: his whole immediate family in the Ukraine was murdered by the Nazis; and, understandably, his Hebrew poems through the late forties and fifties reflect considerable preoccupation with the Holocaust, though they remain distinctly personal poems, and he has never attempted a sustained poetic work on the subject. I might add that stylistically Gilboa moved from a tendency to excessive ornateness in his earliest verse of the forties to a distinctive kind of cultivated simplicity. The poem I would like to cite, "By the Waters of Babylon," is a radical reworking of Psalm 137, which begins with those words. It reassembles principal elements of the psalm—the sitting and weeping by the waters, the hanging up of harps on the willows, the mockery of the captors—in a new order of meaning which is, from one point of view, a vivid image of the predicament of the bereaved poet in a world of holocausts:

> On the willows we hung our harps. I mean the grown-ups.
> As for me, I had a little harp and I hid it under my cloak.
> On the far side of the river the victors lit fires and wild with
>   joy they reveled.
> Evening fell and fell. The grown-ups sat crying. A big fire
>   over there.

Uri Zvi Greenberg: A Poet of the Holocaust 111

And the guards assigned to us, not taking part in the
   dancing,
Reviling us out of impatience, raucously,
Aping our language in grotesque ways.

The grown-ups listened, and looked at their harps. The
   waters filled with tears.
And I out of sorrow dared to cry out: Who is grotesque here,
You wild beasts, and how can you mock us with gibberish?
For there is no language like ours for color and sound, for
   depth and distance.

And they laughed louder, their mouths gaped at me.
They began chasing me, getting entangled in darkness.
I would stop to rest a brief moment briefly to pluck my harp,
They would swell like sacks, glow like copper.

This is, of course, rather strange, but the strangeness
seems to me arresting and suggestive. By casting himself in
the role of a helpless child menaced by cruel captors, the poet
closes the distance between himself and the biblical scene,
making it pulse with the immediacy of a contemporary event,
despite the archaic harps. The wavering of the language between a child's speech and formal poetic diction helps create
this bridge, as do the rapid shifts in verb tenses, which move
from past to present to an imperfect that is a virtual present.
What finally drives the child, as the poet's surrogate, to dis-
traction, is the enemy's vilification of his language, which
seems to him a very precious thing, a unique reservoir of
expressiveness. In the face of brutal historical disaster, the
poet has only the resources of his art to cling to, but in the
end these may amount to no more than the pathetic plucking
of harpstrings by a frail figure resting for a moment in desperate flight. Gilboa, like Greenberg, feels the distinctive
beauty and crystallized cultural experience of the Hebrew
that is his instrument, but "By the Waters of Babylon" precisely reverses the idea of poetry's overwhelming power
which is celebrated in *Streets of the River*.

The child seems a particularly plausible *persona* for the
poet confronted with the Holocaust because helplessness,
fear, impotent rage, incomprehension are such likely responses to that unassimilable historical reality, at least when

a writer tries to imagine it personally and concretely, not ideologically. Gilboa in fact uses the child as *persona* in a number of remarkable poems in which biblical figures are appropriated for contemporary purposes. I would like to quote just one of these, before we try to see how all this bears on Greenberg, because it is such a striking illustration of just that quality of poetic authenticity to which I have alluded. The poem, "Isaac," represents Abraham and Isaac on the way to the sacrifice, with one crucial alteration of the original story; but its first-person narration by a child Isaac breaks down partitions between present and past, waking and nightmare, and projects through the prism of the biblical scene one of the most concentrated images of the Holocaust's sheer senseless horror that any Hebrew poet has fashioned:

> At daybreak the sun took a walk in the forest
> Together with me and with Father,
> My right hand in his left.
>
> Like lightning a knife flamed among the trees.
> And I so dread the fear of my eyes facing the
>   blood on the leaves.
>
> Father, Father, quick save Isaac,
> Then no one will be missing at lunch.
>
> It is I who am slaughtered, my son,
> My blood even now on the leaves.
> And Father, his voice was stopped up.
> And his face was pale.
>
> And I wanted to scream, writhing not to believe,
> Tearing open my eyes.
> I awoke.
>
> And the right hand was drained of blood.

Now, if one turns back to *Streets of the River* with the example of Gilboa in mind, one sees the strategic importance of the fact that over against the patriarchal-prophetic stance of the poet who calls himself *Avleshonram*, Father of the High One's Tongue, there is another speaker, an orphaned child lost in the world and aching for his parents. Though there are some significant exceptions to this general rule, it is by and large those poems of Greenberg's in which the child is speaker that most fully persuade us of their authenticity as responses to the Holocaust. Even the language in these poems is for the most part noticeably different—not high and hortatory but generally simple, dramatically direct, finely modulated, rich in concrete imagery. Despite Greenberg's dedication to the Tenth Muse of messianic purpose, he has included poems in this volume which are not only highly personal but which are no more than obliquely related to the destruction of European Jewry. Intertwined with the subject of the Holocaust is a mourning over a lost childhood, which occasionally is even cast in "Wordsworthian" terms as a universal experience of deprivation that has no necessary connection with the murder of the parents and the devastation of their world. In "Man Dies in the Valley," a poem that provides one of the conceptual keys to *Streets of the River*, Greenberg imagines every human being descending by stages from infancy's mount of beatitude, where a Jacob's ladder stands by the crib, to a dark valley at the bottom of time, where the exposed child needs his mother terribly but will never find her: "As the cradle days of childhood pass/ The little ladder vanishes,/ The angels of childhood vanish/ Unnoticed. . . . A stillness,/ Like after the playing on strings."

On close consideration, a peculiar paradox emerges from *Streets of the River*. The emotion consciously intended by the poet to inform this large imaginative structure is fiery wrath, but the most convincingly realized emotion in the book—perhaps its deepest feeling—is nostalgia. In this regard, the role of the mother, and the anguish of separation from the mother, are crucially important, as, indeed, they are in much of Greenberg's poetry both before and after *Streets of the River*. It is only a little overstated to say that the sense of reality in Greenberg's poetry radiates out from the remembered image of the mother. Idealized but also often delicately eroticized, she is the poet's one abiding model of a meaningful, happy connection with things outside himself. (The father, though also portrayed lovingly in many of the poems, is less central and more ambiguous, sometimes appearing as an Abraham

sacrificing his son or as a proponent of the ways of exile/emasculation, symbolically taking away his son's sword.) No other woman, the poet tells us several times, can give him the joy and beauty he knew at his mother's breast. In one poem the adult poet, sitting in a bar in Tel Aviv, sadly contemplates his body and wonders how it was once caressed by a mother, gently lifted up by her to the *mezuzah* each night and then laid to sleep in that long-vanished home. Indeed, some of the finest moments in *Streets of the River* are imagined returns to the home in the Galician village, filled with vividly recollected details. Everything in these scenes becomes intensely real because the poet's imagination can focus around the felt reality of loving closeness to the mother. The sham reality of adult experience, scarcely to be credited or honored, falls away, and the palpable substance of living existence is, at least for a fleeting moment, recovered.

I do not want to suggest that the subject of *Streets of the River* is only ostensibly the Holocaust and that the book should really be read as a kind of Hebrew *Prelude,* a study of the tragic growth of the poet's mind. On the contrary, it seems to me that the recurrent stress on the universal human loss of primal harmony is precisely Greenberg's most effective means of making the loss of European Jewry accessible to the imagination. This does not of course imply that the prolonged trauma of "descent" from childhood is in any way commensurable with the horror of a political force that with carefully coordinated administrative and technical machinery could gas and incinerate several million innocent human beings. That horror, however, remains ultimately impenetrable, for all our elaborate attempts to analyze it as being everything from banal to diabolic, because the very idea of its possibility reduces all we would build in our lives individually and collectively to rubble. To impose upon the Holocaust in a long series of poems some large symbolic scheme must to some extent falsify our perception of it by trying to elicit an eschatological clash between evil and good from facts too abysmal for any notions so traditional, so implicitly hopeful. What the poet is likely to find more within the reach of thought and feeling artfully ordered through language is not the horror itself, not the broad workings of history by which it came to be, but his own sense of loss and consternation after the awful fact.

To the Jews as a people, the element of irrevocable loss is bound to be particularly salient for the obvious reason that the whole variegated cultural world, from the Volga to the Garonne, from which a large part of living Jewry derives its values, its distinctive identity, and its physical parentage, was in less than six years destroyed for all time. In *Streets of the River* the loss of the parents flows directly into the loss of the world whose exemplars they are for the poet. The inevitable estrangement from the realm of childhood is of course made overwhelmingly sharper, more anguished, by the cataclysmic destruction of everyone who belonged to that realm, and the poet's personal bereavement becomes a concrete, imaginable instance of the bereavement of the entire people.

The laments over the precious world of childhood lost are more than exemplary, for in them the poet succeeds in achieving on a small scale what elsewhere he does rather less convincingly on a more grandiose scale—the creation of a myth to give emotional coherence and dramatic definition to the experience of loss. This myth works, I suspect, because its *dramatis personae* are figures intimately known and felt by the poet, now enlarged and made luminous as they are interwoven with strands of legendary lore and set in a timeless perspective. The murdered mother, father, and sister become a kind of Holy Family, undergoing through martyrdom a celestial Ascension, concentrating in their transfigured presence all the beauty that was cut off, all the felt pain of their separation from the surviving son. In one of these personal visionary poems, Greenberg imagines the celebration of a ghostly Sabbath in heaven, his mother standing protectively over the naked, bloodied figure of his sister, who seems to be purposely confused with the Sabbath itself: "The heavens are hushed . . . and so one can hear the sound of stars whispering/ Like coals of fire murmuring Aramaic:/ *Betulta Kadishta Shabbat Malketa.* Holy Virgin Sabbath Queen." The ingenious device of the Aramaic line makes the image sound like something straight out of the *Zohar,* but in fact there is no *Betulta Kadishta,* no Holy Virgin, in classical Jewish sources, and the seemingly Kabbalistic mythic figure is a direct borrowing from Christianity. This minor detail is worth noting because it points to the fact that the indigenously Jewish character of Greenberg's poetry is not quite so "pure" as he would lead us to think, and in a similar way, the personal impulse in this book is stronger than we might initially conclude from its insistent national emphases.

One of the lyric peaks of *Streets of the River* is a group of four poems entitled "Songs at the Borders of the Heavens" which finely etches the family myth. In the first poem of the group, the speaker sees his martyred parents sinking into the watery depths, then ascending, on both sides of the setting sun, with the burning sea beneath their feet. The second poem moves from sea-changes to mysterious sea-crossings, and here the particular details of the poet's recollected image of his parents are especially prominent. The poem, called "Silence's Martyrs," is a beautiful example of how the artful rendering of personal anguish can reach beyond itself. The extraordinary delicacy of the language and the plangent musicality of the verse regrettably resist translation, but even in my awkward English version one may get some sense of the poem's quiet strength. If at first glance there seems to be a climactic note of self-pity at the end, the pathos of abandonment has a special resonance, a special justification, precisely because profoundly implicated in the first-person singular of the poem is a first-person plural, the orphaned poet intimating through the dramatization of his own plight that of the orphaned people.

In a poet so imaginatively involved as Greenberg with the historical destiny of his people, at some point the distinction between personal and national obviously breaks down. Nevertheless, one may learn something about the possible relation of modern poetry to national experience from the fact that the most convincing expressions of the fate of the people even in this supremely nationalist poet seem for the most part to come in his most intimately personal poems, like "Silence's Martyrs." One must imagine the poet as lost child, after the Holocaust, standing on the eastern shore of the Mediterranean looking to the west and north into the great empty kingdom of death:

On the moonlit nights my martyred mother says
To my martyred father:
When I gave birth to the boy the moon dropped by in the
    window.
At once he opened his eyes and beheld her; since then
Her brightness has sung in his blood till this day
And the moon has been walking since then in his poems.

Much never-stilled longing there was in my father,
But the magic coach never stood by his house
When he longed.
And so he knew silence and melody
And loved-with-his-eyes the wings of birds.
—"When they want to fly, off they fly, just like that."—

But my mother . . . her longing was hitched to the magical
    coach.
By the beat of the heart every cell of her knew how to walk
With both feet on the sea:
By the path-of-the-moon-on-the-waves
To me, to her son, in Zion—
But she would not find me in wait at the shore,
She'd go back with the path-of-the-moon-on-the-waves:
Weary of wandering, feverish, seastruck.

Now, both my mother and father are silence's martyrs.
There's a path-of-the-moon on glittering waves
And an only son
The remaining one
In the world.

—1973

> Impossible *to communicate anything but particulars—historical and contemporary things, human beings as things, their instrumentalities of capillaries and veins binding up and bound up with events and contingencies.*
>
> —Louis Zukofsky
> "An Objective" (1930)

Charles Reznikoff:
Between Present and Past

When Charles Reznikoff died in January 1976, at the age of eighty-one, he had only recently begun to be generally recognized as an important American poet of the mid-century decades. Until the New Directions selection of his poems in 1962, *By the Waters of Manhattan,* all of the dozen volumes of verse he had up to then produced had been published privately—some actually set in type by the poet himself—or by the small Objectivist Press, "an organization of writers," as its jacket blurb, written by Reznikoff, announced, "who are publishing their own work and that of other writers whose work ought to be read." After the focus of activity in the Objectivist group (to which we shall return) during the thirties, Reznikoff receded as a visible presence in American poetry, and I would suppose that for the next two decades he figured in most readers' minds, if at all, as a culturally pious Jewish genre poet, his verse on topics of Jewish history and

119

on biblical or rabbinic motifs appearing in periodicals like the *Menorah Journal*, the *Jewish Frontier* (which he edited from 1955), *Midstream*, and *Commentary*.

The New Directions selection in 1962 seems to have signaled the reemergence into the light of critical esteem not only of Reznikoff but of the other Objectivists as well. When, for example, *Contemporary Literature*, between 1967 and 1970, conducted a series of eight interviews with American poets of stature, half of them turned out to be Objectivists, including, of course, Reznikoff. In the *Times Literary Supplement* (October 1, 1976), the poet Anne Stevenson actually described Reznikoff as "one of the finest writers of his generation," on a par with and in certain respects even superior to William Carlos Williams. The first volume of an edition of his complete poetry, handsomely printed and edited with scrupulous care and tact by Seamus Cooney, was published in the year of the poet's death, so Reznikoff's long inaccessible work is at last available in an attractive and readable format.

The literary enterprise of Charles Reznikoff is an instructive test case for the whole phenomenon of American Jewish writing because no one has gone farther than he in the explicit effort to be both a conscious Jewish writer and an emphatically American one. His parents were immigrants from Russia who worked in the garment industry; he grew up in Brooklyn and more briefly on the East Side with the usual passive knowledge of Yiddish and no instruction in Hebrew—he would first acquire the elements of that language only when he was in his thirties. After completing a law degree, he began working at a series of odd jobs, for a while in business, then, steadily, in literature, as a researcher, editor, translator, freelance writer. He moved through the Greenwich Village literary bohemia of the twenties, sat, sometimes sympathetically, on the sidelines of the radicalism of the thirties, but was also a member of the *Menorah Journal* circle in its heyday during these years, was preoccupied with Jewish themes—at first chiefly in his verse plays rather than in his poems—from his early twenties, and finally was bound to Jewish institutional life through his Labor Zionist commitments, his marriage to the Zionist writer Marie Syrkin, his undertaking of projects of historical research and historical fiction for the Jewish Publication Society, his acute concern for the collective fate of the Jews after 1933.

Apart from a sojourn in Hollywood at the beginning of the forties, Reznikoff remained a lifelong New Yorker, and New York, the Jews, and America are the three matrices of his poetry, both early and late. When he identified his writing in a note for a 1970 London anthology, *Contemporary Poets*, these are the terms he chose: " 'Objectivist,' images clear but the meaning not stated but suggested by the objective details and the music of the verse; words pithy and plain; without the artifice of regular meters; themes, chiefly Jewish, American, urban." The relationship among these three chief themes deserves some reflection, and, still more crucial for an assessment of Reznikoff is the question of how the Objectivist method, here succinctly described, lends itself to an imaginative engagement in these three realms of experience.

The Objectivists, as wavering and elusive as their collective character may have been, were the closest thing to a modernist movement in poetry that America produced—especially if one considers that the other obvious candidate, Imagism, was, after all, an Anglo-American, partly transatlantic, phenomenon. Pound and the Imagists were the chief inspiration of the Objectivists, but in contrast to the Imagist world of visual surfaces, "the mind," as William Carlos Williams later put it, "rather than the unsupported eye entered the picture."[1] The five poets most frequently identified with the group are Louis Zukofsky, George Oppen, Carl Rakosi, Reznikoff, and William Carlos Williams. All but Williams were Jews, and all but Williams and Reznikoff were Communists, but neither Marxism nor Jewishness had any impress on their aesthetic ideology. Zukofsky seems to have been the organizer and promoter, and behind him, Pound, from abroad, the tutelary spirit. It was Pound who persuaded Harriet Monroe to devote a special issue of *Poetry* in 1931 to the Objectivists, with Zukofsky as guest editor, and three years later Pound was listed, with Williams and Zukofsky, on the Advisory Board of the newly launched Objectivist Press. (There is, of course, an irony in

[1]"Objectivism," *Princeton Encyclopedia of Poetry and Poetics*, ed. Alex Preminger (Princeton University Press, 1965).

Pound's involvement with all these offshoots of the Jewish immigrant milieu, but it would appear that Pound was, in diametric contrast to Eliot, an ideological anti-Semite but not a social one. In 1948, Zukofsky vehemently defended him, claiming that Pound had never exhibited the slightest personal anti-Jewish sentiments, and that his ideological aberrations would in time prove to be only an odd footnote to his great contribution to poetry.)

The term "Objectivist" was apparently invented by Zukofsky, without consultation with the others, for the purposes of the special issue of *Poetry*, borrowing from the Sixth Movement (1930) of his lifelong, *Canto*-like poem, *"A"*: "An objective—rays of the object brought to a focus,/An objective —nature as creator—desire for what is objectively perfect." The meanings rippling out from the word were abundant enough for everyone to find something on which to float his own poetic aspirations. In addition to the two notions suggested in these lines, of the poem as a polished focusing lens and the poem as a rigorous reenactment of the objective world, there is at least one further meaning attached to the term by the poets, the idea of the poem as a constructed thing: "[Objectivism] recognizes the poem, apart from its meaning, to be an object to be dealt with as such" (Williams). Zukofsky did not help to clarify matters much in the manifesto he appended to the February 1931 issue of *Poetry*, compounded as it was of ellipses, private references, and other strategies of aggressive bewilderment. ("I confess," Reznikoff said in his 1968 interview, "that I could not follow all that Zukofsky had to say about 'objectification,' or, for that matter, 'sincerity' " —though it was Reznikoff's poetry that served as the principal exhibit of the Zukofsky essay!) These arts of bewilderment are precisely the recurrent characteristics of Zukofsky's heavily allusive, syntactically sliding, punning, self-reflexive poetry, so that for a clear practical demonstration of the Objectivist program, one must look elsewhere—most particularly, I think, to the shorter poems of Reznikoff and Williams.

A few illustrations will be helpful. Here is one poem from a group of seven called "After Rain," which appears in *Jerusalem the Golden* (1934), in many ways Reznikoff's strongest single volume:

The morning light
is dim and blue—
the silent light
of woods;
but now begins
the slight yet multitudinous
noise of rain.

The debt to Imagism is clear in the careful visual definition of
the poem and in its compact, beautifully crafted simplicity.
The Objectivist reach beyond Imagist limits may be marked
by the strategic little explosion of "multitudinous"—a word
that in its polysyllabic Latinity breaks the sequence of iambic
music, tumbles the discourse from sight into sound with a nice
onomatopoeic effect, and, above all, by the slight surprise of
its application as a modifier of "noise," intimates a configura-
tion of the perceiving mind, perhaps an incipient personifica-
tion, in what might otherwise seem a pure representation of
sensory experience.

Occasionally, Reznikoff's short poems do seem entirely
Imagist, haiku-like pieces of two or three lines that achieve
painterly effects, stress primary colors, showing a fondness
for fog scenes and moments of transition from sun to rain or
rain to sun. More typically, however, the presence of the reflective observer is felt in the details chosen and in the way
they are rendered, and is sometimes made explicit with a
first-person pronoun. The process in which personal revelation quietly unfolds from scenic details is particularly evident
in the last four lines of the following poem, also from *Jerusalem the Golden:*

The river is like a lake this morning
for quiet—image of houses and green bank.

A barge is lying at a dock;
nothing moves but the crane
emptying the cargo.

The dark green hill,
the sunset, staining the river—
quiet as a lake;
the tree beside me

Charles Reznikoff: Between Present and Past 123

covered with white blossoms
that cover but cannot hide
the black gnarled branches.

One is reminded here, as in so many of Reznikoff's poems, of William Carlos Williams's evocations of a *paysage moralisé* from the finely attentive rendering of visual detail. (In many of the instances where there are close parallels, the Reznikoff poem is the earlier one, but in any case there is little evidence that one poet actually influenced the other.) Let me cite just one analogous poem by Williams to illustrate the affinities between the two. A brief piece from the group, "The Descent of Winter," it also focuses on branches in seasonal transition, defined by a special quality of atmosphere, in order to intimate a personal apprehension of existence:

in this strong light
the leafless beechtree
shines like a cloud

it seems to glow
of itself
with a soft stript light
of love
over the brittle
grass

But there are
on second look
a few yellow leaves
still shaking

just one here one there
trembling vividly

Reznikoff, I suspect, would have chosen to write the second stanza without the line, "of love," preferring more frequently than Williams to convey such attitudes not by naming them but through the rendering of objective details—like those three consecutive stresses which communicate the ugly insistent presence of "black gnarled branches" beneath the white blossoms. In any case, the similarity in general poetic strategy is apparent, a similarity that extends (though not in this particular poem by Williams) to the creation of a wholly un-ironic urban pastoral mode. In this Reznikoff poem, the crane and barge are perfectly harmonized with the quiet river and green hill. Elsewhere, shining pavements, motor cars, even sewers emptying into glistening rivers and rats creeping through heaps of cans, are integrated with white gulls floating on blue water, the gloom of woods, and other idyllic elements deployed in painterly compositions. In some of these pastoral pieces, the poet taking spiritual stock of his experience enters into the foreground of the perceived scene, but even in these cases the subtle power of delicate intimation is not lost. Here, for example, is a five-line poem from *Inscriptions: 1944-1956* (1959):

> Put it down in your ledger
> among the profits of this day:
> the dark uncertain path of the wind
> on the bright water;
> snow on the yellow branches of the sycamore.

The last three lines alone might be an Imagist poem. It is the ruminative presence in the first two lines that makes the whole an Objectivist piece in a characteristic Reznikoff inflection.

These scrupulously fashioned short poems in the Objectivist manner reveal Reznikoff in the fullest command of his art. The more striking of them—and there are many which could be called that—seem to me quite as fine as anything of the sort that Williams wrote. To these one must add his brief narrative vignettes, mostly of urban and proletarian lives, in which the Objectivist procedures of restraint, seeming impassivity, and precise specification are transferred from nature to the sphere of human actions, with a resultant flatness at times, but also at times with stark effectiveness.

But if these various Objectivist poems mark the height of Reznikoff's achievement, what of his persistent effort to be a Jewish poet? Here some observations are in order about the relation of Objectivist poetry to time, and on Reznikoff's own involvement with the idea of the past. The characteristically Objectivist poem is tightly locked into the moment of experience that it enacts—almost to the same extent as the painted canvases it frequently invokes lexically and by analogies of composition. The Objectivist concentration on the present moment is of course not an isolated instance in the poetry of our century. We should hardly be surprised that some of the most representative projects of modernist verse reflect a breakdown of tradition and the loss of a sense of collective experience, or that the return to tradition after the Imagist experiment of poets like Pound, Eliot, and Zukofsky should often prove to be a self-conscious scissors-and-paste operation of learned citation and pastiche rather than an organic continuation of the tradition. Most of Reznikoff's Objectivist poems are suffused with presentness, and at times he takes positive comfort in that fact, as in this piece from "Autobiography: Hollywood" (in *Going To and Fro Walking Up and Down*, 1941):

> I like this secret walking
> in the fog;
> unseen, unheard,
> among the bushes
> thick with drops;
> the solid path invisible
> a rod away—
>
> and only the narrow present is alive.

More than a decade later, in *Inscriptions*, he provides a gloss on this idea in a four-line aphorism which suggests that the only certain identity, the only ontological security he can hope to enjoy, is in the present time and place, the blessed realm of the known and the determinate:

> The dogs that walk with me are Now and Here
> and a third dog I do not trust at all,
> for he would lead me far into the past
> and there I'd lose myself: his name is If.

Reznikoff's imagination operated on the present moment—which like other modern writers he often felt as a kind of haven in the flux of time—with exquisite poise. What is remarkable is that he nevertheless was preoccupied with the past, felt driven as a Jew to make raid after raid upon it along varying avenues of attack—without, however, any imposing success in conquering it for his imaginative purposes. The same volume in which "I like this secret walking" appears, begins with a sequence of poems entitled "A Short History of Israel: Notes and Glosses." The first long segment of this sequence evinces many of the characteristic faults of Reznikoff's self-consciously Jewish writing. In this historical panorama, Objectivist restraint gives way to "epic" catalogues in which damask, furs, and spice, olive trees, fig trees, and vineyards, figure with a heavy abundance and obviousness. Though such materials are deployed with a craftsman's sense of dramatic appropriateness, there is something inert about the poem as a whole. The chief problem is that this is not the past imaginatively recovered but a series of frozen formulas traditionally associated with the past, the past abstracted into its most familiar literary mediations. And the conception of the Jews themselves is distinctly apologetic—this was, we should keep in mind, 1941—expressed in the anaphoric oratorical rhetoric that apologetics invites: "Among men who gorge and swill/ and sleep in their vomit,/ be temperate and clean; among men who lust and whore/ be true;/ among men in armor/ be men of peace;/ . . . among men who torture/ be Jews."

On occasion, Reznikoff exhibits an acute consciousness of having embarked on a radically contradictory enterprise: to "objectify" in poetry the impelling spirit of a body of historical experience from which he himself, standing on the other side of the chasm of modernity, is alienated. In the concluding poem of "A Short History of Israel," he muses over the very different sense of existence from his own that his grandfathers possessed, living out each act of their lives within a finely-meshed frame of law, in the sight of God: "their past was still the present and the present/ a dread future's./ But I am private as an animal." What introduces a split in Reznikoff's work between a personal poetry of perfect authenticity and a public voice that does not always carry conviction is his repeated uneasiness with being "private as an animal." The need to break out of that privacy into a large historical realm of collective experience moved him to anomalous poetic strategies, at times seemed to encourage the expression of a second self cruder in sensibility, less resistant to the temptations of the obvious gesture.

The end of the poem just cited offers a minor but symptomatic instance of this mechanism. After defining his own private, present-bound condition over against his ancestors' existence as part of a historical continuum, the speaker goes on to resolve, "I will fast for you, Judah,/ and be silent for you/ and wake in the night for you. . . ." I am not, of course, questioning the sincerity of the resolution: it is an understandable and indeed admirable resolution for any Jewish writer to be making in that first year of mass killings as the *Einsatzgruppen* swept eastward. The problem is rather with the imaginative realization of the resolution, which is no more than a rehearsal of ritual gestures, literal and stylistic, a piece of willed piety, the intervention of a kind of poetic superego rather than the expression of an integrated poetic self.

As early as 1921, Reznikoff was engaged with the passion of an autodidact in discovering the Jewish past, and the American past as well, and, with true autodidact intentness, was already trying to make a reckoning with the past, invoking its testimony—a favorite title-word for him—in his writing. His verse plays (collected in *Nine Plays*, 1927) are all based on historical themes, and their subjects constitute a ranging survey of the possibilities of Jewish history and, more fragmentarily, of American history, with dramatic studies of Abraham, Herod, Rashi, Uriel Acosta, Lewis and Clark, Nat Turner, John Brown.

The dramatic genre was clearly not congenial to Reznikoff. These plays, which are sequences of short scenes with little dramatic tension, are not really workable as theater, and the vaguely heightened, unprepossessing verse in which they are cast does not make them viable as poems. The young Reznikoff, already a highly accomplished poet in his pieces based on personal perception, was artistically thwarted by the historical subjects he sought so ardently to embrace. At its worst, as in the play, "Genesis," this poetry is little more than a versified rewording of the sources or a regrettable embellishment of them. When, for example, the annunciating angel tells the childless Abram, "Your spark/ Will light a fire that

Defenses of the Imagination 128

shall burn/ Through every nation,/ And its sparks shall be seeds of fire," the weight and dignity of the actual biblical promise are dissipated by this translation into conventional Romantic imagery, and the verse itself, as elsewhere in Reznikoff's treatment of historical topics, swells to the pomp and ceremony of the text for a cantata. If the Objectivist poet, in Hugh Kenner's fine phrase, "is the geometer of minima," it was Reznikoff's quandary that he was also impelled as a Jewish poet to be a chronometer of millennia, and for that difficult role he struggled to find an appropriate poetic idiom.

The complementary opposite of this effort to work up an exalted poetic vision of the past was a technique of textually incorporating the past with the most limited intervention of the poet. Beginning in the twenties, Reznikoff repeatedly experimented with assembling collages from the sources, using mainly the Authorized Version of the Bible and, occasionally, the available English translations of the Mishnah and Talmud. It is technically interesting to see how he constructs a readable narrative poem by stringing together a careful selection of biblical verses, only occasionally modified, and laid out on the page as free verse, but his retelling in this fashion of Genesis and Exodus, the David story, the life and prophecies of Jeremiah, is less an imaginative achievement than the affirmation of a need to lay claim to the past, to take possession of it in his writing through the simple act of rehearsing it as English verse. His two collages of rabbinic texts, "Palestine Under the Romans" (1936) and the longer "Jews in Babylonia" (1969), are more like original poems because, instead of being anthologies of verses reproducing a familiar storyline, they are collocations of disparate legal and legendary phrases whose concrete language, reassembled in perpetually surprising combinations of fragments, becomes a bold imagery that evokes a whole ancient milieu.

Such felicitous moments of responsiveness to antecedents are rare, however. Reznikoff was fascinated and bedeviled by the past, and he often seemed uncertain as to whether he should be exorcising it, integrating it into his vision, celebrating it, or perhaps perpetuating it for future readers as a kind of curse. The first half of his autobiographical novel, *By the Waters of Manhattan* (1930), is an account of his mother's girlhood in Russia and her early years in America, apparently more or less dictated to him by her, and thus conveyed in a flat, almost affectless prose. The whole section is neither inherently novelistic nor instructively relevant to the account of the dreamy, poetically inclined young man who is the protagonist of this particular novel, but it would seem that Reznikoff could not conceive of telling his own story without including an elaborate report of origins. Later, as though still pondering what might be made out of these origins, he reproduced the entire first half of the novel as the first of three sections in *Family Chronicle* (1963), only transposing the narrative from third to first person in order to make it an integral unit in the tale of his parents' movement from *shtetl* poverty to the sweatshop, boom and bust of the New York needle trade.

In the final decade of his life, Reznikoff returned twice, and at greater length than ever before, to the strategy of textually incorporating the past as verse, first in the two volumes, *Testimony: The United States 1885–1890: Recitative* (1965) and *Testimony . . . 1891–1900* (1968), and then in his last book, *Holocaust* (1975). Both poems—at this point one hesitates a little about using that word—are versifications of documents, in the case of *Testimony*, legal and newspaper accounts of the period, in the case of *Holocaust*, the records of the Nuremberg and Eichmann trials. There is no commentary, no framing or transition devices, no embellishment, only a bearing witness by laying out the language of the documents, with unobtrusive changes, in the typographical and rhythmic emphases of free verse. From one point of view, this is the ultimate Objectivist treatment of the past, perfectly conforming to the definition Reznikoff proposed in his 1968 interview: "By the term 'objectivist' I suppose a writer may be meant who does not write directly about his feelings but about what he sees and hears; who is restricted almost to the testimony of a witness in a court of law; and who expresses his feelings indirectly by the selection of his subject matter and, if he writes in verse, by its music." The problem is that while this technique can yield a chaste precision and suggestiveness when focused on the immediate data of the writer's own experience, its application to historical documents may lead to a kind of helplessness in the face of the raw data of history.

When, moreover, on the large scale of these two long poems, the poet is choosing not a gull or a river rat or a passing cloud to bear witness but a series of publicly recorded incidents, his bias of selection may betray him in more senses than one. These are disturbing poems, less for what they reveal about American history and the program of genocide, which is all too well known, than for what they reveal about the state of the poet's mind.

Testimony is an assemblage of narrative vignettes that almost invariably repeat the same pattern: an anecdotal situation is swiftly defined, then in the last two or three lines, the poem mechanically snaps shut with the same hard bite of disaster on some sort of killing, mutilation, ghastly accident, or brutal deception. One hardly wants to contest the presence of virulent strains of violence in American culture, or argue the fact that workers in the expanding phase of the Industrial Revolution were subject to terribly harsh and dangerous conditions. In *Testimony,* however, the selection of material and the technique of terse deadpan presentation allow nothing but bleak calamity to exist in late nineteenth-century America. This is not, I think, the reflection of any sixties radical view of America but of a mind that had brooded much on American history and had finally come to be obsessed with its destructiveness, mesmerized by images of maiming and killing.

Holocaust bears exactly the same relation to recent Jewish history, where the obsession has a justification of epic scale. I suppose Reznikoff had some conscious notion, in selecting and versifying these documents, of providing "testimony" of the Nazi horrors for future generations, for readers he imagines to be so removed from the subject that he feels obliged to explain in a note what S.S. means, or that *Jude* is German for Jew. These very documents have been widely disseminated in print, anthologized, included in college textbooks, repeatedly discussed, and it is hard to see what is gained by setting them in verse. The poem is one long, unrelieved catalogue of unspeakable torture, degradation, and murder. (One might usefully compare it with Reznikoff's historical novel, *The Lionhearted,* 1944, which recounts in grisly detail the slaughter of English Jewry at the time of the Third Crusade. There the writer tries to set against his piling-on of horrors a final ringing Jewish affirmation, using the hortatory rhetoric we have observed elsewhere. But, as if in the end sensing that such flourishes were no way of coming to terms with a calamitous history, he finally turned to the grimly uncompromising approach of *Holocaust*.) Symptomatically, even a section at the end of the book entitled "Escapes" proves to be mainly about failed escapes, still another series of horrible deaths in infinite variations of cruelty.

I am not, of course, suggesting that the Holocaust was any less ghastly than Reznikoff's version of it, only that there is finally a numbing pointlessness in the constant repetition of savagery and murder without the slightest interpretative response on the part of the poet, without the slightest intimation of historical options beyond or after genocide. One is ultimately led to suspect that this is an extended exercise in masochism conducted under the cover of an act of testimony. History, it would seem, had become a hypnotic vision of unrestrained murderous impulse for the poet: the ultimate breakdown of his whole problematic relation to the past is starkly evident in the flattened landscapes of disaster that take the place of round imagined worlds in these two long poems of his old age.

In all these respects, then, the past proved to be a trap for Reznikoff, but, in fairness, one must also say that there are numerous brief moments in his poetry when the involvement with Jewish antecedents introduces a background of imaginative depth to the enclosed composition of the Objectivist poem. If his affirmations of Jewish allegiance sometimes have a hollow public ring, one hears an authentic resonance in his confessions of personal estrangement from the tradition he would have liked to continue. He is supremely a poet of exile because he frequently senses in his own loving attachment to his chosen medium, the American language, an irreversible abandonment of his Hebrew forebears. The idea of Hebrew, a powerful nostalgia for Hebrew, haunts his poetry (of Yiddish, virtually his native language, no mention is made). A 1927 poem summarizes this feeling:

How difficult for me is Hebrew:
even the Hebrew for *mother*, for *bread*, for *sun*
is foreign. How far have I been exiled, Zion.

And in the same vein, the poem he set at the head of *Jerusalem the Golden* begins, "The Hebrew of your poets, Zion,/ is like oil upon a burn,/ cool as oil," and concludes with this wry commentary on himself as an English poet: "Like Solomon,/ I have married and married the speech of strangers;/ none are like you, Shulamite." Reznikoff was imaginatively at home in American culture, enthusiastically devoted to it, at the center in his generation of poetic experiment in this country. Yet there was a residue of consciousness which did not allow him to sit altogether comfortably in the American scene, and this may well be his most deeply Jewish characteristic.

If Jewishness for Reznikoff is before all else a consciousness of loss, it is also on occasion an imaginative resource, and that is especially evident in the interplay between biblical allusions and personal experience in his poetry. Even in confessing his estrangement from Hebrew origins, he metaphorically invokes, as we have just seen, Solomon and the Song of Songs, shuttling between biblical texts to express his own condition with an almost midrashic deftness. Some of his poems on explicit biblical subjects are not mosaics of verses but vigorous new versions of biblical figures, meaningfully linked with the modern condition out of which the poet writes. A line from a striking early poem of this sort, "Samuel," says a good deal about Reznikoff: "I think in psalms, my mind a psalter." If the Objectivist ideal was to introduce the mind of the poet into the visual scene, this poet's mind was often teeming with remembered biblical images and phrases, which could become apertures in the present time and place looking out on large temporal and cultural perspectives. In one poem a rainstorm merges with Noah's deluge; elsewhere a lovely summer moon recalls the ancient Israelite idolatry of the moon goddess and Jeremiah's stern warnings; or again, still more erotically, the naked moon transforms the speaker in another poem into a David gazing at Bathsheba bathing. At some of its high points Reznikoff's verse focuses its meanings through the kind of imaginative intimacy with the Bible that has been rare in English since the great Protestant poets of the seventeenth century like Henry Vaughan, the Milton of the sonnets, and above all George Herbert. Thus, in an Objectivist rendering of a budding tree, from *Jerusalem the Golden*, the poet's mind is in fact a psalter, crystallizing his perception of the present through a musing upon Psalm 90:

This tree in the twilit street—
the pods hang from its bare symmetrical branches
motionless—
but if, like God, a century were to us
the twinkling of an eye,
we should see the frenzy of growth.

Ultimately, the sense of exclusion from the continuity of Jewish history of which Reznikoff wrote so plangently was not absolute: if you can talk about being in exile with such feeling, that may mean that at least some small part of you belongs, after all, to a realm of rootedness against which the condition of exile is defined. Reznikoff was not an observant Jew and not in any strict sense a religious poet, but the theological perspectives and the ethical values of the tradition he so esteemed do exert pressure at many points in his work, and there are moments when the poet seems to have genuinely assimilated traditional values consonant with his own instead of just ritually affirming them. The still, small reflective voice, hushed with humility, of some of the Psalms and of certain texts from the liturgy, was probably closest to his own, and on occasion he could use it to speak poignantly, as in his cycle, "Meditations on the Fall and Winter Holidays," and some of the related poems that appear with it in *Inscriptions*. A poem entitled "Epilogue" from his last collection of short verse, *By the Well of Living and Seeing* (1969), is a perfect expression of this voice, an apt illustration of Reznikoff speaking as a Jewish poet not in the forensic sweep of a historical gesture but in his fundamental feeling for existence. The poem distills a personal meaning from Ecclesiastes 11:7 ("And the light is sweet, and it is good for the eyes to see the sun"): from the traditional *birkhot ha-nehenin*, the formulas by which a Jew daily blesses what he enjoys in this world; and perhaps also from the Psalmist's sense of human transience. For a moment, the gap closed between his own English and that remembered Hebrew cool as oil on a burn, and with a language wholly his own but also the tradition's, he could sum up his sense of life:

Blessed
in the light of the sun and at the sight of the
world daily,
and in all the delights of the senses and the mind;
in my eyesight, blurred as it is,
and my knowledge, slight though it is,
and my life, brief though it was.

—1977

It is against a background of Christianity that all our thought has significance. An individual European may not believe that the Christian Faith is true, and yet what he says, and makes, and does, will all spring out of his heritage of Christian culture and depend upon that culture for its meaning.

—T. S. Eliot
"Notes Towards the Definition of a Culture"

Eliot, Lawrence, and the Jews: Two Versions of Europe

Whenever traces of anti-Semitism appear in writers of major importance, I suspect that most readers are inclined either to dismiss the whole matter as an inconvenient but incidental prejudice of the author, or, alternately, to respond in mere indignation and, by so doing, to assume that hostility toward Jews is everywhere the same, without significant differences in nuance, motive, or general orientation. However, what a writer has to say about Jews, carefully considered, can sometimes provide a key to underlying aims and even methods in his work, and an insight into his relation to the larger culture around him. To suggest something of the range of the phenomenon, I would like to consider symptomatic works by two English moderns at opposite poles—T. S. Eliot, the Christian conservative militantly defending an ostensibly older idea of European culture, and D. H. Lawrence, the evangelical pagan attacking some of the basic values of Christian Europe.

137

Especially since Lawrence rarely touches on Jews in his fiction with English or European settings, it may seem peculiar that in *Kangaroo,* a novel set in Australia, he should make one of the chief protagonists a Jew and repeatedly draw our attention to the character's Jewish identity. But the choice, as we shall see, has its own logic, given the nature of Lawrence's concerns. This oddest of Lawrence's novels, more preachment and spiritual rumination than novel, records the encounter between a thinly-veiled autobiographical representation of Lawrence and Benjamin Cooley (the Kangaroo of the title), the Jewish charismatic leader of a bizarrely sectarian party with a vague, perhaps ominous, program for redeeming Australia. In the meandering course of the novel, amidst that mixture of claptrap and insight characteristic of Lawrence, reflections on Jews are made by the narrator, by the Lawrencean protagonist Richard Somers, by other characters from both the political Left and the Right, and almost none of it is what one would call complimentary. Nevertheless, it takes some sorting out to see precisely what the novel is trying to do with the Jews. As a clear example of how not to proceed, of how an average liberal reader responds to the first signs of literary anti-Semitism, let me quote a few lines on this novel from John Harrison's survey of political attitudes in Lawrence, Eliot, and others, *The Reactionaries* (Schocken, 1967):

He equated democracy with the rule of Jewish financiers, and he even "gradually came to believe that all Jews, and all Celts, even whilst they espoused the cause of England, subtly lived to bring about the humiliation of the great old England." It needed a Jew, he said, to produce the "last step in liberty," the Theory of Relativity, and like Lewis, Pound, and Eliot, he believed the whole liberal-democratic tradition to be essentially Jewish in nature. Kangaroo, the representative of this tradition, is himself a Jew. He did not mention men like Einstein by name alone; they were "the Jew, Einstein," or "Marx, the Jew."

All this is appallingly careless. It makes *Kangaroo* look like a ranting anti-Semitic tract, which is far from both the intent and the effect of the novel. The subject of these supposed opinions is Richard Somers, not D. H. Lawrence, and though Lawrence himself admittedly tends to blur distinctions between the two, one is hardly entitled to attribute the opinions of a fictional character to the author without the slightest modification. Thus, when Harrison, with no indication of transition, writes, "like Lewis, Pound, and Eliot, he believed the whole liberal-democratic tradition to be essentially Jewish in nature," the real antecedent of "he" has shifted from Somers to Lawrence. In point of fact, Lawrence did not believe this, and it even misrepresents the position of the protagonist of *Kangaroo.* Richard Somers associates democracy and patriotism with commercialism and industrialism, and these in turn he sometimes conceives in the image of the Jewish financier, but he does not *equate* democracy with the rule of Jewish financiers.

Lawrence, we recall, was often preoccupied with notions of racial characteristics and inbred cultural heritages, involving northern Europeans (by no means a positive type in his view), Mediterraneans, black Africans, Australians, Mexicans, Gypsies, Celts, and, of course, Jews. It is almost a matter of course that a Lawrence protagonist, considering the Jews, should connect them with the qualities of driving materialism and disembodied intellectuality that Lawrence himself felt were pervading modern civilization, though Somers also attributes other, rather surprising "racial" characteristics to the Jews, as we shall see in a moment. Finally, it is patently absurd to speak of Kangaroo as the representative of the "liberal-democratic tradition" when the novel clearly presents the movement he leads as a variety of fascism. "I want to keep *order,*" says Cooley with italic emphasis, "and that you can only do by exerting strong, just *power* from above." A moment later, he continues in the tones of a Grand Inquisitor: "Man needs to be relieved from this terrible responsibility of governing himself when he doesn't know what he wants, and has no aim toward which to govern himself. Man again needs a father—not a friend or a brother sufferer, a suffering Saviour." The fact that a reader of even middling intelligence could describe this political outlook as liberal-democratic can only be explained through the blindness of automatic liberal preconceptions: the twin-headed monster of anti-Semitism and reaction is imagined to be everywhere the same, and since

Lawrence dislikes Jews, he must invariably associate them with liberal democracy, which he also dislikes. It would not occur to a writer like Harrison that Lawrence could at once hold Jews in contempt and be powerfully attracted to them, or that he could ultimately reject fascism, for all his cult of "the mystery of lordship," because the fascist idea profoundly violated the proud separateness that was sacrosanct to him, and he sensed that the true nature of fascism was—to borrow J. L. Talmon's telling phrase—"totalitarian democracy."[1]

This brings us back to the central puzzle of the novel itself: why on earth should Lawrence choose a Jew as the charismatic leader of a fascist movement? A moment after Somers's ironic description of the Theory of Relativity as the "last step in liberty" (which is said, by the way, in a spirit of friendly banter to Cooley, who he already suspects is a Jew), he reflects on Kangaroo's racial identity: "Surely . . . it is Jewish blood. The very best that is in the Jewish blood: a faculty for pure disinterestedness, and warm, physically warm love, that seems to make the corpuscles of the blood glow." To this Somers adds another unspoken comment, the aggressive paradoxicality of which should be duly noted: "The man had surely Jewish blood. And he was almost purely *kind*, essential kindliness, embodied in an ancient, unscrupulous shrewdness." Kangaroo exerts considerable magnetism over Somers, yet the Englishman is finally repulsed by the Australian and his political philosophy. Ostensibly, much of what Kangaroo preaches should appeal to a Lawrence hero: he speaks "in the name of living life," and has set his face against "anti-life," denouncing the obscene ant heap of modern civilization. Yet Somers soon realizes that Cooley's doctrine, which he understands to be ultimately Jewish, is death to him.

It is easier to see what *Kangaroo* is all about if one simply recognizes that it is essentially a religious novel and not a political one. Though there are allusions to postreligious Jews who are sensed as a potentially subversive influence in the modern world, the real importance of the Jews in the novel is

[1]Denis Donoghue, in his admirable review of *The Reactionaries* in *Commentary*, August 1967, offers analogous examples of careless reading.

as the living source of the Judeo-Christian religious tradition. Thus, Somers says of the Celts—elsewhere, as we have seen, likened to the Jews—that "they remember older gods, older ideals, different gods: before the Jews invented a mental Jehovah, and a spiritual Christ." The Jews, then, are the ultimate adversary not because of an international Jewish conspiracy to subvert European values but, on the contrary, because the Jews are the source of European values which, in their highest fulfillment, alienate man from his natural world by leading the life of the psyche out of the body through the conduits of intellect and spirit. Although Somers repeatedly speaks of Jehovah and Christ, he is far from following the traditional Christian opposition between the Old Testament God of wrath and the New Testament God of love. Rather, in his own division of Old Testament intellect and New Testament spirituality, love permeates both Laws, love is the essentially Jewish way to redemption, and love asphyxiates, because it is eros ideologized, cut off from its roots in the physical world, reduced to a gospel whose bearer presumptuously violates the order of nature by insisting that he can embrace mankind in godlike compassion. It is this love that the Jewish message of redemption would pour over humanity like treacle, thus denying the individual his individuality, denying him both his connection with and aloneness in a primal world of nature deeper than love. "I know your love, Kangaroo," Somers says in a central renunciation of the new Jewish gospel. "Working everything from the spirit, from the head. You work the lower self as an instrument of the spirit. Now it is time for the spirit to leave us again; it is time for the Son of Man to depart, and leave us dark, in front of the unspoken God: who is just beyond the dark threshold of the self, my lower self." Lawrence's language shows an even more pronounced tendency in this novel than elsewhere in his fiction to adopt biblical cadences and biblical imagery; and this is perfectly appropriate because the book is a new gospel conceived as a radical revision of the old.

The first great religious revelation, as Lawrence views it, came to the West through a people preoccupied with getting God in the head, with subjecting all of life to the rule of will, and love itself to a regimen of will. (This last notion, as a matter of fact, is not so far-fetched: it could be supported by a host of rabbinical statements as well as by biblical injunctions.) The piping insistence of the conscious will falsifies love, deceives man by making him believe he can assume the identity of a God fashioned in his own image, and finds its ultimate issue in a fascist doctrine preaching power from above in the name of a willed love of humanity. The Jew, in whatever sphere he moves, embodies both "essential kindliness" and "unscrupulous shrewdness" because his relationship to life is hyperconscious: with the disposition of will, one can train oneself to kindliness, though never to the deeper impulse of passion; with a will constantly on guard, one responds to enemies not in anger or hatred but with the fine cutting edge of shrewd calculation. In Lawrence's own doctrine, on the other hand, man could be fully man only by renouncing the vision of his own coercive godliness, by slipping out of the constrictive grip of his human will and lapsing into a larger awareness of the magical animal world to which he belongs.

What *Kangaroo* does in effect is to raise the subconscious European archetype of the Jew as father to the level of conscious theological critique. Benjamin Cooley, as we have seen, casts himself as a benevolent All-Father to his future people, and he is ideally suited for this role precisely because he is a Jew. When it is said of Somers's wife toward the end of the novel that she "left Europe with her teeth set in hatred of Europe's ancient encumbrance of authority and of the withered, repulsive weight of the Hand of the Lord, that old Jew, upon it," one can see the serious point of cultural criticism in the remark, however much it may seem merely an unpleasant anti-Semitic slur out of context. For *Kangaroo* is a long, incensed argument against God the Father, and in the Western imagination God the Father stubbornly remains a Jew.

Lawrence's general outlook bears some resemblance, of course, to the neopagan current of German anti-Semitic ideology that attacked both Judaism and Christianity as corrupters of an indigenous Teutonic spirit, but the resemblance is mainly superficial. Lawrence lacks the essential ingredient of a nationalist mystique: all Europeans, Gentiles and Jews, are equally subjected to his scathing criticism, and he attacks what Europe—Christians and their Jewish spiritual forebears

—has made of itself, without imagining a pristine breed of Northern heroes corrupted by a race of Oriental interlopers. He is not impervious, moreover, to the intrinsic appeal of the Jewish character and the Jewish spiritual way, as he understands them—Kangaroo, their embodiment in the novel, is a man of bizarre but very genuine personal charm, and the novelist, in the end unable wholly to exorcise him, must resort to killing him off before the conclusion of the book. Though Lawrence thinks we have had a good deal too much emphasis on reason in our culture, he is not, in the German proto-Nazi style, unreservedly antirational, and the real thrust of his criticism is directed not against reason but the hypertrophied will. It is precisely that critique of will that sets him inalterably apart from fascism, that makes his use of the Jews seem not altogether arbitrary, and that abides, after half a century, as a probing, still unanswered indictment of individual and collective life in Western culture. Careful consideration of the way Lawrence treats Jews and comments on them can help us see these aspects of his novel, and where its deeper intent lies; on the other hand, a stock response of censure or dismissal to the specter of anti-Semitism will only deflect a reader from what the writer is trying to say.

T. S. Eliot clearly brews a very different cup of literary tea from the ingredients of religious prejudice. It is tempting to shrug off all the anti-Semitism in Eliot's poetry as the purely reflexive prejudice of his cultural milieu and therefore of no particular importance in assessing his work. Explicit anti-Semitism in the poetry, after all, is limited to "Burbank with a Baedeker; Bleistein with a Cigar," to the notorious image in "Gerontion" of the squatting Jew "spawned in some estimanet of Antwerp," and to two or three passing innuendos in the Sweeney poems. Yet I would contend that the vehement energy of repulsion one encounters in Eliot when he does mention Jews bears reflection, and that the Jews do in fact constitute a crucial test case for his conceptions of European culture and the nature of literary experience. "Burbank with a Baedeker," then, is not an aberration, as the one Eliot poem wholly devoted to an anti-Semitic subject, but rather it spells out underlying assumptions about poetry, tradition, and modern culture that are operative even when he is not at all concerned with Jews. As such, the poem deserves a careful reading.

For a relatively short poem, it has a rather long epigraph, which we might ponder because it offers at once an image of what Venice will mean in the body of the poem and a model —virtually a self-parody—of the poetic technique Eliot uses here and elsewhere:

Tra-la-la-la-la-la-laire—nil nisi divinum stabile est; caetera fumus—the gondola stopped, the old palace was there, how charming its grey and pink—goats and monkeys, with such hair too!—so the countess passed on until she came through the little park, where Niobe presented her with a cabinet, and so departed.

The intended immediate effect of all this is obviously to impress the reader with a sense of unintelligible jumble, of a collage of snippets and bits and fragments of things, involving some sort of confusion between regal dignity and foul animality or perhaps eroticism; in this way, the whole passage recapitulates the latter fate of Venice, once a splendid center of European culture.

The epigraph is entirely composed of quotations, and a reader with a retentive memory may recall several of them. The clause with the gondola stopping by a grey and pink palace is from the first approach to the Bordereau palazzo in James's *The Aspern Papers*, a story of how great art gets mixed up with sordid commercialism by an interloper in Venice. "Goats and monkeys" is an expletive used by the enraged Othello, that hapless soldier of Venice. Straining a little, one might even recall that "with such hair, too" appears at the end of Browning's "A Toccata of Guluppi's," a poem that uses Venice as an image of the transience of human things: "Dear dead women, with such hair, too—what's become of all the gold/ Used to hang and brush their bosoms? I feel chilly and grown old." Only the energy of a professional annotator, however, is likely to uncover the source of "Tra-la-la" in Gautier's poem, *Variations sur le carnivale de Venise* (allusion here surely on the brink of a dubious joke!), or the original setting of the whole last unit ("so the countess . . .") in the stage directions of a masque by Marston, or the Latin tag

("Nothing but the divine is permanent; the rest is smoke") inscribed around the base of a guttering candle in a Mantegna painting of the martyrdom of St. Sebastian. The epigraph, then, comes close to being a reduction to the absurd of the technique of the poem, which in eight brief stanzas alludes to three different plays by Shakespeare, to Homer, Horace, Ruskin, and one wonders what else.

Now, it is a commonplace to explain Eliot's mosaic method of composition—which he did not entirely abandon even as late as the *Four Quartets*—by referring to his need to reproduce formally the spiritual ruins of modern life, those devastated ruins against which the poet could only shore up fragments. I would like to suggest that this density of discontinuous allusion also has another function in Eliot's poetry, which is to invoke the whole range of the European cultural tradition in a way that suggests the tradition is at once universal and esoteric, impenetrable to the outsider. The Jew in this regard is important to Eliot as the archetypal outsider, a European who is not a Christian, which for Eliot is a virtual self-contradiction. Let us see how this imagination of exclusion works itself out in the body of the poem:

> Burbank crossed a little bridge
>   Descending at a small hotel;
> Princess Volupine arrived,
>   They were together, and he fell.
>
> Defunctive music under sea
>   Passed seaward with the passing bell
> Slowly: the God Hercules
>   Had left him, that had loved him well.
>
> The horses, under the axletree
>   Beat up the dawn from Istria
> With even feet. Her shuttered barge
>   Burned on the water all the day.
>
> But this or such was Bleistein's way:
>   A saggy bending of the knees
> And elbows, with the palms turned out,
>   Chicago Semite Viennese.
>
> A lustreless protrusive eye

Stares from the protozoic slime
At a perspective of Canaletto.
The smoky candle end of time

Declines. On the Rialto once.
The rats are underneath the piles.
The jew is underneath the lot.
Money in furs. The boatman smiles,

Princess Volupine extends
A meagre, blue-nailed, phthisic hand
To climb the waterstair. Lights, lights,
She entertains Sir Ferdinand

Klein. Who clipped the lion's wings
And flea'd his rump and pared his claws?
Thought Burbank, meditating on
Time's ruins, and the seven laws.

Burbank, presumably an American tourist, at least manages to be mock-heroic, abandoned, like Shakespeare's Antony, by the god Hercules, after an assignation at a small
hotel with Princess Volupine, whose name may suggest both
pleasure and wolfishness. Aristocracy has gone all to pieces:
the title of princess, in fact, might be no more than an ironic
epithet for a whore, who hurries on from Burbank to entertain a rich Jew as spuriously noble as herself—for how could
a genuine Sir Ferdinand be Klein? Bleistein is thrust into the
poem against a context of allusions he would not understand,
from which his alien background and nature irrevocably exclude him: *Antony and Cleopatra*, Greek mythology, a Homeric chariot of the sun, an echo of Horace's image of death
beating "with equal foot" on the roofs of rich and poor, an
evocation of Enobarbus's splendid description of Cleopatra
sailing down the Nile, and then the sagging, grubby figure
that is hopelessly incompatible with all this—"Chicago Semite
Viennese." Bleistein is a merchant of Venice—"on the Rialto"
is a phrase from the play—conceived with a nastiness unlike
anything in Shakespeare. Having made his money in the characteristically Jewish fur trade, he continues, ratlike, to gnaw
away the underpinnings of a once resplendent European city,
of European society itself. If Shylock was accorded his mo-

ment of humanity when he could cry out, "Hath not a Jew eyes?," Eliot would seem to answer that the jew—lower-case "j" to suggest it is like the name of some odious animal—has only such eyes as bulge like dull bubbles out of protozoic slime, not civilized eyes that can really see a landscape by Canaletto, a religious painting by Mantegna, the architectural beauties of Venice, the ironic allusions of a poem by Eliot.

Eliot's treatment of the Jews is, I believe, symptomatic of a general dysfunction of humanistic values operating in his work, for all its virtuosity and its power. It may help to see these larger implications in perspective if we recall that Venice had been used by poets as a symbol of transience and the decline of European grandeur for three centuries before the writing of "Burbank with a Baedeker," at least since Ben Jonson's *Volpone.* Eliot is, to my knowledge, the first important writer to introduce the Jews into the picture, indeed, to attribute the final decline of Venice to them—for the clear answer to Burbank's question of who clipped the mighty winged lion of Venice is Klein, Bleistein, and Company. A glance at some earlier images of a fallen Venice will suggest what this innovation means in terms of the poetic act and the poet's imagination of European culture. In the fourth book of the *Dunciad,* Pope sends his prototypical modern fop on a grand tour of the Continent, where, to climax a series of sites of cultural decadence, the young tourist visits "chief her shrine where naked Venus keeps,/ And Cupids ride the Lion of the Deeps;/ Where, eased of Fleets, the Adriatic main/ Wafts the smooth Eunuch and enamoured swain." Pope, too, imagines a Venetian lion stultified, not by the machinations of rapacious foreigners but by the unrestrained sensuality of the Venetians themselves. Classical Italy for Pope, with a remembered Rome of the Augustan age at its hub, is the model of a fully achieved European culture, embodying values of discipline, order, responsibility, public service, magnanimity. In this modern Venice, all of the values of the Latin-speaking peoples have been subverted; and so the machinery of the pastoral tradition—mythological ornamentation and elegant poetic inversions, soft breezes wafting enamored swains—is cunningly used to expose an antipastoral reality of license and perversion.

For the English Romantics, Venice is both the locus of a once magnificent Renaissance art (as in Eliot) and the image of proud freedom crushed under modern tyranny (but Eliot was not interested in republican politics). Wordsworth, in his sonnet "On the Extinction of the Venetian Republic," invokes the city as "the eldest Child of Liberty." The sestet of this sonnet might be instructively set alongside the conclusion of "Burbank":

> And what if she had seen those glories fade,
> Those titles vanish, and that strength decay;
> Yet shall some tribute of regret be paid
> When her long life has reached its final day:
> Men are we, and must grieve when even the Shade
> Of that which once was great, is passed away.

Against this sense of reverence for human greatness passed, Eliot's tone seems thin and self-indulgent, something between a whine and a sneer. "Men are we," says Wordsworth, and it is precisely this awareness of shared humanity in the face of the transience of men's achievements that gives his poem resonance. An implicit sense of "men are we" is what is most essentially lacking in Eliot's poem, which makes clear that European greatness is the property of an elite, and that humanity is not to be accorded so readily to everything that walks on two legs and can smoke a cigar.

Eliot's introduction of an outsider as the principal agent of decay radically shifts the balance of moral meaning in the idea of decline. In order to focus the nature of this shift more sharply, I would like to consider one stanza from Byron's great lament over fallen Venice at the beginning of Canto Four of *Childe Harold's Pilgrimage:*

> Statues of glass—all shivered—the long file
> Of her dead Doges are declined to dust;
> But where they dwelt, the vast and sumptuous pile
> Bespeaks the pageant of their splendid trust;
> Their sceptre broken, and their sword in rust,
> Have yielded to the stranger: empty halls,
> Thin streets, and foreign aspects, such as must
> Too oft remind her who and what enthrals,
> Have flung a desolate cloud o'er Venice' lovely walls.

In contrast to Eliot, who approaches the broken grandeur of the past obliquely and ironically through a jigsaw pattern of allusions, Byron imagines the subject directly in evocative elegiac imagery, the rhythm of decline echoing hauntingly in the falling music of the verse. Byron's file of dead Doges declined to dust makes Eliot's pseudo-aristocrats seem like a flimsy satiric invention, for of the two poets, it is Byron who persuades us that he really knows what aristocracy means. Against Byron's strong sense of present emptiness and his vividly symbolic evocation of greatness shattered, "Time's ruins" at the end of the Eliot poem looks like an abstraction, no more than a traditional poetic phrase appropriately placed by an expert dealer in phrases. But the difference between Byron and Eliot is most crucial in the different identities of the intrusive stranger in the two poems. Byron's reference is historical and political: Napoleon had delivered Venice to Austria in 1797, and so the capital of what had once been a Mediterranean empire was now subject to the very real domination of a foreign imperial power. In the passage from Byron, poetry engages history; in Eliot, it instead conjures with distorted myths about history, for the Jew as the interloper who has subverted Venice, or Europe, is a fantasy of collective paranoia, while the driving commercialism of Venice is very much a home product, from the origins of the city in the Christian Middle Ages to modern times.

The apparition of the threatening stranger in Venice brings to mind an invocation of Venice as an image of decline in a work published just eight years before "Burbank"—Thomas Mann's *Death in Venice*. Mann, too, is concerned with large questions of European culture and values, but his Venice represents a pole of overripe sensuality, joined with the lust for gain, which is not smuggled in from without but is intrinsic to European experience and to human nature, however it may be suppressed: "this was Venice, this the fair frailty that fawned and that betrayed, half fairy-tale, half snare; the city in whose stagnating air the art of painting once put forth so lusty a growth, and where musicians were moved to accords so weirdly lulling and lascivious." We might note that in Mann's story the demonic stranger, who at first seems to be alien and unknown to Aschenbach, the archetypal European, turns out to be a projected image of Aschenbach's own suppressed sensuality, a phantasmagoric inner view of Aschenbach himself. One could not come further from Eliot's vision of the stranger as an utterly alien, pestilential creature penetrating from without into the fastnesses of the European city to gnaw at its foundations.

What I would like to stress in all of this is not that T. S. Eliot had abhorrent ideas about Jews but rather that the ideas he did have about Jews, seen in a perspective of literary history, reveal the defensive strain, the self-consciousness, and finally the externality of his relationship with European culture. There is, I suspect, an element of excessive awareness of tradition as an idea in all of Eliot's affirmations of its importance in his criticism, something that smacks of converting tradition into a literary ideology instead of naturally participating in it and using it, as poets like Pope, Wordsworth, and Byron were able to do. People who shrilly insist on the uniqueness of their own identity are likely to be insecure about it; groups that must forever affirm their own exclusiveness are almost certain to have inner doubts about their coherence or collective validity. It is no accident that the most extreme form of exclusivist nationalism in Europe developed in Germany, the country composed of a congeries of smaller states where a historical unity of national consciousness was most in question. Both *Deutschtum* as a political ideology and Eliot's Christian Europe as a cultural program needed, first, the myth of an ideal past—the Teutonic era and the Christian Middle Ages, respectively—as a prop, and, then, an external enemy, the Jews, to define through opposition their own unsure sense of identity and to explain the fallen state of their present culture. I do not mean to say that Eliot was actually close to Nazism; as a matter of fact, he came to oppose it firmly because of its pagan nature, and he certainly was prepared to make many discriminations and qualifications in viewing the Jew as the symbol of European decadence that would have been beyond the ken of fascism. Nevertheless, the structural analogy between the two is instructive.

The hyperconsciousness with which Eliot ideologizes a tradition and makes himself part of it is observable in the peculiar nature of his poetic achievement. He is a master, but finally a master ventriloquist, speaking in a score of different voices, ingeniously orchestrated, but never fully in a voice of his own. There is almost everywhere something excessively cerebral about the way he uses the poetic tradition, as though he had studied it minutely without ever completely assimilating it. *The Waste Land* is a poem of stunning virtuosity, but one has only to compare its use of the myth of death and rebirth with Milton's handling of the same mythic materials in *Lycidas* to see the difference between a poet who has absorbed the tradition, can freely imagine through it, and one who consciously contrives poetry out of the tradition. Eliot's poetry, to be sure, has its marvelously moving moments, even when it is most synthetic, and I don't want to suggest that he should be written off as "minor." The sense of connection, however, with a real, living humanity is shrunken in him, and because of it he strains and stretches to make himself one with a Western literary tradition that, before all else, expresses just that sense of connection. One suspects that in Eliot an impaired sense of community with the living and the dead is compensated for by the enunciation of Christian community as a program, and by a poetic technique that substitutes an intricate network of insider's allusions for the natural assumption of shared culture and shared humanity. Eliot is often viewed as the paradigmatic poetic spokesman of his troubled period, but it may be equally appropriate to see him as a symptom of the trouble. In any event, his case illustrates how attention to the role of anti-Semitism in a writer's work may lead to a clearer apprehension of his imaginative world. If the Jews have a historical destiny, it is to be at the crossroads of trouble, and that destiny has been fulfilled time after time not only in the realm of geopolitics but also in the Christian imagination.

—1970

3 Fiction
and Historical Crisis

Jewish Humor and the
Domestication of Myth

It is an instructive paradox that one of the grimmest stretches in Jewish history—the recent centuries of Yiddish-speaking culture in Eastern Europe—should also prove to be the period in Jewish history that produced the most richly distinctive humor. Especially since popular stereotypes of Diaspora Jewish history tend to represent it wholly in the image of the ghettos of Central and Eastern Europe and the townlets of the Pale of Settlement, it is worth stressing that rarely before had Jews been so physically constricted, so continuously depressed economically; and perhaps not since the Crusades and the Black Plague did they feel so repeatedly threatened by physical havoc as in Russia during the last decades under the czars. In such circumstances, it has been suggested, a shrewdly ironic humor became a source of necessary inner strength, a mode of survival. Maurice Samuel, the eloquent expositor of East-European Jewish culture, states the case pointedly:

There was nothing jolly and hilarious about the destitution that lay like a curse on millions of Jews in the Yiddish-speaking world; and it would be grotesque to speak of Sholom Aleichem's and Mendele's *kaptsonim* [paupers] and *evyonim* [indigents] as "poor and happy." They were miserable, and knew it; but the question that haunts us historically is, why did they not disintegrate intellectually and morally? How were they able, under hideous oppression and corroding privation, under continuous starvation—the tail of a herring was a dish—to keep alive against a better day the spirit originally breathed into man? The answer lies in the self-mockery by which they rose above their condition to see afar off the hope of the future.[1]

This is beautifully apt, but the implications of "self-mockery," and its relation to a sense of the future, deserve exploration. The European cultural tradition, I would suggest, characteristically conceives suffering as a mystery, beginning with and drawing on the cultic or literary formulation of the mystery of suffering in Greek tragedy and in Christ's passion. Affliction is the medium through which man must realize his humanity, or more-than-humanity; accordingly, he must view both himself and his suffering with the utmost seriousness, defining his time, which is the time of human fulfillment, by the internal rhythm of his suffering. Hamlet, Werther, Dmitri Karamazov, Camus's Stranger, are paradigmatic figures of this European tradition; against them, one might usefully set Sholom Aleichem's Tevye, who acts upon the wisdom of the Yiddish proverb, "Burdens are from God, shoulders, too," never for a moment imagining that it would be appropriate to seek fulfillment through suffering, to create a mythology out of suffering, and who uses his shoulders as much to shrug at adversity as to bear it.

Jewish humor typically drains the charge of cosmic significance from suffering by grounding it in a world of homey practical realities. "If you want to forget all your troubles," runs another Yiddish proverb, "put on a shoe that's too tight." The point is not only in the "message" of the saying, that a present pain puts others out of mind, but also in its

---

[1] *In Praise of Yiddish* (Cowles, 1971), pp. 210–11.

formulation: *Weltschmerz* begins to seem preposterous when one is wincing over crushed bunions. If in the tradition of Jewish humor suffering is understandably imagined as inevitable, it is also conceived as incongruous with dignity—thus the sufferer is at least faintly ridiculous, his complementary comic embodiments of *shlemiel* and *shlimazel* become central in the folk tradition and the literature deriving from it. The perception of incongruity implies the perception of alternate possibilities, humor peeking beyond the beleaguered present toward another kind of man and another kind of time; for the very aura of ridicule suggests that it is not, after all, fitting for a man to be this pitiful creature with a blade of anguish in his heart and both feet entangled in a clanking chain of calamities.

As the sense of inner crisis has deepened in modern literature, one important direction taken by writers beginning with Conrad, Mann, and Eliot, has been a conscious re-mythologizing of literature, usually in order to make it sound the full cultural resonance of our collective disorders. Against this general drift of literary modernism, writers significantly touched by the Yiddish heritage have often been de-mythologizers, using the wryness and homey realism of Jewish humor to suggest that a less melodramatic, less apocalyptic, perspective than that of myth might be appropriate for viewing even the disquieting state of affairs of the modern world.

I would like to begin with an extreme example—a novel peopled entirely by WASPs and black Africans, set in the heart of the dark continent, with not a hint of an *oi* or a *veh* amidst the native ullulations—precisely because it may illustrate the persistence of a Jewish modality of imagination even in the total absence of Jewish realia. The book I have in mind is of course *Henderson the Rain King,* a novel that remains one of the most engaging of Saul Bellow's fictions, despite the flaws of its conclusion. Bellow, it should be observed, is one of the very few American Jewish writers who has more than nostalgic misinformation about the Yiddish-speaking ancestral world: from his ghetto childhood in Montreal he retains enough Hebrew to make proper use of biblical and liturgical motifs in his fiction, enough genuinely literate Yiddish to have produced admirable translations of stories by Sholom Aleichem and I. B. Singer. *Henderson* would seem to be a conscious attempt on the part of a writer who generally uses Jewish milieus and characters to write for once a thoroughly American novel. (In this, and little else, it resembles Malamud's *The Natural* and Philip Roth's *When She Was Good*.) The hero is a strapping Westchester-county millionaire of Protestant descent, first seen wallowing among pigs on his farm. The plot consists of a spiritual safari to Africa—Henderson's initials, Leslie Fiedler has observed, are the same as Ernest Hemingway's—in which the hero eventually tries to prove his manhood and discover wisdom by staring down a lion in an underground cell.

Henderson's irrepressible innocence suggests a kind of aging Huck Finn of the Eisenhower years, yet for all his exuberant Americanism, one is also strongly tempted to apply to him some of the rubrics of Yiddish characterology. An inveterate misadventurer, there is a good deal of the self-perceiving *shlemiel* in Henderson, tinctured with an admixture of the *klots* (clumsy oaf) or the eternal *grober yung* (slob, boorish young man). Following parodistically on the trail of Conrad's Marlow, Lawrence's Kate Leslie, and other modern questers into dark regions, Henderson clearly carries along a very different apparatus of imagination, and it is worth observing precisely how his mind copes with the unspeakable mysteries of the jungle. His version of a native ceremonial procession is characteristic: "amazons, wives, children carrying long sheaves of Indian corn, warriors holding idols and fetishes in their arms which were freshly smeared with ochre and calcimine and were as ugly as human conception could make them." So far, this seems a factual enough evocation of a primitive rite, and might easily fit into a narrative by Conrad except for its avoidance of those Conradian adjectives of looming immensity and ominous things impending. Immediately, however, something peculiar begins to happen to the exotic scene: "Some were all teeth, and others all nostrils, while several had tools bigger than their bodies." The conversational hyperbole ("all teeth," "all nostrils") of course heightens the grotesqueness of the idols while suggesting a quality of ironic observation or perhaps even wondering amusement which separates the speaker from the savage rite, and that quality is reinforced by the use of the familiar-colloquial (but not obscene) "tool" to describe the carved phalluses. Henderson, who has excruciating difficulties with a broken dental bridge, who feels the world's beauty through a tingling in the gums, to whom even the African mountains look as though they might have bad teeth, is struck first by the apparition of toothy gods: as with the pinched feet in the proverb, the novel as a whole tends to shrink suffering and sensitivity to the realistic dimensions of a homey physical detail. Henderson goes on to render his response to the African scene through a rhetorical device that he uses repeatedly elsewhere:

The yard suddenly became very crowded. The sun blasted and blazed. Acetylene does not peel paint more than this sun did the doors of my heart. Foolishly, I told myself that I was feeling faint. (It was owing to my size and strength that this appeared foolish.) And I thought that this was like a summer's day in New York. I had taken the wrong subway and instead of reaching upper Broadway I had gone to Lenox Avenue and 125th Street, struggling up to the sidewalk.

The energy of the style makes Henderson's experience seem very "real," but in a way that violently assimilates Africa to an American metropolitan landscape. Henderson's narrative is a continual farce of deliberately gross similes: acetylene torches and peeling paint, bubbling percolators, baseball stadiums, limousines to La Guardia Field, the smokestacks of Gary, Indiana, cover the African vistas of the novel. The technique effectively destroys any possibility of using exotic climes as a vehicle for myth. Henderson is in his own way open to new experience, as his friendship with King Dahfu demonstrates, but he remains imaginatively anchored in a world of familiar places, objects, and implements; and he cannot be drawn into a yawning abyss of the unknown because his first mental reflex is to domesticate the unknown with a comparison. (The deflation of mysteries through an attachment to the familiar also operates in his sense of who he is. Whatever bizarre roles in which circumstances cast him, he knows that Henderson the clumsy clown is no mythic Fisher King. Here, he maintains the comic self-consciousness of a knowing *shlemiel,* which enables him in the midst of his account of a wild ceremony to note how absurd it is that such a hulk of a man should think himself on the point of fainting.) Many a newcomer to New York has undergone the inadvertent *rite de passage* of neglecting to change trains at 96th Street and thus discovering himself in the heart of Harlem instead of Morningside Heights. Henderson's invocation of that experience at this point vividly conveys a sense of sudden disorientation in an unfamiliar crowd of Negroes, but there is an underlying congruity in the comic incongruity of the comparison that might best be paraphrased with a Jewish verbal shrug: "Natives, shmatives, there are people everywhere. So maybe someone can tell me where I should go?" The point of the comedy of similes throughout *Henderson* is to banish from the protagonist's world the possibility of a primordial Other Side of human life. We deceive ourselves, the novel suggests, with the drama of a return to archaic origins. Through Henderson we are led to acknowledge the home-truth that we have only our civilized selves to work with. Appropriately, Dahfu, Henderson's spiritual guide, turns out to be a former medical student with looney theories about the road to inner transformation—more or less, a black cousin germane to the New York Jewish intellectuals (like Bellow's friend, Isaac Rosenfeld) who, for example, plunged into Wilhelm Reich and built themselves orgone boxes to hasten a personal redemption.

A similar process of ironic or playful domestication of myth is often observable when Jewish writers deal with heaven, hell, and the realm of fantastic creatures in between. Though it is customary to think of Judaism as a this-worldly faith, Jews in fact have often believed fervently in reward and punishment after death, in ministering angels (invoked by name in the bedtime prayer) and lurking demons. Nevertheless, all these other-worldly paraphernalia never quite attained what would be canonical status in another religion, a fact that has given the folk imagination and writers inspired by it considerable freedom in treating these materials. Thus, the charm of Itzik Manger's *The Book of Paradise* (1939) depends upon the completely uninhibited way in which the celestial Eden is recast in the image of the Rumanian *shtetl* Manger knew as a boy. The first glimpse of the streets of Eden at nightfall is of a piece with everything that follows: "Bearded angels were bent over yellowed holy books. Fat lady angels with triple chins were patching shirts; young mother angels were rocking cradles, lulling the first-born little ones with song," while at the local tavern, named after Noah, the proverbial biblical drunkard, angels of the coarser sort "were sitting at small tables, drinking spirits, smoking cheap tobacco, and continually spitting at the floor through their teeth." Manger's translation of a spit-covered tavern floor into the fields of paradise has an imaginative affinity with Bellow's conjuring up Lenox Avenue and 125th Street in the supposed heart of darkness, though the emotional effect is rather different: Bellow transports a zest for things familiar into the scary realm of the unknown, while Manger, equally moved by affection for the familiar, introduces into the True World *(di emese velt)* the grossness, the poignancy, and the sadness of things flawed in the world below. In both cases, humor is generated by the disparity between our expectations of an ideal type (the primordial African, the paradisiac soul) and what the writer actually invents for us, but Manger's comedy is tinged with wistfulness, for if indeed we have only our familiar world to imagine with, then wherever there is life, schoolboys are whipped, poor tailors starve, parents and children bicker, and the spiritual magnates *(tsadikim)* lord it over the common people.[2]

Something of this mood of soberly realistic humor touched with sadness is present in Bernard Malamud's naturalization of fantasy to the American Jewish immigrant milieu. Malamud has his own vividly humanized angels—the black Jew from Harlem in "Angel Levine" who, trying to earn his wings, comes to the aid of a poor Jewish tailor, and Ginzburg, the ominous Yiddish-accented figure in "Idiots First" who turns out to be the *malekh-hamoves*, the Angel of Death. At the penultimate moment of "Idiots First," Mendel, the distraught father, seizes Ginzburg in anger, crying, "You bastard, don't you understand what it means human?"; and a moment later

[2]Manger, *The Book of Paradise*, translated by Leonard Wolf (Hill and Wang, 1965), p. 8.

Ginzburg is actually shocked into relenting, despite himself allowing Mendel's idiot son to depart for California. This final turn of the plot could serve as an emblem of how this whole mode of imagination works, wresting a kind of concession from the ultimate powers by the very act of humanizing them, conceiving them in such a way that they will understand what it means human.

A related translation of the fantastic into the familiar is effected, perhaps with more artistic success, in another Malamud story, "The Jewbird." It becomes evident very soon in the story that this remarkable talking bird—*"Gevalt,* a pogrom" are its first words, when the Jewish pater familias takes a swipe at it—is virtually an allegorical figure of the wandering Old World Jew. Its name, after its color, is Schwartz, and in the eyes of its unwilling host it is clearly what is known in the vernacular as a *shvartser yid,* a Jew who is "black" not in the racial sense but in the foul oppressiveness of his crude manner and his religious obscurantism. "The Jewbird," in fact, deals in its peculiar way with essentially the same predicament of identity as Philip Roth's "Eli the Fanatic"—the ambivalence, guilt, and impulse to rejection aroused in an American Jew by the confrontation with a black-garbed survivor of the ancestral world. Without the fantasy of the talking bird, and the muted comedy generated by that incongruity, this would be merely a sour story. As it is, the conclusion is bleak enough, Schwartz finally being cast out and ending in the snow with a twisted neck. Without the grubby realism in which the fantasy is embodied, the bird would be only a contrived symbol and the story would lack conviction. Malamud's invention engages the imagination precisely because the black bird of exile is able to assume so persuasively the habits and accents of a familiar milieu and a familiar type. He has a fondness for herring and schnapps, his breath stinks of garlic, his speech is a chain of wry Yiddish twists, only minimally conforming to the prevalent syntactical and lexical requirements of spoken English.

Now, one might be tempted to dismiss all this as a compound of anecdotal affectation passed off as fictional invention were it not for its necessary function in the Jewbird's relation to his host, Harry Cohen. For Cohen, the "Americanized" frozen-food salesman, the bird must embody in all its details the stigmatized stereotype of a kind of Jew that he emphatically wants to leave behind. Cohen is really attacking a part of himself in his hostility toward Schwartz, as becomes clear at the end of the story when, swinging the bird around his head, he enacts a parody of the ceremony of *shlogen kopores*, in which a rooster was whirled in the air before being slaughtered on the eve of the Day of Atonement, while the person holding the bird recited the formula, "This is my surrogate, this is my atonement." What the reader quickly realizes is that Cohen is by far the grosser of the two figures, and that by contrast, Schwartz, in the very pungency of his garlic-redolent Yiddishisms, possesses a certain quality of nobility. He is a creature who lives meagerly, but lives nevertheless, by his wit, and even though this resource finally fails him, the impress he makes is of a shrewd, engagingly stubborn survivor. He knows too much of the hardships of surviving to have any grand expectations of future circumstances, but his mental shrugs help him maintain some sort of inner equilibrium through his difficulties by ceding their inevitability while contracting their ruinous nature to imaginable dimensions. The very first words of the story, where the narrator seems to move immediately to a rendering of Schwartz's interior speech, briskly define the use of a kind of acerbic stoicism as a means of coping with adversity: "The window was open so the skinny bird flew in. Flappity-flap with its frazzled black wings. That's how it goes. It's open, you're in. Closed, you're out and that's your fate." As we perceive from the grief to which the Jewbird finally comes, this is hardly a way of overcoming disaster, but it does provide a strength of resolution to go on.

The procedure of amiable domestication to which Manger and Malamud subject their angels is happily applied by Isaac Bashevis Singer to the multitude of demons who variously prance, slink, and amble through his stories. One of the most memorable of all these is the nameless narrator of "The Last Demon,"[3] a story in which the immense sadness of matter and the delightfulness of manner constitute a paradigm for the

---

[3]English translation in *Short Friday* (Farrar, Straus & Giroux, 1964).

use of comedy as a last defense of the imagination against grim fate. This story is one of the rare attempts anywhere in Singer's work to respond to the horror of the Holocaust, and it is effective precisely because of the brilliant obliquity of its method. The demon briefly alludes to the Holocaust in the opening words of his tale but then promptly drops the subject and seems to forget about it until the last three paragraphs of the story: "I, a demon, bear witness that there are no more demons left. Why demons, when man himself is a demon? Why persuade to evil someone who is already convinced? . . . I board in an attic in Tishevitz and draw my sustenance from a Yiddish storybook, a left-over from the days before the great catastrophe." The original is less ambiguous, since *khurben*, the word rendered as "catastrophe," is the accepted term for the Holocaust. In any case, our immediate attention is caught less by the magnitude of the catastrophe than by the amusing, cool-headed logicality of the speaker—"after all, should I go convince someone that's already convinced?"— who at once proceeds to affirm by statement and demonstrate by tone his authenticity as a familiar folk figure: "I don't have to tell you that I'm a Jew. What else, a Gentile? I've heard that there are Gentile demons, but I don't know any, nor do I wish to know them. Jacob and Esau don't become in-laws." Tone, of course, is tied up with language, and so "What else, a Gentile?" catches only part of the homey nuance of *"vos den bin ikh, a goy?"* while the humor of Jacob and Esau as in-laws is largely lost because there is no English equivalent for the Yiddish *mekhutonim*, which implies an elaborate and dignified sense of social alliance and extended kinship, and is sometimes also used jocularly or sardonically to suggest a dubious or presumptuous relationship.

The demon-narrator is thoroughly engaging not only in his easy command of the comic inflections of the folk, sharpened in the Yiddish by his talmudist's fondness for Hebraisms and Aramaicisms, but also in the way he maintains the jaunty posture of a city slicker (from Lublin) condemned by the infernal powers-that-be to cool his heels among the hayseeds. He has a worldling's contempt for Tishevitz, a one-horse, mud-choked town so small, he claims, that "In the tailors' synagogue a billy goat is the tenth in the quorum." He can only condescend to the resident imp of Tishevitz, a hopeless yokel who "cracks jokes that didn't amuse Enoch" and "drops names from the Haggadah," to whom he charitably proposes the possibility of a devil's position elsewhere: "We have an opening for a mixer of bitter herbs. You only work Passovers." Alongside the breezy urbanity of the demon, the virtuous young rabbi whom he chooses as his target seems a pale figure. The minimal plot of the story consists of the demon's futile effort to tempt the rabbi. The implicit point of that action is its very humanity: this is a world where good and evil are still struggled over and the rules of the game are familiar to both sides, where the rabbi is truly saintly and the demon one of the old school, the sort that can quote Bible and Talmud with the best of them, conjure up for his victim visions of sex and power and even a chance at messiahship, who preens himself on his abilities but is smart enough to know when he has met his match. Then, in a few swift sentences, with no transition and without the hint of an appeal for pathos, this whole world is wiped away:

The rabbi was martyred on a Friday in the month of Nisan. The community was slaughtered, the holy books burned, the cemetery desecrated. The *Book of Creation* has been returned to the Creator. . . . The generation is already guilty seven times over, but Messiah does not come. To whom should he come? Messiah did not come for the Jews, so the Jews went to Messiah. There is no further need for demons. We have also been annihilated. I am the last, a refugee. I can go anywhere I please, but where should a demon like me go? To the murderers?

Tempting though it may be to read the last word of the passage as it appears in English with a throat flooded with outrage, it seems to me that what the whole context of the story calls for is another sardonic shrug, closing the circle of those with which the story began—"What do you think, a self-respecting demon like me should go mix with murderers?" The consideration of tone is essential because the tone suggests that even after genocide—and the entire story, we must recall, is told retrospectively after that ghastly fact— the demon maintains his humanity (what else, devilishness?) by preserving his knowing, ironic sense of things, though tinged now with bitterness. Significantly, the story ends with the narrator's attention wholly absorbed in the Yiddish story-book he alluded to at the beginning. The book is an old-fash-ioned compilation in the best demonic manner, filled with blas-phemies, denials of God's justice, invitations to transgression and despair. "But nevertheless the letters are Jewish," the last demon affirms, and he lingers over them, torturing each one with the traditional *pilpul* of interpretation, drawing nurture from them. In kabbalistic lore, the twenty-two letters of the Hebrew alphabet, the letters through which God created the world, remain ontological constituents of reality. Through their combinations and permutations man can tap sources of cosmic power, establish connections with the ulti-mate ground of being. The Yiddish black book over which the demon pores represents merely a reversed mirror-image of that kabbalistic tradition: the narrator concludes with the recitation of a demon's alphabet, from *aleph* to *yod*, in which each sacred letter is made to spell disaster but nevertheless remains a sign in a system of cosmic orthography, a key of meaning, though the meaning is dismal. Humor collapses in the face of utter chaos, and the characteristic Jewish humor of shrewd observation especially needs to assume a realm of meaning accessible to intelligence, even if it suspects that whatever meaning it unearths will be perverse, unconsoling.

Something of the general function of the comic domestica-tion of myth may be revealed by the fact that in Singer's story the surviving demon proves in the end to be a surrogate for the writer—a wry teller of tales in the old way, steeped in the values and traditions of a vanished world, conjuring with the letters of the lost in the sickening vacuum left by their de-struction. My description, of course, of the narrator's final predicament is a little misleading because it neglects his en-gaging buoyancy of tone in all but the three concluding para-graphs of the story: the last demon is not a self-dramatizing Survivor[4] but, almost eerily, an enlivening voice from the Old World, demonstrating the peculiar vitality of its values through his own person. Instructively, writers who draw on

[4]The hint of melodramatic tremolo in the title is absent from the Yiddish, in which the story is simply called "A Tale of Tishevitz."

this whole mode of folk imagination tend to create fictional events that are not impersonally conveyed but manifestly *narrated*, as though the act of narration and the presence of a narrator sane enough to be funny in a mad world were a way of hanging on to lucidity.

If much modern writing, from Rimbaud's attempted *dérèglement de tous les sens* to the jumbled hallucinations of William Burroughs, has conceived radical disorientation as the necessary path to reality, the legacy of Jewish humor, by contrast, seems to encourage a kind of traditionalism in writers, leading them to draw even the realms of the ultimate unknown into a comfortable human space warmed and worn by long usage. This imaginative at-homeness with the experience of a personal and collective past generally implies a stubborn if cautious hopefulness about the future, or perhaps simply the ability to imagine a human future. Thus Singer's demon draws "sustenance" from the letters, knowing that when the letters are gone, he will be gone, too, and the imaginable world at an end. If disaster, whatever the scale, seems to be our general fate, the persistence of the comic reflex is itself evidence of the perdurability of the stuff of humanity: a shrug is a small and subtle gesture, but, in the face of the harshest history, it may take a world of strength to make.

—1972

> *The novelist of today . . . cannot quite believe*
> *in . . . his finite world. That is, the existence of*
> *Highbury or the Province of O—is rendered*
> *improbable, unveracious, by Buchenwald*
> *and Auschwitz, the population curve of*
> *China, and the hydrogen bomb.*
> —Mary McCarthy
> *The Humanist in the Bathtub*

A Novel of the Post-Tragic World

Anyone for whom novels have mattered must surely at times be troubled by the sort of doubt Mary McCarthy raised some years ago in one of her most intelligent, and disquieting, essays, "The Fact in Fiction." In a century of scarcely imaginable historical outrages, what, after all, is one to do with a literary form so sturdily commonsensical, concerned as it traditionally has been with the realistic rendering of ordinary experience, the potential of revelation in trivia, the gossipy side of human intercourse, the petty frustrations, sordidness, or sheer banality of local scenes and personal relations? Mary McCarthy states this dilemma of the contemporary novelist with painful sharpness: "If he writes about his province, he feels its inverisimilitude; if he tries, on the other hand, to write about people who make lampshades of human skin, like the infamous Ilse Koch, he feels still more the inverisimilitude of what he is asserting."

The work of S. Y. Agnon provides an especially instructive instance of the difficulties of the novelistic imagination in engaging modern historical reality because there is such a peculiar and baffling duality in Agnon's relation to the twentieth century. Stylistically, of course, he made a point of seceding from his own age, insisting on a meticulously classical Hebrew, even, for example, in the speech of a kibbutznik or the dialogue of a very contemporary lover and his mistress— a language that goes back many centuries to the formative texts of rabbinic tradition. Both early and late in his career, he sometimes chose to write about what was, literally, his province (Galicia) before its familiar forms of Jewish life were obliterated by the onslaught of modern history. Turn-of-the-century Buczacz remained a favorite setting for his shorter fiction, in his declining years occasionally inviting something like pious reminiscence, and his first big novel, *The Bridal Canopy*, takes us all the way back to a Galicia of the eighteenth century. Yet Agnon could not, I think, have written at all without in some way using his work to sound the abysses of modern history, for modern history constituted a ruthlessly uncompromising challenge to the validity of the language, values, and traditions from which he shaped his fiction.

As an ironist and a brilliant fabulist, he preferred to approach the menace of recent history obliquely, often displacing the raw terror of contemporary experience into various kinds of symbolic images and parabolic intimations that could be held at an intellectual distance. Thus, the book that seems to me his most original and powerful novel, *T'mol Shilshom* (*Just Yesterday*, a work that has not yet been translated into English), though conceived and written as the crematoria roared, took for its setting the distant and comparatively placid historical period of Palestine in the first decade of the century. The utter bleakness, however, of this novel's vision of man and God may be, after all, a direct response to the nightmare of the Hitler years, as Arnold Band has plausibly argued. The grotesque "dog's death" of the protagonist, described in hideous detail, is by no means a symbol of the fate of European Jewry, but it does suggest itself as an analogy, generating in the reader a sense of outrage and helpless dismay that would be appropriate responses to a senseless catastrophe that is historical, not merely individual. Agnon can produce this double effect all the more readily because one of the central impulses of *Just Yesterday* is to give the lie to theodicies, and God as an object of radical critique remains conveniently timeless. When a pious woman cries out in anguish at the end of the book, "After all, we know the Holy One's mercies are many, but why doesn't he have mercy on us?" her words, pronounced in a fictional time, circa 1910, resonate over an actual 1945 landscape gray with human ash and clotted with mass graves.

A novel so grim and uncompromising as *Just Yesterday* could hardly be called an evasion, but it deals with contemporary history only by indirection, while in the foreground it focuses on less apocalyptic, more manageable, processes of historical decline: the decadence and petrifaction of Orthodox Judaism, the erosion of traditional Jewish values in the new secularist milieu, the crippling disorientation of an individual cut loose from the moorings of the Old World and unable to find himself in the new one. It remained for Agnon to attempt a direct, full-scale novelistic rendering of the contemporary Jerusalem he knew as it was gripped by the historical violence immediately surrounding it and shaken by the shock waves of the much vaster movement of violence that swept over Europe from 1933 to 1945. This was the major task that occupied him—sometimes, one is tempted to say, as a kind of labor of Sisyphus—for the last twenty years of his life. In 1949, four years after the appearance of *Just Yesterday*, Agnon published in the *Ha-aretz Yearbook* the first chapters of a new novel, *Shira*. From 1949 to 1955 some two hundred pages of the novel appeared in the same annual publication. After that the publishing of portions of the work in progress stopped, until two more chapters appeared in 1966. Throughout this period, as one might imagine, there was a continual hum of rumor in the Israeli literary world about the scope of the novel, its ultimate direction, about whether, as Agnon occasionally hinted to visitors, an immense magnum opus lay finished in one of his drawers, awaiting the whim of the master to be revealed to the world. According to the testimony of Agnon's daughter, he set aside the manuscript after the mid-fifties and then began again to work on it seriously in the last years of his life. During his final illness, he gave instructions for the manuscript to be published, indicating certain chapters in manuscript that were to be omitted, others to be included. Now, a year after Agnon's death, *Shira,* his longest novel and his most contemporary in setting and personages, has finally been published in Israel. The novel is still without an ending, and at a number of points obviously still in need of the author's editing (particularly in the overabundance of anecdotal digressions), yet with its flaws it is a compelling—at times, haunting—book that confronts directly problems Agnon was content merely to allude to elsewhere in his writing.

The materials of *Shira* more closely resemble those of the traditional European novel than do the materials of any other long work of fiction by Agnon. The social milieu in which the action is set is the best approximation of a bourgeoisie offered by Jerusalem on the eve of World War II—the highly Germanic academic community of the Hebrew University, with its acute consciousness of rank and status, its rituals of social propriety, its squabbles and intrigues, its constant institutional fuss and bother, all seen here in a caustic, satiric light. The action itself pivots upon the most traditional of novelistic subjects, adultery, though, as I shall try to show, Agnon does some rather peculiar things with this subject. The protagonist, Manfred Herbst, a lecturer in Byzantine history, is a scholar capable of the most selfless dedication to his work, but while he endlessly accumulates notes and references and index cards for that big second book, a study of the burial of the poor in Byzantium, the book itself never materializes and his professorship remains a distant mirage. Herbst is decidedly an autumnal figure, as his German last name suggests, soul-weary from years on the academic and domestic treadmills: one is a little startled to learn near the end of the novel that he is only forty-three, which would make him perhaps barely forty when the action starts. "Action" is something of an exaggeration, since we first see Herbst and his wife Henrietta lapsing into somnolence in the reception room of a maternity ward. Herbst watches his pregnant wife doze between contractions, studying her faded, distorted features, and then he himself nods. He is awakened by the entrance of a nurse named Shira, "tall, masculine, wearing glasses that jutted out impudently in front of her eyes, making the freckles on her gray cheeks rise like nailheads in an old wall."[1] Hardly an alluring bedmate, one would think, but within a few hours, while Henrietta, presumably, is giving birth, Herbst will find himself alone with Shira in her room where she, changed now into a light blouse and tight blue slacks, uncannily becomes a potent sexual presence and quickly moves the shy academician from caressing touch to naked embrace. The surge of guilt Herbst feels after the encounter is predictable, and so his subsequent visits to Shira are intermittent, ambivalent, driven. She on her part allows him to go to bed with her only two or three times more, choosing for inscrutable reasons to tantalize rather than satisfy him. Eventually, she disappears without a trace, leaving him his obsession with her, his violently erotic dreams, a recollected line of Hebrew verse that insistently repeats itself in his head: "Flesh like your flesh will not soon be forgotten."

This exploration of the poignancy of banal experience is very much in keeping with the traditions of the realistic novel, and the plot itself—the futile attempt to escape the aridity of bourgeois life by pursuing a will-o'-the-wisp of passion—is virtually the archetypal plot of the classical European novel. What makes *Shira* crucially different is the fact that this familiar domestic drama is enacted against the obtrusive background of a world in flames. All around Herbst and his books, wife, and mistress, Arabs are killing Jews. (These were the grim days, in the years between 1936 and 1939, of murderous assaults by Arab bands on the Jewish settlement, during which the Haganah followed the policy of *havlagah*, or non-reprisal.) A Jewish boy murdered by Arabs is mentioned on the first page of the novel, later Herbst himself is barely missed by a sniper's bullet, and painful reminders of the unending killings are repeatedly thrust upon him in a variety of ways. At a greater geographical distance, Hitler is preparing his death camps. Jerusalem is flooded with refugees, many of them broken inside by the violent wrench from their

[1]The translations throughout are my own.–R. A.

old way of life. Henrietta Herbst has aged prematurely from the frantic, unavailing effort of running from office to office to obtain immigration certificates for her otherwise doomed relatives in Germany. Ironically, Herbst, the man of sedentary learning and vagrant passion, heads a household of activists—his wife trying to intercede with the authorities, one grown daughter joining a kibbutz, the other becoming a terrorist, while he, like most of the world under the shadow of apocalypse, continues to read, write, think, brood, and lust.

I have called the plot of *Shira* a "domestic drama," but in fact Agnon takes pains to emphasize the utter aimlessness of the events narrated, thus carefully destroying any dramatic urgency they might generate. The story breaks down into a series of deliberately repetitious, rudderless circlings: Herbst at his desk, hovering over his mounting stacks of notes; Herbst drifting through the streets of Jerusalem, going round and round Shira's apartment, now always locked and empty; Herbst going over and over in his mind the memory of the soft flesh that will not soon be forgotten. This quality of drift is, of course, partly a function of Herbst's indecisive character, but the narrator himself ultimately connects it with the general impact of public experience upon private life in an age of historical enormities: "Ever since the wars began coming one after the other, with killing upon killing upon murder, shrinking the value of man, the power of the moral qualities has been drained, the sting of hatred blunted, the honeyed taste of love gone, and everything follows the impulse of the moment." The comprehensiveness of this catalogue is noteworthy. All the moral qualities *(midot)*, good and bad, have lost their urgency; hatred as well as love is insipid. The point is not, as in the cliché, that man has become a monster but rather that his moral life does not seem to matter to him any more in an era of global massacres. An Emma Bovary or an Anna Karenina could believe passionately and take fierce delight in her illusions; Manfred Herbst lives in a world where grand dreams are absurd, and the would-be heroic individual is no longer capable of morally challenging the accepted order of things by casting up against it an intense vision of private fulfillment. In stark contrast to the hero of the traditional novel, Herbst has no illusions at all about his

Defenses of the Imagination 174

mistress. He stumbles into her path quite accidentally, is attracted to her entirely by "the impulse of the moment" *(yetzer
ha-sha'ah)*, and afterward experiences not love but a sour
and distracting erotic obsession. Even in his guilt, moreover,
he wonders whether the whole affair really amounts to anything, whether moral consequentiality is not entirely a matter
of convention. The "honeyed taste of love" appears once in
the novel, retrospectively, when Henrietta recalls an idyllic
swim in the nude with Herbst during their courtship in Berlin
almost a quarter of a century earlier; but such Edenic love
clearly has no place in the "war years" which are the setting
for the main action of the novel.

Yet, peculiarly, there abides in Manfred Herbst's private
experience, however circumscribed and frustrated, a stubbornly human value, something that at moments seems almost precious. Politics for Herbst (and, one assumes, for
Agnon) is a realm of futility, unmanageable, unimaginable,
inhuman. "Through politics," he bitterly announces to a
young girl whose father has been murdered by Arabs, "one
dies and through politics one is killed, through politics one
gets sick and through politics speeches are made and shots
fired." Though he has occasional misgivings about his own
stance, politics is simply not a sphere with which he can deal;
however insistently it impinges on him, he remains a
thoroughly private person. Man as a private creature rather
than a strictly political animal is impelled by three age-old
drives: to seek knowledge, to make beauty, and to gratify his
senses. All three of these impulses are strong in Herbst, and
it is through an insight into the dynamics of their interrelation
that Agnon manages to articulate in *Shira* an immensely
suggestive statement about the place of fiction, and of art, in
an age of endemic disaster.

At first glance, the pursuit of knowledge—and for the most
part, it is the knowledge of distant antiquity—in this novel
may seem merely grotesque. On occasion, the harshly sardonic satire is quite explicit: "Wechsler sits as is his wont
doing his own work, classifying talismans and seals and family insignia and putting them into bags and leaving Hitler to
kill and the Jews to save themselves." Now, in interpreting
the harshness here, it is important to note that Agnon distin-

guishes crucially between the disinterested pursuit of knowledge and the exploitation of supposed knowledge for selfish
ends. The academic profession here, like most professions
everywhere, is filled with singleminded careerists, opportu-
nists, and charlatans, playing all the old academic games with
doctored footnotes, unacknowledged borrowings from colleagues and students, selective use of documents, and slick
restatements of worn ideas. The cutting edge of Agnon's
satire is directed not against the academic enterprise as such
but against those manifestations of it which are really a kind
of confidence game and not a pursuit of knowledge at all.
Wechsler, for example—his name means "changer" or "bro-
ker"—has made a brilliant career out of the discovery and
purported deciphering of a scrap of ancient leather on which
appear three fragmentary letters so obscure that no one is
sure whether they should be read from right to left or from
left to right.

By contrast, the book repeatedly alludes to Professor Neu,
Herbst's teacher in Germany, as the model of a superbly
perceptive mind unswervingly devoted to the discovery of
truth, and it is clearly felt in the novel that such devotion is
one of the preeminently human activities, becoming in its pure
state a moral achievement on its own account. Just before the
point where the narrative breaks off, Herbst meets a medical
researcher who had infected himself with a highly dangerous
disease in order to discover a cure for it. Deeply troubled,
Herbst wonders whether he and his fellow humanists would
be capable of such sacrifice for the knowledge they seek, and
he concludes that there are rare men like Neu who would not
fail even that test. For those who can carry on the academic
enterprise in such a spirit, their persistence in it even at a
moment of historical cataclysm is not selfish privatism, like
Wechsler's, but the affirmation of a basic value of civilization.

Agnon is concerned, however, to suggest the ultimate limits of historical knowledge, which is quite a different matter
from satirizing the self-seeking practitioners of a bogus historiography. One reason for Herbst's failure to finish his book
is his acutely honest sense of the tentativeness of all our
knowledge of the past. A magisterial intelligence like Neu's
can, after painstaking research, illuminate whole regions of

the past that were previously cloaked in darkness—might Agnon have had his friend Gershom Scholem in mind?—but nagging doubts persist about the ubiquitous necessity to work from partly suppositious evidence, incomplete documents, chains of inference, and possibly faulty hypotheses. Historical investigation, moreover, even when it is disinterested, is seen to involve a special sort of self-absorption without genuine self-knowledge. It seems to promise but never really delivers the kind of truth one needs to live with at a moment of universal mayhem. This point is clearly suggested by the very remoteness of the materials studied by these Jerusalem scholars (patristics, Byzantine history, proto-Sinaitic literary remains); and Herbst's own preoccupation with ancient practices of interment obviously suggests that the past available to historical research is, literally and figuratively, dead and buried.

Against this large sense of the limits of scholarship as a source of existential truth, imaginative literature is presented in the novel almost polemically as the alternative to the scholarly way. There is more direct discussion of the value and nature of literature here than anywhere else in Agnon's work. *Shira* completely drops the characteristic Agnon affectation of independence from the corpus of European literature: Goethe, Rilke, Stefan George, Strindberg, Balzac, Tolstoy are on the lips and minds of both the characters and the narrator; Herbst himself has been a careful student of the literary classics and is an avid reader of contemporary fiction and poetry. More than once the novel comments ironically on the multitudes that read literature for all the wrong reasons—for moral edification, for the imbibing of a grand "message," for the understanding of social problems, for the revelation of erotic mysteries, the excitement of the plot, the richness of the language, or simply to while away the time. For Herbst, on the other hand, "the essence of any book was in the power of its poetry, in the living spirit it embodied, in its imaginative power, in its truth." It is hardly accidental that this series should begin with poetry *(shira)* and end with truth *(emet)*, and some clue to the concrete meaning of those large, ringing terms may be grasped if one recalls that they are the equivalent of the German *Dichtung und Wahrheit.* That, of course, is the title of the work of Goethe's old age, not a theoretical statement but an autobiography, an elaborate literary experiment in self-knowledge, a study of the making of a poet which is, incidentally, divided into four parts, like Agnon's novel. The story of Manfred Herbst also turns out, somewhat surprisingly, to be about the making of a poet. Nearly halfway through the book, the diligent historian, pondering the intrigues of the Byzantine court, is seized with the sudden realization that what he must make of them is not another article for the learned journals but a tragedy. Comically, he grabs a notebook and begins to jot down a thumbnail bibliography on tragedy: Aristotle's *Poetics*, Sophocles's *Antigone*, *Wilhelm Meister*, Lessing, Herder, Schiller, Schlegel, Jean Paul. One can already guess that Herbst will never actually write the tragedy, though the reasons for his failure lie less in his academic work habits than in the reticence of his moral imagination.

It is only after his involvement with Shira that Herbst conceives the idea of becoming an imaginative writer, and the reader of the novel can scarcely forget that her name means "poetry." Yet, paradoxically, Shira is the most thoroughly unpoetic of "muses," not only in her aggressive manner and her often sloppy appearance but in the open contempt she shows for literature, literati, and all lofty aestheticism. If it were not for the distracting thoughts about Shira, the narrator observes, Herbst would be able to write his tragedy (which is, of course, another kind of *shira*, of poetry). Nevertheless, it is appropriate that this harsh and elusive mistress should bear the name of poetry, for the inflaming, exacerbating relationship she offers Herbst is the gateway to the difficult world of artistic creation, a world of imperious, passionate experience, of naked confrontation with self and other, outside the rules and restrictions and protective structures of bourgeois society. *Shira* is more openly concerned with sexuality than any of Agnon's other novels because it is a study of the intimate and intricate connection between sexuality and artistic creativity, between both those terms and self-knowledge.

In this connection, it is important to note that the sexuality operating in the relationship between Herbst and Shira and ramified in a variety of dreams and narrative insets throughout the novel is, by conventional standards, perverse. Shira's masculinity, as we have seen, is observed the moment she enters the novel, and Herbst quickly realizes that she appeals to him precisely because she vividly embodies the radical ambiguity of male and female roles and identity. When she slips out of her nurse's uniform into "man's clothing" (the blue slacks), he discovers that her womanliness is suddenly enhanced. Later, in dream and waking experience, he will encounter other women whom he confuses with men. At the feminine end of the spectrum, Lisbeth Neu, a niece of the great professor and the delicately idealized alternative to Shira in Herbst's fantasies, arouses his desire because of the shadow of downy hair on her upper lip. "Women with a faint sign of masculinity," Herbst observes of Lisbeth, "can drive us wild. Look at Shira, she seems half-man, but when you know her better you realize that no one is more womanly." In the great climactic dream that concludes Book One of the novel, the opposites of masculine and feminine, scholarship and poetry, Herbst and Shira, Shira and Lisbeth Neu, all merge phantasmagorically. Shira, in her blue slacks of the first night, appears before the scholar in a form so threatening that his teeth start to chatter and he cries out, "If you insist on living my life, you will have to turn into a man." The still-dreaming Herbst then encounters a friend from his student days, a classics major who "used to correct Wilamowitz's translations of the Greek tragedies." The two begin to talk about "the limiting of genders in language, and especially about those words which are masculine in one language and feminine in another. Herbst wanted to mention the word *poeta* as Neu interpreted it." In the final sequence of the dream, Herbst stumbles through a series of grotesque frustrations and in the end buys a silver knife as a wedding present for the marriage of Shira to Lisbeth Neu.

All this, of course, reflects the neuroses of Manfred Herbst, but even more interesting is what it suggests about the relationship between erotic experience and art. The realm into which Shira introduces her lover is a realm where all fixed roles are denied. Herbst's bourgeois-academic milieu, by contrast, is a sphere where personal and professional roles, not to speak of rank, are utterly determined and scarcely to be questioned. The academic mind itself tends to work with a neat classroom logic that excludes the paradoxical identity of antinomies. Thus, in formal grammar masculine and feminine are mutually exclusive, though language itself, mirroring more complex human realities, presents anomalous exceptions to the rules, and a scholar of the stature of Neu is able to perceive that the Greco-Roman word for poet crucially crosses the ordinary demarcations of gender and morphology. The realm of poetry—in Agnon's Hebrew either *piyut* (masculine) or *shira* (feminine)—is a realm of the polymorphous perverse imagination, which can assume either sex, any identity, the most exalting and the most degrading of relations and activities. It is a far more dangerous, disturbing sphere of existence than the four-square world of the solid burgher, but precisely for that reason it can embrace more of the truth, though it also makes exacting demands of the individual who would attain that truth. In the world of *shira-piyut,* sex is a plunge into the unknown. In bourgeois academe, it is a utilitarian act of biological procreation: Henrietta conceives on each of the two occasions in the novel when Herbst is said to have had intercourse with her; he habitually addresses her as "Mother"; and when, at the midpoint of the novel, he presses against her in bed, desperately calling "Mother, Mother," we see that this kind of sex is an escape from experience and a return to the womb.

One highly significant detail in Herbst's dream that I have not yet commented on is his choice of a silver knife as a wedding gift for Shira and Lisbeth Neu. In the suppressed inner life of this quiet academician, there is a progressively insistent association between sex and violence. Not long after her first meeting with Herbst, Shira has a sado-masochistic encounter with a certain genteel engineer equipped with an exquisitely cunning whip. As Shira begins to report this experience to Herbst in languorous detail, she coyly challenges him: " 'And you, my dear little boy, tell me, aren't you capable of hitting a woman?' Herbst, shocked, answered no, while he felt himself close to raising his hand and slapping her across the face." Later, Herbst will begin to have recurrent nightmares of rape and dismemberment. In the most significant version, Shira goes for a walk on the beach with the engineer

—now a dream-surrogate for Herbst—who, deprived of his whip, is forced to flee and watch from a hiding place while Shira is stabbed and raped by Arabs, and the unforgettable "flesh like your flesh" of the line of verse, recalled in the dream, is reduced to butchered meat.

The "political" implication of this descent into the nether self is virtually the same one that emerges from the sexual portrait of a pacifist girl in *I Am Curious (Yellow)*, though the novel is entirely free of the Swedish film's heavyhanded didacticism. Herbst, by background and temperament inclined to pacifism, has been peripherally involved in Brit Shalom, the pacifist binationalist movement led by Martin Buber, Judah Magnes, and other Hebrew University figures, but he remembers another time, when he had to "wade up to the knees in blood" as a German soldier in World War I. In fact, pacifism for Jews at a time of bloody assaults against Jews is clearly seen as a suicidal retreat from history for the sake of a self-congratulatory posture of higher morality. Yet in the novel, in any case, Agnon is not interested in making a programmatic political statement but in penetrating human nature at a time of bewilderingly murderous politics. Herbst, the well-meaning, peace-loving *homme moyen sensuel*, proves in the depths of sexual violence pent up inside him to be profoundly implicated in the world of "killing upon killing upon murder" from which his conscious mind recoils. Thus, the psychic energies that issue in global slaughter are sounded in the novel as they pulse through a private life, the insight of art becoming a first condition for the realistic imagination of politics.

The hiatus in Herbst between unconscious and conscious self is the most essential reason for his failure to write the tragedy of which he dreams. If, as I have suggested, poetry is seen as the realm of the polymorphous perverse imagination, it also requires, paradoxically, imaginative discipline and an unblinking courage of vision, and these are beyond Herbst. Early in the novel, the scholar proudly shows to a friend a copy of the first edition of Nietzsche's *The Birth of Tragedy* which he has discovered in a used-book shop in Jerusalem. The frustration of Herbst's ambition to become a tragedian can be explained directly in terms of Nietzsche; indeed, much of *Shira* might usefully be viewed as fictional variations on themes from *The Birth of Tragedy*. (In all this, I would be inclined to suspect an ultimate indebtedness to the imaginative use of Nietzsche in the fiction of Thomas Mann, though Mann is never alluded to by Agnon and the two writers have not generally been linked by Hebrew critics.) For Nietzsche, one recalls, the roots of tragedy are in the connection it maintains with that chaos of human nature and of existence which is usually masked by the institutions and psychology of life in culture. Herbst, in Nietzsche's terms, is neither an Apollonian nor a Dionysian but a Socratic type, "Socratic" culture being the falsely optimistic culture dedicated to science rather than to wisdom, to the rationalized accumulation of knowledge. The Socratic impulse, in Nietzsche's view, dominates modern Europe, making it the antitragic culture par excellence. The ultimate implication of *Shira*'s satire on the academic world is Nietzschean, for in the tragic vision of life, the bearded satyr is the true archetype of man and, as Nietzsche writes, "Confronted with him, the man of culture shriveled into a mendacious caricature." The real Shira of the flesh and, still more, the protean and menacing Shira of Herbst's imagination introduce the scholar to the realm of Dionysian experience. The various avatars of Shira seem "to whisper to us," as Nietzsche says of the tragic myth of the Sphinx, "that wisdom, and particularly Dionysian wisdom, is an unnatural abomination; that he who by means of his knowledge plunges nature into the abyss of destruction must also suffer the dissolution of nature in his own person." Herbst, as a would-be tragedian, must be able to contain this dissolution in Apollonian form. (His daughter sends him a postcard from Greece with a picture of Apollo and an inscription on the statue's arm, "greetings from Apollo"; comic mention is made more than once of Tchernichovsky's Nietzschean poem, "Before the Statue of Apollo," in which Apollo turns out to be Dionysus as well.) But Herbst cannot contain what he cannot confront.

Near the end of the novel, the historian comes to the conclusion that, "Modern poets may be experts on the ingredients of tragedy, some of them perhaps more than the early poets were, but because the ancients were believers, the creation of tragedy was granted to them." The idea is, of course, a familiar one, but it is worth trying to see the specific meanings given to this lost state of belief within the context of the novel. In the tragedies of Aeschylus and Sophocles, an inexorable principle of *diké*, or divine justice, works through the resistant medium of humanity, making possible some ultimate reconciliation at the end of the tragic agony—in terms of the literary form, making the tragic plot possible. For the moderns, who have seen "the power of the moral qualities . . . drained" by one wave of killings after another, divine justice is the most difficult of all beliefs, and so writers cannot imagine true tragedy but only, as Herbst puts it, "the narration of tragic events." More specifically, a modern intellectual like Herbst is no longer capable of absorbing the shattering impact of Dionysian return to primordial unity which, according to Nietzsche, was the basis for the tragic experience in a cult attuned to primal unities.

Since the fragmentary details of Herbst's plan for his tragic play indicate it is a projection of his obsession with Shira, one can infer that he is unable to write the play because he is finally too committed to the surface-world of his Socratic self to enter into the Dionysian depths intimated by his experience with her. In the projected tragedy, the emperor of Byzantium has designs on a young noblewoman which he plans to carry out when the pregnant empress goes into labor, thus leaving him free of her scrutiny. The parallel to Herbst's own story is clear, but the playwright has an even more important surrogate in the play, a slave named Basileios, who is the only character of the tragedy invented and not taken from history. This slave is in love with the same noblewoman the emperor desires—his predicament suggests Shira's unattainability for Herbst, the abject submission she demands of the scholar—but he contracts leprosy and is placed in quarantine outside the walls of the city. Significantly, the narrator of the novel notes that it was a tactical error for the playwright to make Basileios a leper, since Herbst was a man of delicate sensibility and could not bring himself to imagine concretely the physical appearance of leprosy, "how lepers treated one another and what their sexual practices were like."

The difference between the occurrence of disease here and

in classical tragedy is basic to the "death of tragedy" theme in the novel. *Oedipus the King* begins with a plague hanging over Thebes sent by the gods for the sins committed unknowingly by the king. When the full price of tragic suffering has been exacted, the plague will be lifted, the city purged. In Herbst's antitragic world, on the other hand, disease is not an instrument of divine justice but a correlative of the consciousness of guilt: it does not chastise or purge but lingers, loathesome. Herbst associates Shira (who is, of course, a nurse) with disease from the beginning of the novel. He has a recurrent hallucination of Shira enveloped in the polluted flesh of a blind beggar from Istanbul. (Istanbul, one should note, stands on the site of ancient Byzantium.) At one point, he convinces himself that he has contracted a venereal disease from her and lives for days in fear of infecting his wife and children. Nothing can be resolved through such disease because it is the image of an unhealthy soul incapable of facing its own experience squarely. (The parallels here with Mann's *Death in Venice* are suggestive.) Herbst, therefore, can be neither a participant in nor a creator of tragic experience. What the art of the novel—an essentially post-tragic art, Agnon seems to imply—can do is to use such images to illuminate the condition of particular figures like Herbst, communicating a unique sense of coherence through the very act of artistic illumination.

The novel offers one striking paradigm for the mode of communication of art, the meaning of its "poetry and truth," at a historical moment when disease has touched the inner nature of human reality. Herbst, rummaging through an upstairs room in a bookstore, comes across the reproduction of a large panoramic painting by an artist "of the school of Breughel." The subject is horrifying, and utterly mesmerizing: a leper, his eyes and hand eaten away by the disease, is ringing a bell to warn people off. Herbst is seized with the uncanny conviction that the infection emanates entirely from the bell, clear and bright at the center of the picture:

Who painted this picture? What was the name of the master artist who was able to infuse the spirit of life into an inanimate object? The men and women of the city could barely be seen, while the image of the diseased man, his hand and bell, were visible in great clarity. Despite this, you could see that everything in the town, the men and the women and the houses and the marketplace and the well were almost entirely tranquil, without the slightest apprehension, but the sound of the bell had already started out from the bell, clanging and reverberating and moving outward from the diseased man's hand, and a great dread was drawing near. Herbst looked at the picture again, looked at the leper and his hand but not at the bell, for now he realized that the sickness could not be in the bell. All the while he avoided touching the picture as if its form had been smirched like that of a living leper. . . . At that moment it was clear to Herbst that he heard a sound emanating from the bell in the diseased man's hand proclaiming a warning, "Get away, don't touch me." Herbst observed the warning voice and did not touch the picture but he looked and looked again with terror-stricken eyes and an eager soul.

The Breughelian painting—like a few of the greatest modern novels—combines an intense quality of apocalyptic vision with painstaking, almost clinical realism in the rendering of individual detail against a large social background. At the center of vision is the uncanny bell, a visible token of the true artist's ability to focus the reality he represents, to give it formal coherence and thus significance. What the bell communicates as its presence radiates out to the limits of the scene and beyond cannot be conveyed discursively, for it is the kind of immediate insight into the nature of things available only to the artist and realizable only in his chosen medium. The corresponding immediacy of communication through the achieved work of art is of course clear in the hallucinatory way the painting becomes a living, speaking presence to its observer. The complacent burghers in the background of the painting register no response to this resonating center of disease and impending dread at the heart of their world because their deafness is itself an essential and highly realistic part of the artist's subject. The same opposition between complacent trust in a false order and probing insight into radical disorder is the central opposition of this novel, as it is of so many serious works of fiction in our century. Agnon is not, I think, suggesting a necessary association between artistic creativity and neurosis (here he differs from Mann) but rather between art and the perception of human reality—which, as a rule, involves neurosis, and in our age, often worse. (The medical researcher at the end of the novel may hint at Agnon's ideal of the artist: the healthy man who has the courage to take disease into himself in order to discover a necessary truth.) Instructively, Herbst's eyes are "terror-stricken" but his soul is "eager" to take in the painting, because the soul is avid for reality and the great artist gives us as much of it as we can bear. In a moment, Herbst will quiet his agitation by examining some Rembrandt reproductions with their "inner sadness that brings with it inner rest—the rest which is called harmony but which I call growing wise and knowing."

Clearly, the painting from the school of Breughel with its silent pulsations of disaster is the more characteristically modern, but, however different in feeling, its function as a work of art is not finally different in kind from that of the Rembrandts—to make possible through the rigorous translation of insight into formal order a true perception of man's estate. *Shira,* then, proves to be very much an artist's personal testament, which may be why it was so difficult a book for Agnon to resolve. That may also suggest why he was hesitant about having the entire work appear in his lifetime, for it would have impaired the misleading image he liked to preserve as a writer whose fundamental points of imaginative reference were God, Torah, and Israel. In any case, *Shira,* even unfinished as it is, succeeds in being a plangent response to the modern writer's quandary about the improbability of his own province in a world of Ilse Kochs. What Agnon has done is to give that improbability a visible body by a satiric novelistic study of the figures and folkways of the province, while in the foreground, his rendering of the inner life of his protagonist hints at subterranean connections between the province and the heart of historical darkness. To place the diseased hand and the dire bell of warning at the center, the townsfolk half-glimpsed in the background, is to reverse the proportions of most traditional novels, but it makes *Shira* one of the few major works of fiction since the last world war that manages to speak knowingly from the depths of our century's grim history.

—1971

*There is nothing for which you feel such a
great longing as for the sea. The passion of
man for the sea . . . is unselfish. He cannot
cultivate it; its water he cannot drink; in it he
dies. Still, far from the sea you feel part of
your own soul dying, disappearing, like a jel-
lyfish thrown on dry land.*

—Isak Dinesen
"The Monkey"

Agnon's Mediterranean Fable

S. Y. Agnon was a writer often fascinated with fabulous
antiquity, but what is peculiar about "Betrothed,"[1] one of his
most intricately devised and original tales, is its seemingly
promiscuous intermingling of different ancient worlds. The
story is set in the early Zionist community at Jaffa, all its chief
characters are Jewish, and the language of narration is of
course the richly traditional Hebrew, with predominantly me-
dieval-rabbinic tonalities, that is Agnon's stylistic hallmark.
Yet the protagonist, in his student days an impassioned
reader of Homer, freely invokes "the good gods" in his speech
(though when the whim moves him he also calls on a monothe-
istic "God"); has Zeus and Esculapius on his lips; tells the local

---

[1]An apt English translation by Walter Lever is available in *Two Tales* by
S. Y. Agnon (Schocken Books, 1966). Subsequent quotations are from this
version.

187

girls in Jaffa stories about Sappho and Medea. He is pledged to a woman whom he remembers rising out of the waters of a pond, half-mermaid, half-Aphrodite; and, finally, in the climax of the story he becomes the prize in a weirdly reversed reenactment of an ancient Greek race for athletic laurels. Beyond this circle of allusions to ancient Greece drawn around the protagonist, we get momentary but significant glimpses of other ancient or exotic cultures. There are weighted references to the Egyptian art of mummification; a symbolically important invocation of Semiramis, mythological queen of Assyria and supposed founder of the garden-city of Babylon; a bizarre tale about a black African queen who rides the back of one of her ministers; and strategic reminders of the presence of Islam in the city of Jaffa.

"Betrothed" is a muted psychological study of one Jacob Rechnitz, who is the powerless captive of a profound Oedipal impulse, and, simultaneously, it is an "Oedipal" story in a rather different sense, of a geographical and imaginative return to the womb of Western cultures. It is this latter aspect of the story that I shall try to describe, though the symbolic argument is so intricately articulated that I can only sketch the general outline of a development that must be followed through minute attention to a whole series of interlocking passages in the actual experience of reading. The opening lines of the story set it in a broad perspective as a tale of the encounter of cultures: "Jaffa is the darling of the waters: the waves of the Great Sea kiss her shores, a blue sky is her daily cover, she brims with every kind of people, Jews and Ishmaelites and Christians. . . ." The use of the biblical term Great Sea for the Mediterranean in itself has the effect of shifting the viewpoint backward toward the ancient Mediterranean world, where this was the great sea of all the earth (for Odysseus as for Jonah), and of course these three peoples are all groups whose faiths first flourished at the eastern end of the Mediterranean basin. In the Hebrew, the first two words of the story are a pointed pun: *Yafo yefat yamim*, literally, "Jaffa, beautiful one of the seas," calling our attention to the supposed etymological derivation of *Yafo* (Jaffa) from *yafeh*, the word for beautiful, and reminding us that Japheth *(Yafet)*, the biblical progenitor of the Greeks—a people associated with the ideal of beauty—is also according to one tradition the founder of the city of Jaffa. Later in the story, when Rechnitz is taking his fiancée Susan Ehrlich around town, he points out to her "the 'Nine Palm Trees,' planted by Japheth, the son of Noah, when he founded Jaffa: one for himself, one for his wife, and seven for his seven sons." It is clear that one of several central polarities with which the story elusively plays is that of Hebraism and Hellenism, or, to put it in more indigenously Hebrew terms, Shem and Japheth, the two cultural archetypes of Israel and Greece. The "Seven Maidens" who run the race for Jacob stand in strangely suggestive correspondence to the seven sons of Japheth, as do past and present, Hebrew and Greek, to each other in the tale.

"Betrothed" records the subtle but profound assimilation of the world of Shem by the world of Japheth through the character of Jacob Rechnitz. According to Noah's blessing to his two more fortunate sons in Genesis, "the Lord will deal bountifully with Japheth"—in another traditional interpretation of the enigmatic verb-form *yaft*, "will grant beauty to Japheth"—"and he will dwell in the tents of Shem." Rabbinic tradition understood the tents of Shem as an epithet for the talmudic academies or study-houses of the Law, and imagined the offspring of Greek aesthetic culture coming to learn the moral law of the Jews, thus realizing a cultural ideal by combining "the loveliness of Japheth" *(yefeifiuto shel Yephet)* with "the Torah of Shem." Jacob Rechnitz—his first name, of course, is a biblical synonym for Israel—represents a reversal of this ideal: he is a Shem in the tents of Japheth, an amateur of ancient Greek culture, a sedulous student of the natural sciences that derive from Greece, pursuing his own specialty of marine biology in an eerily erotic fashion. "Another young man would ask for no more than such a life [walking by starlight with beautiful girls]; but as for Rechnitz, another world lay in his heart: love of the sea and research into her plants." And as his eyes feast on the magical marine world of colors and shapes and textures, his response is amorous rapture: " 'My orchard, my vineyard,' he would say lovingly." It is not surprising that, when he comes to Palestine during the pre-World War I period in which the tale is set, he should settle in Jaffa, the city that has a mythological "Greek" founder. Japheth planted seven palm trees for his seven sons; Rechnitz at the end of the story will be trapped by a shimmering vision of seven girls on that same Jaffa shore. The switch from masculine to feminine is thoroughly appropriate for the passive, woman-ridden Rechnitz (is it any wonder he tells stories about Medea and man-bestriding queens?); and one even suspects that, despite the masculinity of Japheth and his sons, the story ultimately associates the Greek world into which Rechnitz moves with a female principle that stands opposed to the masculine world of the Semites. Jaffa is a city founded after the flood, yet Rechnitz chooses it for his residence not because it is the entrance to the Promised Land but, on the contrary, because it faces out on the verge of the ever-returning, never-receding flood of ancient waters.

The world of "Betrothed" is a remaking of the old biblical creation according to the ambiguous design of gods other than the Lord of Genesis. One of the two, seemingly disparate, ultimately complementary reasons given in the story for Rechnitz's interest in the sea is a kind of vision he has one night while reading Homer:

He heard a voice like the voice of the waves, though he had never yet set eyes on the sea. He shut his book and raised his ears to listen. And the voice exploded, leaping like the sound of many waters. He stood up and looked outside. The moon hung in the middle air, between the clouds and stars; the earth was still. He went back to his book and read. Again he heard the same voice. He put down the book and lay on his bed. The voices died away, but that sea whose call he had heard spread itself out before him, endlessly, while the moon hovered over the face of the waters, cool and sweet and terrible.

The vision of the sea transmitted to Rechnitz by Homer is of a sphere of tremendous primal power, echoing in the power and vitality of Homer's own poetic creation. Rechnitz thus associates the sea simultaneously with the vital source-culture of early Greece and with the evolutionary source of life itself: "off he would sail to where, as he told himself, the earliest ancestors of man had their dwelling." But, in Rechnitz's Homeric vision, as the pounding of the waves dies down, he becomes aware of the moon (an actual moon outside his window) hovering over the face of the waters (waters conjured up by the lines of poetry before him)—not, as in Genesis, the spirit of the Lord, but the *moon*, "cool and sweet and terrible," like the call of sirens, like the allure of eros itself to this threatened male. The evocation of Genesis I by way of the Greek Homer becomes a new, stirring but ambiguous creation presided over not by the forthright biblical God but by an erotic lunar demiurge, associated with the female principle, with imagination and beauty, with a world of shadows and wavering reflections. The reverberations of this moment are heard again in an exchange between Rechnitz and the pious Yemenite caretaker of his school which he reports to the Consul:

"Once he asked me, 'Why is it that King David says: *Thou hast set a boundary, they shall not cross it, they shall not return to cover the earth; thou hast set a boundary to the waters of the sea, that they shall not go up on the dry land?* And yet we see that the waters of the sea do go up on the dry land.' "

"And how did you answer the Yemenite?"

"What could I reply?" said Rechnitz. "I didn't give him any answer, but I sighed deeply, as one does when regretting that things are not as they should be."

The Psalms, here quoted by the Yemenite, are full of allusions to a primordial conquest of the intransigent sea by the Lord of Creation (in its ultimate derivation in Canaanite religion, it is the conquest of the sea god by the land god). The reality, however, inhabited by both the pious caretaker and the freethinking teacher, seems to contradict the authority of the Psalms. For, in the story, it is the sea that repeatedly asserts its dominion over the land, and that whole solid biblical world of divinely-set demarcations and boundaries dissolves into a marine flux where opposites merge. Shem and Japheth are fused—to borrow Joyce's phrase—into Jewgreek and Greekjew, life looks like death, or love becomes death (the climactic race that begins at the Hotel Semiramis ends by the old Muslim cemetery; the solemn pledge of betrothal between Jacob and Susan is itself renewed in the cemetery), and even the dividing line between personalities blurs, with Susan fading into her mother and her mother into Jacob's mother, in the sea-and-moonstruck mind of the protagonist.

For Rechnitz, the confusion of realms and identities is doubly appropriate. Whether life-spawning sea or womb, the primal source to which he is drawn implies a denial of the principle of individuation. And because that to which he would return is an ultimate taboo, it is fitting that he can make the approach only through a series of surrogates. Thus, the narrator suggests early in the story that Susan's mother becomes an uncanny substitute for Rechnitz's in his own mind: "Jacob's mother, too, had loved him as a mother should love her son, and he had returned her love in a son's normal way; but his affection for Frau Ehrlich was something apart. It was a love that could be accounted for by no natural cause, though there was reason for it, no doubt, as there is reason for all things; yet the reason was forgotten, the cause was lost and only the effect remained." Rechnitz, impelled as he is by longings for this mother-figure, is the very type of a man caught in a web of motives that remain obscure to him, but hardly to the narrator and his audience. Agnon's technique for suggesting this condition is to set up a kind of verbal smoke screen, a merely seeming obfuscation, through which, however, the lineaments of Jacob's predicament are visible to the discerning eye. Characteristically, just a moment later in the narrative, Agnon conveys the transference of Jacob's affection from Susan's mother to Susan after the mother's death with a gesture of mystification that only partly hides the explicitness of his statement: "It was rather like a new motion of the soul, when the soul attached itself at once to one who is absent and another who is present, and is taken up into both as one." Years later, in a garden in Jaffa, Jacob will gaze at Susan's lovely hands and think, most unsettlingly, of "her mother's hands when she would place them on the table and his lips would long to touch them."

It is significant that the awareness of this chain of surrogates, always powerfully subliminal in Rechnitz and always ultimately associated with the sea, should reach the verge of consciousness in the penultimate moment of the story, when

he closes his eyes to the limitless expanse of sea and listens
to the pounding of the waves as the girls run down the beach:

He saw his mother kneeling down before him. He was a small boy;
she was threading a new tie round his collar, for it was the day Susan
was born and he was invited to the Consul's house. But surely,
thought Jacob to himself, she can't be my mother, and it goes without saying that she isn't Susan's mother either, because one is far
from here and the other is dead; if I open my eyes I shall see that
this is nothing but an optical illusion. The illusion went so far as to
present him at once with his own mother and with Susan's; and since
one object could not be two, it followed of necessity that here was
neither his own mother nor Susan's. But if so, who was she? Susan
herself, perhaps?

The threading of the tie around the collar looks forward to the
moment when Jacob will crown Susan with a circlet of sea-
weed at the end, and catches up a series of images of circles
and encirclement linked with women and water—the circular
pond in the garden, the wreaths of flowers on Frau Ehrlich's
bier, the entourage of girls on the beach, the golden ring of
Susan's eyelashes that captivates Jacob, from which her voice
seems to emanate at the end.

It is no wonder that Rechnitz, for all his love of the sea, is
moved to pensive regret by the idea that its waters go up on
the dry land. The sea is a never-forgotten presence in the
story, effectively dominating all the action and all the personages. In various evocations of Susan Ehrlich, her mother, the
moon, and Rechnitz's algae, water is associated with erotic
experience, and both water and eros are linked with the imagistic motif of "the blue distances" intimating death. At the
beginning of the story, Jacob observes in the Consul's office
portraits of mother and daughter, before which is set "a moist
rose in a glass of water"—the Hebrew for "Susan" means
"rose"—and both female figures in the pictures seem about
to disappear into blue mists. Later, when Susan herself identifies the blue distances with a nirvanalike death, she "seemed
to hover over those blue distances she had spoken of," and she
invites Jacob to kiss her closed, tear-moist eyes, his lips at

once touching her flesh and salt water in a dream of love and death.

Elsewhere, less passively, the sea, glimpsed through the hotel windows or heard in the dark of a summer evening, is "like some being that lacked peace in its depths," the sound of its waves "like the distant roaring of beasts of prey," ominous, alien, ready to pounce. These are not the "mighty breakers of the sea" in Psalms whose might is as nothing before "God Who is mighty on high," but rather the savage man-breaking waves of Poseidon, if not the dark waters of still older Greek gods, Chaos and Old Night.

Why should the ancient Greek Mediterranean culture exert the seductive, perhaps fatal attraction that it does within the world of the story? The answer has to be sought, I think, not so much in the intrinsic nature of Greek culture as in the peculiar condition of the twentieth-century world to which Rechnitz, the Consul, Frau Ehrlich, and Susan belong. Perhaps the best way to see that condition is through the strange relationship of the principal characters to both personal and historical time. Though only Susan is afflicted with sleeping sickness, father, daughter, and lover are all weighed down in varying degrees and manners with an enormous sense of weariness and ennui. "There is nothing new," sighs the Consul, echoing Ecclesiastes, "the world goes on as usual," and he is by no means the only character who perceives time in the manner of Ecclesiastes as endless cyclicality with no meaningful progression or innovation.

If experience merely repeats itself endlessly, it is endlessly fatiguing, and so the two lovers of the story, Susan and Jacob, are seen in repeated flight from the time of adult experience into the timelessness of sleep or longed-for death, or into the radiant atemporality of remembered moments from early childhood or the mythic past. It is significant that the narrative is marked by a number of trancelike moments of vision when a fragment of the past seems to erupt into the present as though untouched by the flow of time. On the personal level, this occurs in Rechnitz's visions of the garden of his childhood, fixed forever with its pond, its flowers, its iron gate. On the cultural level, the same pattern is observable, for example, in the still presence of the Nine Palm Trees, which tremble slightly in the brilliant sunlight before Rechnitz's eyes as they must have done at the beginning of history before the eyes of Japheth and his seven sons.

Jacob Rechnitz, the most representative figure of the modern age in the story, is bloodless, will-less, directionless (except for his attraction to the vegetation of the watery depths) —in sum, the very image of an enervated humanity that has lived beyond its historical prime. The Consul's absurdly inappropriate remark to Rechnitz, "You look as fresh and blooming as a young god," accompanied by the old man's own wistful longings for a renewal of youth, point up the essential irony of Jacob's relation to Greek antiquity, for it is precisely his anemic character that explains both why he is drawn to the Homeric sea and why that magnetism is finally so dangerous to him. Like Dr. Ginath, the scientific seeker in Agnon's later story, "Edo and Enam,"[2] Rechnitz tries to penetrate the mysteries of a primeval realm of vitality as the representative of an age sapped of vitality, an age out of touch with the inherent mystery of man, the gods, and the natural world. But any attempt to seek "renewal" in this way—as, for example, in the notable modern cults of archeology and anthropology, in the various modern spiritual flirtations with the carnal gods of the ancient Near East or of ancient Greece—is futile and may also be fatal, for man is no longer capable of belonging to the archaic world, however powerful his nostalgia for it. Too many centuries of accumulated cultural experience intervene, experience which, for better or for worse, has gradually modified man's nature and estranged him from his own beginnings. The fate of anyone who essays this route of no-return is likely to resemble that of the venerable sage Gevariah in "Edo and Enam," who climbs to the top of a mountain to learn from the eagles the secret of the renewal of youth and instead receives from them his mortal wound. Agnon himself makes a point of comparing the magical appearance of the charmed leaves brought down from the mountain in "Edo and Enam" with the algae Rechnitz hauls up from the depths in "Betrothed," and with "the silver strands we observe on the moon," as if to say: what is sought up above in the later tale

[2]The companion piece to "Betrothed" in *Two Tales.*

is sought down below in the earlier one, and the fate of the seekers may be the same.

In "Edo and Enam" the quest for cultural origins leads clearly to death. In "Betrothed", the story ends in poised ambiguity, with death lurking as a teasing spectral possibility —or is it a presence? The lovely lyric spookiness of the closing moments of the tale is a function not only of Agnon's peculiar sensibility but of the perilously seductive meaning that the pagan past and the primal sea must have for Rechnitz:

Sea and sky, heaven and earth, and all the space between were grown into a single living being; a luminous calm enveloped by azure, or an azure transparent as air. Up above, and under the surface of the sea, the moon raced like a frenzied girl. Even the sands were moonstruck and seemed to move perpetually. Like the sands, like all the surrounding air, the girls, and with them Rechnitz, were taken up into the dream. If they looked overhead, there was the moon running her race, and if they looked out to sea, there she was again hovering upon the face of the waters.

This is beautiful, but it is the precarious beauty of a dream that can dissolve momentarily. Precarious, too, is the paradox of delicate balance between luminous calm and frantic, driven motion. The hovering upon the face of the waters from Genesis is once more invoked, for this is a grand final recapitulation of that pagan lunar cosmos where boundaries vanish and opposites fuse—sky and sea, heaven and earth, dry land and water. We can hardly forget that the double moon racing above and below here was first described as cool and sweet and terrible. Rechnitz is ready, then, for the eery race along the seashore in which he will at the end be claimed by a moonstruck girl—the Hebrew for sleepwalker also means moonstruck—who would call him on an impossible road back to another image of watery origins, the pond in the long-locked garden. Are Susan's night clothes her shroud? Has she arisen from a sickbed or the grave to fulfill her pact with Jacob? Agnon is careful to draw a veil of ambiguity over the conclusion by the suggestion of a possible continuation in the studied anticlimax of his final paragraph. Whatever the literal answer to these questions, such life as Susan can offer Jacob must be a kind of death, for what invites him to her is a return to the womb, as what draws him to the sea is a longing for the womb of human culture, and to man born of woman, the return to the womb can only mean in the end a turning to death. One understands, then, why an ambiguous hint of a dybbuk-motif—the spirit of the plighted bride returning to claim her own—is appropriate for the ending, and why the whole tale should be a reversal of the Sleeping Beauty legend, the kiss of the entranced maiden conferring on her redeeming prince a breath of eternal sleep.

The anticlimax of the last paragraph deserves reflection, because it suggests Agnon's conception of the nature of his fiction and perhaps something also of the larger use such fiction might serve:

Here, for the time being, we have brought to an end our account of the affairs of Jacob Rechnitz and Susan Ehrlich. These are the same Susan and Jacob who were betrothed to one another through a solemn vow. Because of it, we have called this whole account "Betrothed," though at first we had thought to call it "The Seven Maidens."

At the very end, the artificer asserts what is in two senses his authority over his artifice, calling it a "composition" (*hibur,* rendered freely above as "account"), reminding us that the conventional matter of title is entirely the author's decision. The two titles are linked by an etymological pun, *SHEV'UAT Emunim* (literally, "The Solemn Vow") and *SHEV'A HaNe'arot* ("The Seven Maidens"), pointing to the connection in Hebrew between the taking of vows and the magical number seven. But this thematically central play on words also makes us aware that the absorbing reality of the tale is itself a construct of words—words, in the shimmering perspectives of Agnon's double vision, being both the stuff of their own reality and the means through which our historical reality is made accessible. It is hard to think of another extended piece of fiction by Agnon where the artistic control is so unflaggingly sure, its exercise so intricately consistent. That quality of control, surfacing in the placid authorial "we" of the final paragraph, constitutes an implicit affirmation of a confident life-making impulse even in a tale that lingers so

hauntingly over the watery depths. It is through the control-
ling intelligence of the writer's imagination that the story
makes real for us the ultimate abyss at the brink of which our
culture stands, and any truth the tale conveys could hardly be
a consoling one. Yet the self-delighting, reader-delighting
control of the artist, asserting itself openly at the end, cunningly shaping a narrative structure where no simple conclusion, whether apocalyptic or naively optimistic, can be drawn,
is an intimation of possibilities beyond the sea of nothingness
that beckons to the protagonist, and is a demonstration of the
imagination's ability to cope with the world by being both in
it and outside it. The switch in mood at the end to the prosaic
reality of the writer's workroom is in its peculiar way tonic as
well as anticlimactic. The ontological duality of all imaginative works is felt with especial sharpness here: inventing
fictions, we conclude, is an arbitrary act but it may somehow
also be, in the quandary of our whole culture, a necessary act
as well.

—1972

Shtetl and Revolution

Paris in 1923 hardly seems a likely place for the gestation of a novel written in Hebrew that would offer a searching panoramic vision of the *shtetl*'s disintegration in the historical maelstrom of the Russian Revolution. The last volumes of Proust were still coming out; Gide was working on *The Counterfeiters*; Surrealism was about to be born out of the aftermath of Dada; and at that time and place, a twenty-five-year-old Ukrainian Jew, who having fled Russia two years earlier had arrived in Paris by way of Constantinople, began to ponder the fate of Jewry and Judaism in the age of revolution, using a mode of fiction that harked back to Dostoevsky and to the cognate traditions of social realism of the nineteenth-century Yiddish and Hebrew novel.

Haim Hazaz had nearly half a century of activity as a novelist still ahead of him, and after his emigration to Palestine in 1931, his work, with varying artistic success, would eventually reach out to encompass other continents, other cultural spheres, other communities of Jews. The traumatic events, however, that he had witnessed in Russia in the fateful winter of 1917–18 were to remain at the heart of his imaginative world, for he would continue to brood over the Jewish hunger for redemption and the modern attempts to realize redemption through politics. In 1923, the Revolution was still being almost universally celebrated by the intellectual avant-garde in the West. Hazaz as a Hebrew writer was, one might say, acutely advantaged in being able to see not only the vastness of the Revolution's messianic hopes but also its murderously destructive possibilities. If the Revolution, catalyzed and to an appreciable degree implemented by Jews, meant the end of the Jewish people, it might also mean the end of humanity as we had been accustomed to think of it. Over the years, as historical experience confirmed the rightness of this grim perception, Hazaz returned to the fictional material he had conceived in that distant Paris, working and reworking it.

The kernel of his novel, *Gates of Bronze*,[1] first appeared in print in 1924 in the periodical *Ha-Tekufa* as a series of fictional vignettes entitled "Revolutionary Chapters." In 1956 Hazaz radically revised and expanded these chapters into a short novel. In 1968, four years before his death. he published a new version of the novel, almost twice as long, with certain significant additions to the historical picture presented in the earlier material. As the book grew in length, Hazaz's conception of how he must handle his subject became firmer, moving away from effects of decorative elaboration through imagery and flaunted grotesquerie in the first version (qualities he would remain addicted to in other works) to a spare, concentrated representation of the conflicts among classes, generations, and ideologies in the second version, finally rounded out with greater novelistic specification of scene and subsidiary characters in the final version. Specific episodes and characters, however, remain substantially unchanged through all three treatments of the subject; and there is one scene, I would like to suggest, retained from the 1924 story, that is the

[1]Translated by S. Gershon Levi, Jewish Publication Society, 1975. This essay forms the introduction.

vital central point from which this whole Hebrew imagination of the Revolution radiates.

A small knot of young comrades in the Ukrainian village of Mokry–Kut has just emerged from a political meeting held in the heady period of fervid debate and confusion of tongues that marked the first winter of the Revolution. At the meeting, there has been a collision between Communist and anarchist views of the revolutionary situation. As these Jewish revolutionaries make their way through a midnight blizzard, the town itself seems to disappear in the storm. Then a spectral voice reaches them from behind the clouds of wind-whipped snow. It is, we will learn in a moment, the drunken chanting of Heshel Pribisker, pathetic, uprooted Hasid, a religious instructor by profession with no children to teach any more, who has left his own wife and children and now dangles in desire for one of the young Communist girls while the iron wheels of revolutionary change move rapidly down upon him. At first, however, Heshel's voice alone is detectable, as though this sorry representative of the twilight of traditional Judaism were a mere sounding-box for visionary words first intoned 2,500 years earlier. The words chanted by the stranded Hasid through the all-enveloping storm are those of the prophet Ezekiel: "One third of you shall die of the pestilence . . . and shall perish of hunger in your midst, and a third shall fall by the sword round about, and a third will I scatter to every wind, and the sword shall pursue them."

Hazaz, let me hasten to say, was by no means a symbolic writer, and the midnight encounter between Heshel Pribisker and the young comrades is in context entirely continuous with the verisimilar representation of historically plausible figures and actions out of which the whole novel is shaped. The very choice, however, of the Hebrew language to enact the clash between two generations of Jews in the throes of the Revolution produces certain symbolic overtones, the words themselves sometimes leading us to see the paltry events of a few months in this forsaken *shtetl* though the magnifying prism of ancient visionary perspectives. It is precisely this peculiar feature that gives Hazaz's account of the crisis of Jewish values in the Revolution unique worth as historical testimony.

Hebrew literature on European soil had rarely been very

subtle in the nuanced discrimination of character and motive, largely because it had no vocabulary for such fine discrimination and perhaps also because there was little in the culture from which it derived that might have trained writers to Jamesian or Flaubertian niceties of perception. (Hazaz is no exception to this general rule.) By way of compensation, Hebrew, because its own adaptation to secular literary ends sharply reflected the contradictory struggle with modernity of Jews steeped in tradition, provided an ideal instrument for probing the pathologies and potentials of historical Judaism in the modern era, and also for measuring the modern world against the values of historical Judaism. The effectiveness of this recurrent literary focus on a critical stage of historical transition was enhanced, for Yiddish as well as for Hebrew writers, by an accident of sociology—the fact that the Jewry of Russia and Poland typically (though by no means exclusively) lived in *shtetlach*, provincial townlets of predominantly Jewish population. The *shtetl* was for the Hebrew and Yiddish writer more or less what the ship was for Melville— a readymade microcosm, a social unit of limited scope, with established hierarchies and conventions, within which opposing views and conditions could be set in coherent relation as part of a cohesive fictional structure. Thus, the imponderable forces of modernity could become fictionally manageable in the microcosmic conflict between the study-house hangers-on and a local *maskil*, or proponent of Enlightenment, in the grudging decision of a pious householder to bypass the matchmaker and allow his daughter to choose her own husband, and so forth. This concentration on the microcosm of the *shtetl* leads Hebrew and Yiddish writers in precisely the opposite direction from the European novel, which is impelled by the titanic aspiration to embrace, encompass, dominate in language the vast inchoate reality of the modern metropolis, from Balzac's Paris and Dickens's London to Joyce's Dublin and Biely's St. Petersburg. The two novelistic traditions are, one might say, ways of scrutinizing the dynamics of history from the two opposite ends of the telescope.

Historical change is generally a corrosive presence, inexorably encroaching on the enclaves of piety, in the late nineteenth-century Hebrew and Yiddish fiction about the *shtetl*.

In the revolutionary moment in which the action of Hazaz's novel occurs, such change becomes literally explosive: the first illumination of the *shtetl* in the book is from the flames of the aristocratic manors put to the torch by Sorokeh, the Jewish anarchist. *Gates of Bronze* explores the tensions and discrepancies between two competing views of the Revolution, one messianic and the other apocalyptic, both rooted in the language and concepts of Jewish tradition. The most dramatic expression of the messianic construction is voiced by Sorokeh at a New Year's party held by the young revolutionaries to inaugurate 1918. As the midnight hour strikes, Sorokeh announces that "At . . . this very moment, the whole world is crossing a frontier, traversing a line that divides all of human history into two. . . . The sun of capitalism has set— a new world has come into being—a world of social justice, of freedom and happiness, a world celebrating the grandeur of man." Sorokeh's image of history cut through by a critical dividing line at the point where he stands, with "everything that has gone before, the entire past for two thousand years, four thousand years . . . on one side," is central to the novel and to Hazaz's general perception of the modern predicament. What is at issue is whether the other side of the line hides the *atkhalta degeula*, the dawning redemption, as Sorokeh imagines, or universal doom, as the Ezekelian vision of Heshel Pribisker darkly intimates.

Lionel Trilling once suggested, with an allusion to Dostoevsky, that the future of the novel, because the old conflicts between social classes had become blunted and blurred, might lie in the study of conflicting ideologies. *Gates of Bronze* is a rather pure example of this sort of ideological novel. Hazaz in fact sharpens the focus on ideological conflict by devoting so much of the novel's bulk to dialogue, with a bare minimum (particularly in view of his narrative procedures elsewhere) of authorial obtrusion around and between the long exchanges among the characters. What makes this book especially distinctive, however, as an ideological novel is the way in which the ideologies articulated by the characters repeatedly impose themselves as theologies in political guise. The choice of Sorokeh, the utopian anarchist, as the central character is wonderfully effective in precisely this connection because Sorokeh in himself is a "one-man party," a busy intersection of different ideologies with their sundry theological freight. It would have been temptingly easy for Hazaz, a Hebraist and a Zionist, to have introduced a clear spokesman for his own commitments in the novel, a Zionist Positive Hero anchored in the Hebrew heritage who could reprove the waywardness of the young Jewish Communists. Something of this is in fact done through Sorokeh, but in a historically complex, psychologically convincing way, because Sorokeh embodies so many of the baffling contradictions and ambiguities of trying to persist as a Jew on the other side of that great dividing line of history.

The young Communists who quickly become the administrators of the local revolutionary government have only a tenuous connection with their Jewish antecedents, while their professed ties with the Russian people are even more dubious, as Hazaz made clear in the final version of the novel by confronting the Jewish comrades with anti-Semitic Russian peasants (there are scarcely any Gentiles to be seen in the two previous versions). Sorokeh, by contrast, recapitulates the various stages of ideological modernization undergone by Russian Jewry without really abandoning the earlier stages as he goes on to later ones. He is, then, the son of a yeshiva director, the grandson of an illustrious talmudist. Trained from an early age in rabbinical lore, he had lost the old faith, seized upon the new secular Hebrew literature, afterward Russian literature, then the Social Revolutionary party, as modern instruments of salvation. But when, on the verge of World War I, the Social Revolutionaries renounced terror as a weapon of revolution, Sorokeh turned anarchist. Psychologically, he is a new kind of Jew, measuring the length and breadth of the *shtetl* with a machine gun tucked under his arm, answering a demand from the local revolutionary committee chairman to show his arms permit by coolly drawing his pistol and pointing it with a smile at the head of the Bolshevik authority.

And yet, we are reminded that his revolutionary fervor is continuous with the mystical fervor of his pious forebears; he quotes Judah Halevi as passionately as he does Kropotkin; and the interludes to his dreams of sweeping the world with a cleansing fire of destruction are the idyllic fantasies he entertains of going back to a sun-drenched bucolic haven in the Land of Israel. Sorokeh's fitful imaginings were the only voice of Zionism in the two earlier versions of the novel. In the book's last revision and expansion, however, there is actually a Zionist movement in Mokry–Kut, the *Tzeirei Tziyon*, and its presence gives greater substance and balance to the conflict of ideologies among the young generation of Russian Jews. Nevertheless, Hazaz remains true to the soundness of his first intuition in keeping Sorokeh with his confusions at the center of vision, so that in this historical maze of contradictory longings Zionism is plausibly an alluring—perhaps quixotic—possibility, not a pat solution.

Sorokeh the anarchist is driven on an unchartable zigzag course by passionate impulse; his Communist rivals follow a straight line of murderous abstraction. In the foreground of the novel, we see the purity of Sorokeh's motives; in the background, we get an occasional glimpse of the awful consequences of his utopian activism—in the rape and destruction unleashed upon the countryside by the anarchist bands he has helped to organize. As a voice in the ideological debate, what sets him apart from the Jewish Bolsheviks most decisively is that his feelings are still palpably in touch with the living Jewish people caught between the millstones of the Revolution. The older generation of that people is almost entirely a gang of bourgeois counterrevolutionaries, running-dogs of capitalism—which is to say, they are more or less the *shtetl* Jews of Mendele and Sholem Aleichem, only a little more prosperous, not *shnorers*, petty conmen and ne'er-do-wells, but small shopkeepers, grain merchants, economic middlemen of varying sorts. They still have the same verbal mannerisms, the same comic nicknames, the same daily regimen of pious practices as the Jews of Mendele and Sholem Aleichem, but now they flounder in a bog of desperation, for everything on which they lived is being destroyed, with their own children zealously executing the iron purpose of the new regime. Incomprehension is their primary response to the revolutionary moment, and it is in its way a historically illuminating incomprehension. They simply cannot understand why their shops should be closed, their stock confiscated, why their homes should be invaded for a general search on the holy Sabbath itself, why some among them should be summarily arrested, beaten, even shot.

The Hebrew words they use in the novel to express their bewilderment impart to it a special historical resonance. In point of fact, such Jews would of course have been speaking Yiddish to one another. Hebrew literature in Europe, following the masterful example of Mendele, made the most of a supreme gesture of stylization, putting Hebrew in the mouths of speakers of Yiddish, exploiting the older language's rich texture of literary associations while trying to simulate in Hebrew the nuanced liveliness of the actual vernacular. Hazaz's novel is a culminating instance of this peculiar literary tradition, which means that even though the book was completed by a writer who had been living for decades in the new Hebrew-speaking cultural milieu, it is by no means modern Hebrew that the characters use with one another but the language of the Mishnah, the Midrash, the medieval exegetes, and the Bible, as it would be embedded in a Yiddish consciousness.

This exchange between two study-house faithfuls at morning prayers is typical: " 'They just don't want us to live,' said Yankel Potchar hoarsely. 'I've heard that their *rebbe*, Karl Marx, was himself an apostate and a Jew-hater, and said all kinds of terrible things about Jews, as renegades always have. They say he left the Bolsheviks a torah called *Kapital*, where he preaches hatred for mankind, and permits stealing and bloodshed.' " The translation clearly suggests the unbridgeable chasm between the mental world of, say, Rashi's commentary and Left Hegelianism, though certain important overtones are necessarily lost in the English. "Apostate and Jew-hater" is *meshummad v'sonei yisrael* in the original, two Hebrew terms naturalized in Yiddish usage, habitually invoked in both languages with a kind of spitting emphasis of contempt that could only be guessed at by speakers of a genteel language like English. The conversational "said all kinds of terrible things . . ." is in the Hebrew *amar dilatoria kasha al yisrael*—roughly, "viciously maligned the people Israel"—a turn of old-fashioned literary phrase that, with the key Latin loanword, *dilatoria*, calls to mind early rabbinic contexts and thus suggests that Karl Marx is only the most recent version of an archetypal line of plotters against Jewry going back to Hellenistic times. Yankel Potchar's Hebrew formulation of revolutionary Marxism is obviously a terrible simplification, but it is a simplification that firmly catches a brutal historical truth which somehow continued to slip through the fine mesh of immeasurably more sophisticated intellectual vocabularies even during the Great Terror, the Doctors' Trials, and more recent barbarities.

The response in context to Yankel's observation then moves the argument from rabbinic lore and law to the Bible and its exegesis: " 'Ye shall sow your seed in vain, for your enemies shall eat the fruit thereof,' quoted Reb Avrohom-Abba, holding his beard and swaying mournfully. 'Scripture is talking about our children. We toil to bring them up, and they turn around and choke us.' " In the Hebrew here, every single phrase, except of course for the biblical quotation, is in perfect Midrashic idiom: the mentality nurtured by a long tradition of exegesis naturally applies biblical texts to the present predicament, though there is sour irony in that mental operation, in the use of that vocabulary, since the present predicament threatens both to extirpate the tradition and to hound to death its upholders.

Sorokeh, as the chief focusing device of the novel's historical vision, provides a lucid perspective on these Jews of the old world under the shadow of extinction precisely because his feelings about them oscillate between critical distance and intimate identification. Broadly, his sense of solidarity with the Jews is expressed in dialogue, in his debates with the other revolutionaries, while the angry criticism is generally reserved for his interior monologues, his debates with himself. This socialist-anarchist has no use for the Jews in their stance as "otherwordly spectators of history," alienated from nature, enmired in petty trade, adept in a thousand varieties of verbal ingenuity but impotent in the realm of practical action. His indictment is one that had been familiar in Hebrew literature since the days of the Haskalah; it shares the vehemence of those early Hebrew-Enlightenment critiques, but the vehemence is now qualified with compassion. The obvious and sufficient reason for that change is the fact that in the historical moment of 1918 these idlers and obscurantists of the *shtetl* culture are catastrophically threatened by forces whose ruthlessness is infinitely more pernicious than their own shambling impracticalities. Indeed, Sorokeh is able to perceive in the Jewish fathers a kind of quixotic integrity that seems almost noble in comparison with the motives of their revolutionary sons and daughters. If the traditionalists with their long-deferred messianic hopes have an imperfect knowledge of their complicity in history, the revolutionists, giving their own lust for power the name of humanitarian idealism, exhibit an even more disastrous lack of self-knowledge.

I have been speaking of *Gates of Bronze* as an instructive historical testimony, but its assault on the contradictions of Jewish revolutionary universalism also makes it a compelling monitory text still relevant in the last decades of the twentieth century. The ideological debate between universalism and particularism is at the root of all modern Jewish history, and it is a debate that has had literally deadly consequences. Because this debate involves a collision between general ideas of history and concrete, individual human predicaments, perhaps the most effective formulation it could receive is in fiction, where fully imagined personages can struggle with ideas against a background of highly specified human situations. In the novel, Sorokeh himself has universalist aspirations, feels torn between them and his persistent Jewish loyalties, but he serves primarily to confront the young Jewish Communists with an inexorable historical fact: that national consciousness remains a stubbornly potent element in all human identity, including that of self-professing universalists; and therefore the Revolution, in which the Jews imagine they enjoy an equal role, is as Russian as the spires of Moscow, or the knout.

"In the end reality will catch up with you," Sorokeh tells the Bolsheviks, "you'll have to pay for your illusions. The bill will be paid by the Jew each of you carries hidden within himself. These *goyim* will take it out on him with axe and pitchfork, as they have from time immemorial!" These words were first devised for the 1956 version of the novel; in the 1968 revision, Hazaz underscored this general emphasis by having a Russian peasant later in the book fire into the Revkom office, killing a Jew, with the cry, "Down with the commune of the

Zhids! Long live the rule of the Soviets!" The basic insight, however, was already present in Hazaz's first conception of the novel a scant half-dozen years after the Revolution, and subsequent history has proven to be a series of terrible footnotes to this observation, from the countless Jewish universalists who died as Jews in the gas-chambers and before the firing squads, to the hundreds of thousands of Russian Jews in the 1960s and 1970s desperate to leave the country at any cost because there is no place for them in Soviet society.

Both Sorokeh's special interest as a psychological type and his peculiar value as a voice of ideological critique derive from his cool confidence in the rightness of his own perceptions. This confidence is unshaken even when his perceptions lead him to be stigmatized with the labels that modern Jews fear above all else: chauvinist, nationalist, reactionary. He is, in other words, impervious to that force of moral blackmail which in our century has so often cowed intellectuals into positions of base political conformism, and he is able to bring to bear a fine lucidity in the debate with the partyline Marxists.

One exchange between Sorokeh and Leahtche Hurvitz, the rather conventional Jewish girl turned Bolshevik who is the erotic center of the novel, brings us to the heart of his quarrel with the universalists. The dictatorship of the proletariat, he has been arguing from his twin vantage-point as anarchist and self-respecting Jew, is a dictatorship like any other, and its moral character is especially transparent in the way it has set about crushing the pathetic, befuddled Jews of the *shtetl.* "These poor people have to pay for the sins of the bourgeoisie! Tell me, what hope is there for these poor lost Jews, what have they got to look forward to?" Elsewhere, Leahtche Hurvitz, like the other Communists, is willing to contend that the Revolution is beyond all considerations of morality, that if it requires colossal injustice, its redemptive power lies precisely in thus trampling upon the jaded values of the dead past. (The claim sounds like a late echo of Sabbatian theology.) In this particular discussion, Sorokeh's polemic insistence on the suffering of the Jews, always an irritant to leftists, triggers a classic leftist response: " 'I'm not a nationalist,' she shook her head solemnly. 'I'm for humanity as a whole.' " This grand declaration induces a peal of laughter in Sorokeh, then a dismissal of her words as foolish cant. Leahtche, much offended, reaffirms her position: " 'I don't care what you say ... but I'm not a nationalist. I'll go further, I'm an antinationalist. I'm a Communist.' 'What a Jewish answer!' Sorokeh laughed again. 'No *goy* would say, I'm not a Russian, I'm not a Ukrainian. Only Jews talk like that.' "

Certain words and ideas find uncanny echoes in unexpected places, perhaps because of their inevitability as historical perceptions. Cynthia Ozick, in a grimly powerful essay on the Jews, the world, and past and future Holocausts, evokes a ghastly vision of the universalist victims of the Nazis, refusing to be categorized as Jews, their "charred bones . . . cry-[ing] out from the gut of the ovens, 'You cannot do this to me! *I am a member of all humanity!'* " To this Cynthia Ozick adds, "Only Jews carry on this way," and then a devastating epigrammatic summary: "Universalism is the ultimate Jewish parochialism."[2]

What a novel like *Gates of Bronze* might well do is lead us to reconsider the meaning of parochialism. If to be parochial is to be hedged in by the mental assumptions of your own limited parish, whether geographical, cultural, or ethnic, that in turn implies some grotesque, perhaps calamitous disparity between the terms through which you conceive the world and the way it really is out there, in the historical moment which is yours to confront. The study-house Jews of Hazaz's novel are obvious and familiar parochials, almost comically so when they talk of the Bolsheviks' *rebbe* Marx and his torah, or when they imagine writing a letter to their Jewish brother, Lev Trotsky, to redress the injustices done them. Their Communist sons and daughters are far more self-deceived in their parochialism, but they, too, apply to the alien world a grid of assumptions unwittingly taken from their own group's experience and needs, and so in certain crucial respects they are even more incapable than their elders of seeing what is actually going on in the movement of history around them. Sorokeh angrily accuses them of being all too eager to make themselves the lackeys and mindless functionaries of a revo-

[2]"All the World Wants the Jews Dead," *Esquire*, November 1974.

lution that is not ultimately theirs. As a point of historical fact, when the nativist managers of the Revolution no longer needed such a class of "universalist"—that is, non-Russian—zealots to do their administrative dirty work, that class was ruthlessly eliminated. The iron boot of Cynthia Ozick's epigram fits these young Jews of 1918 with painful precision.

The issue of revising notions about parochialism is raised not only within the novel itself but also by the anomalous facts of its composition in Hebrew. Hazaz's commitment in the Paris of 1923, after his flight from multilingual Russia, to go on fashioning an imaginative world in Hebrew—an eminently "parochial" language and at the time hardly a spoken one—must surely seem a peculiar choice to conventional ways of thinking. (It might be worth recalling what an illustrious line of East European expatriates—playwrights, poets, critics—has come to Paris in this century and adopted French as its means of expression.) When "Revolutionary Chapters" first appeared, Hazaz could have hoped at best for a couple of thousand readers—a few brave coteries of Hebraists in Paris, Berlin, Vilna, New York, and the new, small centers in Tel Aviv and Jerusalem. Even by 1968, the likely readership for a Hebrew novel would not have increased by more than a few thousand. Yet after half a century, this fiction first conceived in an almost lost language for the perusal of the not-so-happy few possesses a cogent timeliness, and from our own vantage-point seems to render the fateful historical juncture which is its subject with a persuasive fullness of vision. The same could hardly be said of the now quaint reams of effusions by "progressive" intellectuals in the sundry European languages during the twenties and thirties written to celebrate the achievements of the Revolution.

Hazaz, as I have tried to suggest, needed Hebrew in order to define his Jewish material with some profundity of historical dimension, in order to take its measure through and against the accreted meanings of its own distinctive terms; and, of course, he needed his Jewish material in order to describe the full impact of the Revolution at the point he knew most intimately, could probe deeply. Historically and imaginatively, there is a way of seeing out and around by first seeing within very keenly. The availability in English of *Gates of*

Bronze offers American readers a valuable opportunity to observe the operation of that paradox in fiction, for it is a novel which, by making scrupulous use of its inherited cultural and verbal materials, vividly shows how a supposed backwater of history could be a point where the most portentous historical currents converge.

—1975

One should present the great and simple things, like desire and death.

—Amos Oz

Fiction in a State of Siege

Something new has clearly been happening in Israeli fiction. Literary generations of course never really correspond to those symmetric schemes in which writers are seen marching past the review-stand of criticism in neat rows two decades apart; but now that twenty years have elapsed since the emergence of the first generation of native Israeli writers, one becomes increasingly aware of new Hebrew writers who have grown up with the accomplished fact of Jewish sovereignty in a state of seige, and whose attitudes toward language and literary tradition, as well as toward the social realities around them, are often strikingly different from those of their predecessors.

The writers who first came to prominence in the later forties are generally referred to in Hebrew criticism as the Generation of '48, sometimes even as the Palmach Generation, and there is a certain justice in the fact that their literary

213

effort should be linked in this way with a historical event and a national—necessarily, military—institution. Historical trauma was a first fact of manhood for many of them; public events had irrupted into their lives with all the imperiousness, the ugly violence, and the moral ambiguity that such events can assume in a time of war, against a background of ideological stridencies. The act of writing fiction, then, was frequently the direct critical response of a troubled individual consciousness to the political and social realities that impinged upon it, pained it, threatened its integrity. Consequently, the most common mode of Hebrew fiction throughout the fifties and early sixties was social realism, usually of a drably conventional sort, however strong the moral impulse behind it. Such writing was often primarily an examination of the problematics of self-definition through a repeated sifting of the various social, political, and ideological materials that were the particular circumstances of the Israeli self at a fixed point in time. Thus, the nature of the kibbutz, the army, the youth movement, the new urban milieus, was sometimes almost as much the "subject" of this fiction as the lives of the characters, or, at any rate, individual lives were conceived in terms of their entanglement in these social spheres, and the social setting in turn was implicated in the destiny of the nation.

Such characterizations of whole generations, to be sure, easily lapse into caricature and in fact one can find a few exceptions to my generalization among books written by members of the Generation of '48, but the broad orientation of the group toward social realism seems to me undeniable. On the other hand, there were a few writers old enough to have fought in the War of Independence whose cultural background, personal experience, or sensibility set them quite apart from this group; who have been attracted to symbolic, parabolic, or expressionist modes of fiction; and whose writing looks beyond the historical situation to trans-historical questions about human nature, value, existence itself.

Perhaps the earliest and most peculiar Israeli book of this sort is Pinhas Sadeh's *Life as a Parable* (1958), the autobiographical record of a Rimbaud-like spiritual quest beyond the limits of conventional morality. One might also mention Yehuda Amichai's first volume of experimental stories, *In*

This Terrible Wind (1961), his remarkable symbolic novel, *Not of This Time, Not of This Place* (1963),[1] and Yoram Kaniuk's Agnonesque first novel, *The Acrophile* (1961). Kaniuk's second novel, *Himmo, King of Jerusalem* (1966),[2] is an especially clear illustration of the distance between this middle group of writers and the Generation of '48 because, like many of the earlier Israeli novels, it is set in the War of Independence, but with a startlingly different perspective. (It might be noted that both Kaniuk and Sadeh are in their late thirties, while the typical Palmach Generation writers are now in their late forties or early fifties.) The substantive action of the Kaniuk novel—the eery, ambiguous love of an Israeli army nurse for a hideously mutilated casualty—could have taken place in any war, at any time. The novel is actually a kind of clinical investigation into the extreme limits of human love, into the moral ambiguities underlying our ultimate categories of life and death.

Pinhas Sadeh's second prose work—he published poetry earlier—provides an even more dramatic antithesis to the fiction of the Generation of '48. The first volume of a projected longer novel, it is called, apparently without either irony or allusion to Malraux, *On the Human Condition* (1967). Deploying its characters in a recognizable Jerusalem setting, often with persuasive fidelity to details of milieu, the novel and its protagonists conjure with such terms as the image of God and the image of man, divine jest and cosmic dread, infinity and finiteness, loneliness, lust, the hunger for beauty, and their dialectic interrelation. Sadeh's radically antinomian religious vision—both Sabbatai Zevi and Joseph Frank are invoked in the argument of his novel—is admittedly rather special, perhaps finally private, but his explicit insistence on using the medium of fiction as a means of confronting nothing less than "the human condition" is shared by the two most original and highly regarded of the new Israeli writers, Amos Oz (who is just twenty-nine) and Avraham B. Yehoshua (who is now thirty-two). Like Sadeh, like Amichai and Kaniuk, both Oz and Yehoshua are capable of precise observation of Israeli

[1]English translation, Harper & Row, 1968.
[2]English translation, Atheneum, 1968.

actualities, but their real interests, too, lie far beyond or below the particular structures of Israeli society.

At first thought, it may seem a little odd that Hebrew writers should permit themselves the "luxury" of contemplating man as a moral, spiritual, or even metaphysical entity rather than as a social-political agent at the very moment when the vise of historical necessity has gripped Israel's national existence more tightly than ever before. On reflection, though, one can see a kind of logic in this whole shift of perspective. For Israelis who have grown up with the State, harsh historical necessity has lost the upsetting impact of traumatic surprise. Statehood and armed confrontation with the Arabs are basic facts of existence, no longer new crises that throw into question the whole moral and political vocabulary with which one has been raised.

There is even a sense, I would argue, in which Israel's continuing existence as a sophisticated technological society and parliamentary democracy in a state of siege becomes a sharply focused image of the general conditions of life in the second half of the twentieth century. Israelis live with a full sense—at times even a buoyant sense—of realized "normalcy," committing their constructive energies to the continuing development of a civilized order of existence, while the contradictory awareness of the menace of the abyss on the other side of the border has itself become a part of normalcy. The insistent presence of the Palestinian landscape, moreover, with its startling topographical contrasts and its complex web of historical associations, amplifies and complicates this sense of looming oppositions in the Israeli situation.

For Amos Oz, and in a more restricted way for A. B. Yehoshua, there is something uncannily semantic about Israeli reality. Topographical, architectural, even institutional actualities allude to things beyond themselves, and though both writers have been guilty on occasion of symbolic contrivance (Oz much more glaringly), one gets some sense that their cultural predicament has made symbolists out of them. One of Yehoshua's narrators in fact comments on the temptations of symbolism which the setting offers: "For everyone here is addicted to symbols. With all their passion for symbolism the Jerusalemites imagine that they themselves are symbols. As a result they speak in symbolic fashion with a symbolic language, they walk symbolically and meet each other in symbolic style. Sometimes, when they lose their grip a little, they imagine that the sun, the wind, the sky above their city, are all merely symbols that need looking into." There is, patently, an acerbic ironic perspective here on the excesses of symbol-hunting and symbol-making; the ironic intelligence points to the admirable artistic restraint with which Yehoshua, in his second volume of fiction, *Opposite the Forests* (1968),[3] develops a distinctive mode of symbolism that is quietly suggestive and for the most part not obtrusive.

Perhaps the best way to see what Yehoshua and Oz do with their local surroundings is to observe an instance of their treatment of Jerusalem. For Jerusalem, as the passage quoted from Yehoshua suggests, is the most portentously "symbolic" of Israeli realities, its streets and skyline and natural setting a crazy-quilt pattern of all the profound antinomies of Israeli life—modernity and antiquity intermingled; brisk Western energies amid the slow, patient rhythms of the Orient; incessant building on a landscape that remains fiercely unbuilt, or somehow in ruins; the seat of Jewish sovereignty hard against the presence of the Arab antagonist. Here is Yehoshua, in as long a descriptive passage as the taut surface of his writing will permit: "Apartment buildings all around, bared rocks, crimson soil. Half city, half ruin. Jerusalem in her sadness, her unending destruction. No matter how much they build, there will always be within her a remembrance of the destruction." And here is Oz, with somewhat untypical conciseness, reflecting on the same setting in a novel where the presence of the city dominates the action: "On winter nights the buildings of Jerusalem seem like mirages of coagulated gray on a black screen. A landscape of suppressed violence. Jerusalem knows how to be an abstract city: stones, pine trees, and rusting iron." Or, later on in the same novel, when political boundaries—they are those of the period before June 1967—give a special resonance to the sym-

[3]An English translation was published under the title, *Three Days and a Child* (Doubleday & Co., 1971). All translation of Yehoshua and Oz cited here are my own.—R.A.

bolism of the landscape: "Through the defiles of the streets in Jerusalem at dusk one can see the mountains growing in obscurity as though waiting for the darkness in order to fall on the drawn-in city."

The opposition between Yehoshua and Oz is roughly that between daytime and night world. Though Yehoshua's first volume of stories, *The Death of the Old Man* (1962), draws frequently on fantasy, with signs of influence from both Kafka and Agnon, his world is characteristically one of bright Mediterranean daylight, and it is instructive that the principal action in three of the four novellas grouped together in *Opposite the Forests* takes place during a *khamsin*, when the pitiless summer sunlight gives an astringent definition to surfaces, contours, colors, people. The swift staccato phrases quoted on the paradox of Jerusalem occur in the first-person narration of an aging, long-silent poet who has just come to leave his retarded son as an apprentice with a Jerusalem bookbinder. The city quite naturally becomes a voice in the frustrated poet's disheartened meditations on the futility of all creative activity, the ambiguity of speech, the eternal dead ground of silence from which language arises and in which it is absorbed again. The harsh peculiarities of the local landscape are a means of giving shape and solidity to the harsh contradictions of being a man, a speaking creature in a universe that cares nothing for speech.

Oz's vision of Jerusalem is also seen through the eyes of a first-person narrator, in this case a young married woman obsessed with death, the passage of time, the threat of violence, and dreams of sexual debasement. The perspective he tries to establish, however, for all his fiction is ultimately not clinical but mythic: Jerusalem the city surrounded by ancient mountains and enemy forces, as it is mediated through the consciousness of his protagonist, becomes the flimsy structure of human civilization perched on the lid of a volcano of chthonic powers, and so the "true" city emerges in the developing solution of darkness as a coagulated mirage, while the sinister darkling mountains all around prepare to pounce, to destroy.

The work of both Oz and Yehoshua raises an interesting question about Israel's peculiar cultural situation. Their concerns, as I have already intimated, are if not quite apolitical then metapolitical, seeking to come to grips with the ultimate facts about human nature and social existence which issue in political events, institutions, and conflicts. But given the explosively charged nature of Israel's political situation, it is not surprising that a good many readers should see directly political, even "subversive," implications in this new kind of Hebrew fiction. Oz's books and the response they have elicited are especially instructive in this connection because his imagination has been powerfully attracted to visions of Dionysiac release which he has repeatedly translated into local social situations and political terms.

The plot of his first novel, *Somewhere Else* (1966)[4] is a writhing tangle of adulterous and quasi-incestuous relationships in a kibbutz near the Syrian border. (Oz himself has been a member of Kibbutz Hulda near the old Jordanian border since 1957.) Some reviewers, reading Oz's novel as though it were one of the novels of kibbutz life of the preceding generation, denounced him for sensationalistic distortion, even accused him of attempting to discredit Israel's noblest social experiment. The real function, however, of the kibbutz for Oz is as a focused, dramatically tractable image of the fragile and precarious nature of all civilized order. His fictitious kibbutz sits under the shadow of enemy guns, with the murky realm beyond the border almost a kabbalistic Other Side, or, to use the animal imagery in which Oz delights, a howling, primeval "jackal country"—the title of his first book, a collection of short stories issued in 1965—that both entices and disturbs those who dwell within the tight geometric boundaries of the kibbutz.

The collective settlement, then, is more a convenient microcosm than the "representation" of an actual institution: a small, rationally ordered society, explicitly idealistic in its purposes, where roles and relations are sharply defined, and where forced proximity can serve as a social pressure-cooker for petty jealousies and instinctual urges, the kibbutz becomes in Oz a kind of schematic recapitulation of civiliza-

[4]An English translation called *Elsewhere Perhaps* was published by Harcourt Brace Jovanovich, Inc., in 1973.

tion, its self-delusions and discontents. The Israeli critic Gershon Shaked has stated this same point succinctly in a cogent argument against the conception of Oz as a tendentious social realist: "His kibbutzim are human islands in a 'jackal country' that breaks into the islands and destroys them from within." This process of the symbolic transmutation of the political may become clearer through example. Here is a description of night on the kibbutz, in fact part of a short chapter devoted solely to such description, which occurs about half-way through *Somewhere Else:*

Now the crickets. The crickets exchange secret signals. The distant motor of the freezer-shed slips in among their voices. The swish of the sprinklers tricks you and falls into the camp of the crickets. The crickets are discovering your hidden places, giving away your fear in sound-signals to their friends who listen to them from the enemy fields.

And what is in the howling of the dogs? There is a dark nightmare in the howling of the dogs. One must not trust the dogs. The howling of the dogs goes whoring after the mountains.

The mountains are unseen but their presence weighs on the valley. The mountains are there. Wanton gulleys descend and charge against this place. Somber masses of rock hang by a thread on the heights. Their connection with the mountain range is suspect. A kind of muted stirring, a restrained patient murmur, glides down from somewhere beyond. The mountains are there. In absolute stillness they are there. In a position of twisted pillars they are there, as though an act of burning lust had taken place among the eternal elements and in the very moment of heat it had petrified and hardened.

This remarkable piece of disquieting prose catches up most of the important elements of Oz's distinctive world. One notes a strange interplay between descriptive specification and looming vagueness, between massive solidity and wraithlike elusive substance and sound. The stately, repetitive, almost incantatory movement of the prose points toward the revelation of some dimly impending cataclysm, prefigured here in the violent image of the last sentence. Oz is a poet of fluid and disruptive energies, and for him the solidity of the "real" world—whether natural scene or man-made object and order or human nature—is illusory, merely the temporary hardening of volcanic lava that seeks to become molten again, or, as in his vision of Jerusalem, merely a mirage of "coagulated gray on a black screen." Significantly, the violent forces locked up in nature are linked with wild sexuality: the gulleys storming down on the kibbutz are "wanton," the contorted forms of rock are testimony to a primordial past of vast orgiastic dimensions. Correspondingly, in the action of the novels and short stories, it is chiefly through his sexuality that man answers the call of the darkness "out there." The howling dogs of this passage are a dramatic model of the human response to the darkness within. In proper biblical language, their cry "goes whoring after the mountains," for one assumes it is an answer to the howl of their untamed cousins, the jackals, out beyond the pale, where human restraint and discipline are unknown, where every instinct to raven and destroy, to sate all appetites, is, quite literally, unleashed.

The scene, of course, has a direct relation to recognizable political realities. The mountains are forbidding not only because of their ontological otherness from man but because they are in Syrian territory, and they hide an armed human enemy waiting for the chance to attack the kibbutz. What should be noted, however, is the way in which the Arab military adversary has been completely assimilated into the mythic landscape, interfused with it. As a matter of fact, actual Arab antagonists do not appear in this passage at all (though they do frequently elsewhere in Oz), but nature here has itself become the invading threat—the spy network of crickets, the treacherous dogs howling up to the mountains— and the Arabs when they are imagined directly are merely extensions, embodiments, of an inimical yet seductive nature. Oz's imaginative rendering of the state of siege, in terms of its origins in his private world of neurosis, is an Israeli's nightmare of life in a garrison-state, but as a component of a realized artistic whole, it has very little to do with the actual conditions of the state of siege, whether political, moral, or even psychological.

All this needs to be clearly stated in order to see in proper perspective Oz's most fully realized book to date, *My Michael*

(1968).[4] The novel, which was a spectacular bestseller in Israel in 1969—over 30,000 copies sold in a country where the Hebrew-reading public can scarcely number a million—has enjoyed the peculiar fate of being at once a *succès de scandale* and a *succès d'estime*. The critical esteem seems to me warranted because *My Michael* is an arresting novel in itself and represents an impressive advance in artistic control over its author's two earlier books. For Oz's brooding lyric prose, as one might infer even from the passage just quoted, is often in danger of breaking out into purple patches; and his intense desire to connect characters with elemental forces sometimes leads him into blatant melodrama or painfully contrived symbolism. (Some of the early fiction makes one think of the most sophomoric things in D. H. Lawrence, like "Nomads and Viper," the story of a kibbutz girl who, repelled, frightened, and attracted by a dusky, potent bedouin, imagines she has been touched by him and is racked with physical revulsion, then is bitten by an all-too-phallic snake and dies in sweet waves of ecstasy.) In his latest book, Oz demonstrates a new sureness of touch in arranging a suggestive dialectic between fantasy and outer reality through the language of his first-person narrator.

Hannah Gonen, the protagonist, the wife of a graduate student in geology at the Hebrew University, is, as at least two reviewers have observed, a Madame Bovary of the interior world. Trapped in the flat bourgeois existence of a Jerusalem hausfrau, her isolation ironically reinforced by the good-natured devotion of her systematic, practical-minded, "achievement-oriented," hopelessly unimaginative husband, she escapes into an inner realm of fantasy, compounded of early memories, juvenile literature, and suppressed desires, where she can reign as a splendid queen and abandon herself to lovers who exist solely in a subterranean sphere of the imagination. What Oz has done in this novel is to find a fully-justified location within character for that chthonic world to which his own imagination is drawn. As Hannah Gonen's narrative shuttles between outer and inner worlds, the quality of the prose itself oscillates—on the one hand, a parade of

[4]An English version was published by Alfred A. Knopf, Inc., in 1972.

brief, factual, elliptic sentences whose flat rhythms and direct unqualified statements precisely define the deadness of the external world for Hannah; on the other hand, in her interior monologues, a haunting florescence of language, highly colored with emotive adjectives and vivid sensory imagery, run-on sentences spilling from fantasy to fantasy through underground caverns out of Jules Verne. It is precisely because Michael, her husband, has no access to this private world, is incapable even of imagining its existence, that conjugal sex itself is finally adulterous for Hannah. She clings to her husband's body in fear and desperation, as Emma Bovary grasped at Rodolphe and Leon, but he cannot release her from the prison of her isolation even when he gives her ecstasy. Thus, after a pyrotechnic description of the heights and depths of orgasm with Michael, Hannah tells us, "And yet I evaded him. I related only to his body: muscles, arms, hair. In my heart I knew that I was betraying him, over and over. With his body."

Hannah's maddening desire to break loose from the trap of her own existence is, like the dark urges of the characters in Oz's previous novel, a response to the basic condition of civilization, but it is presented in a familiar social context, and this is what has given the book a certain degree of notoriety in Israel. For the Israeli, Jerusalem is the political center, the key historical symbol, and since June 1967, the chief non-negotiable fact, of national existence. (One notes that the draft of the novel was completed just weeks before the war broke out.) In *My Michael*, however, Jerusalem, the illusory, unknowable city of congealed nightmare and suppressed violence, is the principal symbol for the protagonist's state of alienation. The single moment in the novel when she can pronounce the words, "I belonged," is during a visit to a kibbutz in the Galilee, where "Jerusalem was far away and could no longer pursue." But a glimpse of Arab shepherds on an opposite slope is enough to remind her of her lack of connection with the world around her, and at once a vision of the somber, forbidding Jerusalem of her fears rises before her again.

Oz thus puts the materials of the Israeli scene to darkly suggestive use in a mythic drama, but it is clear why some readers should feel at least uneasy with what he has done.

Such uneasiness becomes acute in the response to his treatment of Arab terrorism in *My Michael*. Hannah Gonen remembers a pair of Arab twins, Halil and Aziz, with whom she used to play as a child in Jerusalem during the period before 1948. Halil and Aziz return now in her fantasies to break into her house and violate her, and it is evident that she is far more fascinated than frightened by them. She imagines them as having become terrorists, and it is in this guise that they appear in the climactic fantasy of destruction which concludes the novel, and which more than one reviewer quoted in outrage: Hannah sees Halil and Aziz gliding across the Judean Desert toward their objective within Israel, daggers in hand, submachine guns and explosive devices on their backs, so thoroughly part of the natural setting that their movements are pure feline grace and fluidity, and, like the crickets in *Somewhere Else*, their communication an exchange of guttural "sound signals," not human language. The alluring alien twins are in some way an uncanny and piquant doubling of the male principle for Hannah; she imagines both their animal grace and their capacity for violence in erotic terms: "Theirs is a language of simple symbols—gentle touches, a muted murmur, like a man and woman who are lovers. A finger on the shoulder. A hand on the nape. Birdcall. Secret whistle. High thorns in the gulley. The shadow of old olive trees. Silently the earth gives herself." Thus there is an almost exhilarating feeling of release in the explosion that culminates this fantasy, and the chill silence that afterward descends on the land, in the final sentence of the novel, brings with it a curious sense of relief for the protagonist.

Now, it is obvious that this dream of terrorists flowing across the desert in perfect catlike motion "that is a caress full of yearning" corresponds faithfully only to Hannah Gonen's fantasy world, not to the actual motley collection of unstable, deluded, and generally inept types that have tried to carry out the fundamentally ineffectual program of Al Fatah. As some of the response to the novel indicates, Oz is playing with explosive material in more than one sense by pulling these political actualities into the warp of a mythic confrontation. What should be noted is the peculiar double edge of his whole literary enterprise. In one sense, it can legitimately be conceived as a document, and a very troubling one, of Israel's state of seige; but at the same time, paradoxically, it bears witness to the complete freedom of consciousness of the Israeli writer, who does not feel compelled to treat the conflict with the Arabs in a context of political "responsibility" but may reshape it into an image of human existence quite beyond politics.

Avraham B. Yehoshua writes a much cooler, more understated kind of fiction than Oz, sometimes arranging his narrative materials in generalizing designs that place them almost at the distance of parable from the reader; but there are certain affinities in theme between the two writers. Several of Yehoshua's protagonists, like those of Oz, bear within them a deep sexual wound that humiliates them, drives them to acts of hostility. Without a trace of Oz's mythopoeic imagination or his interest in an erotic underworld, Yehoshua also often sees lurking animal instincts beneath the façade of the civilized self; his educated, ostensibly pacific, ineffectual personages frequently harbor a murderous impulse to destroy whatever stands in their way or whatever is associated with those who have given them pain. "Three Days and a Child," the last story in *Opposite the Forests,* is the account of a bachelor who agrees to take care of his former mistress's son and then struggles—in quiet ambivalence, never melodramatically—with the desire to do away with the child as an act of vengeance against its mother, who has dared to prefer another man.

Peculiarly, but most appropriately, this tersely-reported first-person narrative proves to be a kind of submerged animal fable. If we translate the rather common Hebrew names of the protagonists—all of them are graduate students at the Hebrew University and none is overtly "animalistic"—we find that Wolf the father brings his small son (whose garbled name remains a puzzle) to Bear, his wife's former lover. Bear has a new mistress, Gazelle, a naturalist devoted to the collection of thorns, and he shares with her an odd friend, a gentle, slightly daft herpetologist named Hart, who gets bitten by one of his snakes during the course of events because he refuses to crush it when it slithers away. Near the end of the novella, Bear tells the child a story about a bear, a fox, a wolf, a hart, and their wives who go off to the forest where they carry on "cruel wars." The boy is especially moved by the little wolves that are drowned in the river; and at the end of the tale, when the teller decides to destroy every living creature, leaving only one little wolf-cub, we infer that an ambiguous reconciliation has been effected between the man and the child he thought of killing: Bear (is he also the ravening fox of his tale?) identifies with his rival's son, the wolfling, out of self-pity, and so allows him to live, in story and in fact. The scheme of the animal fable here may suggest how Yehoshua deftly defines an intricate constellation of ambiguous motives and relations with great economy of means.

Also like Oz is Yehoshua's fascination with destruction for its own sake, the desires civilization breeds in people to escape its imposed order and rational framework. Yehoshua treated one variant of this condition in an early story, "The Tropville Evening Express," about a quiet little town that is pitifully *de trop* in a world of vast wars and so its citizens conspire to cause a trainwreck simply to make something happen in the dead air of their empty existence. More memorably, this time using materials from Israel's political situation, Yehoshua deals with the same problem in the title story of *Opposite the Forests*. A quick summary will reveal the direct thematic connection with Oz. The protagonist, a badly-blocked graduate student in history, has taken a job as a fire watchman at a Jewish National Fund forest so that he can have the uninterrupted solitude to write an essay on the Crusades. (In order to see the full point of the story, one must keep in mind the comparison between Israelis and Crusaders frequently drawn in Arab propaganda.) The man-made forest has grown up over the site of an Arab village that was razed in the fighting of 1948. One of the villagers, however, an old mute, remains as caretaker of the ranger's station together with an enigmatic little girl who seems to look after him. At first the new ranger strains every nerve watching day and night for a sign of fire in order to call in the alarm, but imperceptibly it becomes clear to him and to us that he really wants the fire to break out, and when the Arab mute finally puts the forest to the torch, the watchman is a passive accomplice, exhilarated by the all-consuming flame and by the vision of the long-destroyed village he sees rising in the tongues of smoke and fire.

The political application of the story is transparent, and for anyone accustomed to thinking of Israel in official Zionist terms, it may seem more comprehensively "subversive" than anything in Oz. Yehoshua, let me emphasize, is unswervingly committed to Israel's survival and to the constructive development of Israeli society—he is, of all things, Dean of Students at Haifa University—and the story must properly be seen as an unflinching exploration of the shadowy underside of ambivalence in Israeli consciousness within the state of siege. A more general human ambivalence is also implied in the story's use of the local situation; as we move in a typical Yehoshua pattern from the frustrations of impotence—here, the unwritten paper—to the thirst for destruction, we get a sense of the balked consciousness of civilized man secretly longing for the cataclysm that will raze all the artificial hedging structures of human culture. The steadily generalizing perspective of all Yehoshua's fiction is clear from the opening sentences of "Opposite the Forests":

The last winter, too, was lost in fog. As usual he did nothing. He put off his exams, and the papers, of course, remained unwritten. Yes, he had long since finished hearing everything, that is, all his lectures. A chain of signatures in his dog-eared registration book certified that everyone had fulfilled his obligation toward him and had disappeared in silence, and now the obligation was left in his hands alone, his slack hands. But words make him tired; even his own words, and certainly the words of others. In the world around him he drifts from one apartment to another, without roots or a steady job.

The unnamed graduate student at once becomes an exemplar of contemporary futility, purposelessness, deracination, but with none of the self-conscious reaching for the effects of a Kafka parable that one finds in some of Yehoshua's earlier stories. The language is unpretentious, the diction largely colloquial, the references to the details of student life factually precise yet formulated to make their paradigmatic implications evident. The first sentences of the story introduce us immediately to the characteristic Yehoshua world, which is, in a word, a world of incompletions. Characters undertake all kinds of projects which they are incapable of seeing to an end—a thesis, a poem, a love affair, the building of a dam in Africa. As this protagonist's fatigue with language suggests, the individual is confirmed in his radical loneliness because the instruments of communication seem so pathetically inadequate, or futile. "Is it still possible to say anything?" asks another Yehoshua protagonist at the end of his disillusioning experiences. Most of Yehoshua's stories are models of the difficulties of communication; as we have seen, he delights in juxtaposing mutually incomprehensible figures—an Israeli student and an old Arab mute, a poet father and a retarded son, a bachelor and a three-year-old, and, in the fourth story of this volume, an Israeli engineer and a hostile, mocking African doctor. In each of these cases, communication of sorts does take place, but it is generally an ambiguous, troubling communication, sometimes with ominous results, destruction becoming the final language. I alluded earlier to Yehoshua's ironic intelligence; one is especially aware of its presence in the wryly comic effects of poignant farce through which he frequently conveys the breakdown of communication, the failure of human relation. An ultimate act of derisively inadequate communication is the visit paid to the fire-watcher in his lonely station by a former mistress, the wife of a friend:

Only toward sunset does he succeed in stripping her. The binoculars are still hanging on his chest, squeezed between them. From time to time he coolly interrupts his kisses and embraces, lifts his binoculars to his eyes, and peers into the forest.

"Duty," he whispers in apology, with a strange smile, to the naked, embarrassed woman. Everything intermingles in the illumination of the far-off, reddish sun. The blue of the sea in the distance, the silent trees, the drops of blood on his bruised lips, the despair, the insipidness, the loneliness of naked flesh. Unintentionally her hand touches his bared skull, and recoils.

Such a bleak view of humanity as this would be utterly depressing were it not articulated with a quality of imaginative wit, as a critique of mankind's inadequacies, a sort of ultimate satire, that is finally moral in purpose. If, as I have suggested, there is some relationship to Kafka in the earlier Yehoshua, he stands at about the same distance from the

German writer as Isaac Rosenfeld. Like Rosenfeld, he offers us in place of Kafka's neurotic visionary intensity a critical shrewdness in the manipulation of narrative, a certain muted intellectual verve, an ironic perspective in which sympathy for the characters and their predicaments is continuous with rigorous judgment of them. Because of this effect of broad critical overview in his fiction, Yehoshua is able at times to project with the greatest naturalness a general image of human existence out of the particular tensions, strains, fears, and ambiguities of life in an Israel surrounded by enemies. The suggestive connection between particular and universal is especially clear in a story called "The Last Commander," which is included in *The Death of the Old Man*. This is how the story begins:

Since the end of the war we have been sitting in gloomy offices, gripping pencils and sending each other chilly notes on matters we regard as important. Had we lost, we would now be cursed. Called to account for murder, for theft, for our dead comrades. Having won, we brought redemption, but they must keep us busy with something; if not, who would get down from the swift, murderous jeeps, piled high with their machine guns and bands of bullets.

At once we are presented with a world that is based on Israeli reality but not a direct representation of it. Reflections and refractions of particular facts of Israeli existence glimmer through the story: the veterans are called on annual reserve duty to maneuvers in a blistering desert where two or three of the enemy, "wrapped in black," are occasionally glimpsed disappearing into the distant hills; a staff officer descends in a helicopter from the pitiless desert sky to supervise the reservists; even the transition indicated in the opening sentence from military service to bureaucracy is an especially characteristic fact of Israeli life. However, only one place name, presumably Arab, is given in the entire story, the few names of characters offered have no clear national identity, and the war that has been fought is not specifically the war of 1948–49 but an archetypal "seven year's war" with an anonymous enemy who remains completely faceless.

The story finally is not "about" Israel's security situation but about human effort, will, and the strain of maintaining the disciplines of civilization in an utterly indifferent cosmos. The veterans are deposited in a completely isolated desert camp-site where they find themselves under the command of an enigmatic officer named Yagnon who promptly sprawls out on the ground and goes to sleep, very quickly inducing his men to follow his example. Long undifferentiated days of languid stupor under the hot desert sun are finally interrupted by the airborne arrival of the company commander, who at once begins to put the men through their paces—setting up tents, building latrines, erecting a flagpole, charging, crawling, scrambling in full battle gear across the sun-baked terrain hour after hour in mock pursuit of an imaginary enemy, even forced to bellow out old battle songs around the campfire at night. Six days the commander works the men, and on the seventh day he allows them to rest while briefing them on a week-long forced march across the desert that he has devised for them. But on the morning of the eighth day the helicopter descends out of the empty sky to take the commander back to the base, and in a single impulse, the men wreck the la-trines, overturn the tents, pull down the flagpole, throw off their battle gear, and fling themselves onto the ground, to return to their previous state of numbed somnolence. "Seven days he was with us," the narrator comments, "and every day he engraved with white-hot iron. He wanted to make order, and what he brought was fear."

If one tried to restrict the story to a purely political frame of reference, it would emerge as a parable of encounter with a fascist ethos. The writer, however, offers a number of im-portant indications that the meaning of the events demands a broader and more complex perspective. We are made signifi-cantly aware of the presence of the elemental desert over against the sky, described at the very end as "the stretches of whitish glare called the heavens"; we note equally the descent of the commander out of the fierce blue like an im-placable god, and the six days of creation through which the soldiers labor on their exhausting and futile tasks. The story might usefully be viewed as an ironic inversion of the great desert myth of modern Hebrew literature, Bialik's *Desert Dead*. In the Bialik poem, the titanic figures who sought to rebel against the Lord of Hosts lie struck to stone, massive granite forms cast by the divine wrath out of the stream of time. In "The Last Commander," rebellion expresses itself not as in Bialik by an assertion of clenched will but in a slackening, a lapse into lassitude. The bodies stretched out on the desert sands represent an ironic victory over the divine imperative in having escaped from the agonizing and abrasive effort of life in history—the seven days of creation—to an unending antisabbath of leaden slumber. The story maintains a fine balance of perspective to the end; the narrator makes us feel the voluptuous attraction of sleep, and more sleep, for the exhausted men, but we are also led to see that this orgy of indolence signifies moral and physical paralysis, is finally a sour parody of death.

Both Yehoshua and Oz, then, achieve the widest reverberations of meaning not when they attempt self-consciously to be universal but precisely when they use their fiction as an instrument to probe the most troubling implications of their own cultural and political reality. One is tempted to see them as a kind of Faulkner–Hemingway polarity of talents, Oz having the greater range—in resources of style, in realization of character, in sheer mimetic ability—and Yehoshua a greater degree of poise, efficiency, artistic cunning. Either of them, I believe, would be an exciting writer in any national literature. Their appearance on the Hebrew literary scene bears witness to the ability of Israeli society to maintain under the shadow of the sword a complex culture that is both a medium of self-knowledge and an authentic voice in the larger culture of men.

—1969

Updike, Malamud,
and the Fire This Time

Taking certain striking passages out of context from some recent American novels, one might conclude that white writers in this country have been engulfed by a wave of racial paranoia. To begin with, there is the elegantly dressed black pickpocket in Saul Bellow's *Mr. Sammler's Planet* who exhibits his ropy male member to the panicked Mr. Sammler as an ominous lesson in "lordliness." Still more emphatically, Bernard Malamud's Willie Spearmint, the black novelist in *The Tenants* (Farrar, Straus & Giroux, 1971), stirs an acrid literary brew in which black guerrilla squads round up "wailing, hand-wringing Zionists" to finish them off with pistols or, in another version, stab "Goldberg" to death and taste his sour flesh. In the last confrontation of the novel—or is it only the protagonist's final fantasy?—Willie's slicing knife unsexes Lesser, the Jewish writer, at the very moment, to be sure, when Lesser's ax cleaves the skull of the black man.

John Updike's *Rabbit Redux* (Alfred A. Knopf, Inc., 1971), moreover, demonstrates that these visions of menacing black power unleashed are not restricted to Jewish writers. Updike's working-class white Protestant protagonist, contemplating the eerie, manipulative Negro fugitive he has taken into his home, suddenly sees him as "evil," mentally comparing him to the backyard cesspool he used to poke into as a boy. "Now this black man opens up under him in the same way: a pit of scummed stench impossible to see to the bottom of."

The relationship, of course, between a novelist's fantasies —specifically, the acts and attitudes he ascribes to fictional characters—and his actual views, or those of any group with which he could be linked, is bound to be ambiguous, fluctuating, difficult to chart. Sociological and political perspectives on literature are surely necessary if literature is to be taken seriously as an act of public discourse, but these perspectives easily do violence to the literary work by too crudely connecting fictional invention with social fact. A case in point is John Murray Cuddihy's "Jews, Blacks, and the Cold War at the Top," (*Worldview*, February 1972), an essay that builds upon *The Tenants* and upon a survey of Saul Bellow's work a general argument about Jewish literary intellectuals, their attitude toward black writers, and the problems both groups have with the novel as a form of self-expression. Cuddihy's intellectual earnestness has led him to research the backgrounds of his subject with admirable thoroughness, but in his avowed orientation as "a sociologist of literature" I think he is seriously confused about the implications of Malamud's novel as well as about the larger issue of literary form and group identity.

In *The Tenants*, one recalls, the novelist Harry Lesser, living on the top story of an otherwise abandoned tenement building, is joined on the floor below by Willie Spearmint, an aspiring black writer. The two men pass from mutual suspicion to a distinctly uneasy friendship to violent enmity. Lesser gains the affections of Willie's Jewish mistress; Willie burns Lesser's manuscript; Lesser responds by chopping up the black novelist's typewriter with an ax; and all this concludes in that ghastly vision of mutual destruction. Cuddihy's reading of the novel turns it into a virtual allegory of what he conceives as a cultural struggle between black and Jewish writers for a "room at the top." The struggle is less for power than for status, each of the two minorities seeking cultural preeminence by pressing its claim to the prestigious role of supreme Victim. Lesser is the established figure—he has already published two novels, one of them a critical success—Willie the interloper. Lesser, according to Cuddihy, is willing to accept the black newcomer only on the condition of keeping him literally and figuratively below himself. At Willie's invitation, the Jew tries to teach the black writer something about literary form, ultimately frustrating and infuriating the younger man through his advice. This proffered aid, in Cuddihy's view, is primarily a self-protective affirmation of special privilege on the part of the Jewish writer: "Black experience is eligible for registration in cultural terms only if it assumes proper fictional form. Lesser and his colleagues [presumably, Jewish literary intellectuals in real life] are the self-appointed custodians of these rubrical and civilized matters." Reflecting on Willie Spearmint's resentment against the exigencies of form, Cuddihy contends that the "Wasp art-novel" *(sic)* is in fact "ethnically emasculating" to Jews and blacks alike, and he tries to illustrate this thesis by reviewing the career of Saul Bellow. What Cuddihy describes as the "central insight" of that career is a perception that East European Jewry, in the tenor and texture of its distinctive experience, is not *Romansfaehig*, not susceptible of representation in the modernist novel. Thus, *Augie March*, because it adopts the sprawling, episodic qualities of the picaresque novel, is viewed as an authentic attempt to achieve an appropriate ethnic narrative form, while Cuddihy can assert of the Bellow who wrote *Herzog* that "he has 'sold out' to the good-taste canon of Western modernism."

To set straight the most basic issue first, the notion of a Wasp art-novel is mere nonsense, and it vividly illustrates the absurdity in the new fashion of attributing all cultural facts to ethnic origins. The so-called art-novel, most literary historians would agree, begins with Flaubert, a French cultural Catholic. If one of Flaubert's influential heirs, Henry James, was in fact the scion of a patrician Protestant New England family, the Flaubertian conception of painstaking formal structure and minute attention to narrative viewpoint was equally taken up by Conrad, an expatriate Pole, and most signally by Joyce, a writer who beyond any consideration of faith remained profoundly Irish-Catholic.

On the other side of the question, the literary production of thoroughly Protestant writers is hardly so homogeneous as Cuddihy implies. "The Protestant ethic," he claims, "—impersonal service of an impersonal end—passes imperceptibly into the Protestant aesthetic of restraint and self-effacement. As self-importance and vanity violate the Protestant ethic, exhibitionism and ostentation are the core lapses in the Protestant aesthetic." Wherever this Protestant aesthetic existed, it could not have existed in a once-Protestant country called the United States, or else what is one to make of Poe, Melville, Mark Twain, and, above all, Walt Whitman as American writers, of Faulkner as the major American modernist, of Henry Miller as a self-conscious heir to Whitman and to the Protestant spiritual tradition? Indeed, Bellow's explicit intent in *Augie March* was not to write distinctively ethnic fiction but, on the contrary, to make a mainstream American novel out of Jewish immigrant experience, and precisely for that reason he drew on Mark Twain and Whitman as models for the free-swinging looseness of his narrative form and the flamboyant expansiveness of his style.

Assuming an identity between a putative Protestant aesthetic and the modernist novel, Cuddihy implies that the Jewish protagonist of *The Tenants*, as a self-appointed custodian of civilized matters, has unwittingly "sold out" to the dominant Wasp norms—like Saul Bellow and, presumably, like Malamud himself. The novel, however, makes it quite clear that Lesser criticizes the black writer's work not on the basis of some external norm or fixed model of literary form but for the self-defeating contradictions within the work itself. Willie's weakness for inflated rhetoric, as Lesser sees it, violates the "simplicity and tensile spareness of his sensibility." His impulse to articulate a revolutionary position often sits uncomfortably with his attempt to make sense of his personal experience. Far from wanting Willie to write a Wasp novel, Lesser is simply asserting that art as communication must have internal coherence, that every literary work must integrate the appropriate means to its own specific ends. Not to make this demand is to surrender literature to a chaos of self-indulgence underwritten by a mystique of ethnicity. A few years ago, Richard Gilman was suggesting that no white critic had the right to judge the work of a black writer. Now, Cuddihy's more general argument about ethnic form would turn our national literature into an archipelago of ethnic and racial islands, each speaking according to its own mysterious laws, not to be judged or assimilated by others.

What of the claim that *The Tenants* reflects a conflict between Jews and blacks over cultural status? Obviously, Malamud as a novelist whose own rise to prominence coincided with a vogue of Jewish writing in America must have been very conscious in his choice of subject of black writing as a new literary wave. Nevertheless, there is no evidence in the novel that Lesser conceives his relationship with Willie as a competition for literary preeminence, though the interaction of the two *races* is a central concern. To begin with, the supposed vying for the role of chief victim is nowhere present in the novel. Black victimhood cries out from every page of Willie's writing, but Lesser unhesitantly grants this prerogative to the black writer while his own work is in no way concerned with the Jewish role as victim, and he makes very little of that role outside his work. Indeed, the only references to past persecution of the Jews are introduced by Willie in the anti-Jewish fiction he writes after the deterioration of his relationship with Lesser (he calls one story, "The First Pogrom in America").

More important, there is no real status for the two writers to struggle over, and Lesser's residence on the top floor of the tenement as it is actually described in no way allows the figurative sense of a "room at the top." On the contrary: the tenement is a trap, a self-elected prison-hole, a womb-tomb, still another embodiment of the claustrophiliac vision that informs Malamud's whole *oeuvre*. Lesser's shabby apartment, despite its elevation, is not different in meaning or psychological function from Morris Bober's grocery store in *The Assistant*. Like Bober, Lesser is bound to his place by chains of habit, by fear of the outside world, and finally by the unbending integrity of his commitment to a futile calling.

This psychological deadlock of self-incarceration is stressed in the novel by Lesser's maddening refusal of the landlord's astronomically mounting cash offers and of his mistress's urgent imploring to leave the apartment. He finally renounces material security, love, even the most basic physical safety, in order to stay where he is. "The bribe has increased but this is where Lesser's book was conceived more than a decade ago, died a premature (temporary) death, and seeks rebirth. Lesser is a man of habit, order, steady disciplined work." Willie Spearmint is an apprentice to Lesser not so much in the art of writing—Lesser ultimately fails to teach him anything about that—as in the ardor for self-enclosure. The Negro is a far more obstreperous and hostile disciple than the Italian Frank Alpine in *The Assistant*, but, like Alpine, he finally does become a "Jew" in Malamud's special sense—a man who renounces the great world, accepts the confines of some personal prison, takes up a self-punishing labor of Sisyphus in which the act of commitment itself becomes its own ultimate end. What seems to underlie a large part of Malamud's work is a private obsession presenting itself as a universal moral vision,[1] and this is nowhere clearer than in *The Tenants*, where the urgently topical materials finally fall into precisely the pattern of the fiction he was writing ten, fifteen, and twenty years ago.

The peculiar nature of the white-black confrontation in Malamud, and the limits of its range of implication, will become clearer through a comparison with the encounter between the two races in the Updike novel. It is intriguing that two such different writers should have produced simultaneously novels in which the plotting of the racial situation is so similar. By an uncanny coincidence, the white protagonists of both novels even turn out to be exactly the same age, thirty-six, and to have the same first name, Harry. (Updike's Harry Angstrom is German–American, so the name is as probable for him as for the Jewish Harry Lesser.) In each case, a vague, passive, ineffectual character is discovered trying to hang on to a viable sense of self in the eroding terrain of his

---

[1] I am indebted on this point to the insights of Marilyn Fabe's Berkeley doctoral dissertation, a psychoanalytic study of Malamud's novels.

early middle years, sustaining himself with the fading memory of youthful success (Lesser's first novel, Rabbit's brilliant career as a basketball player that antedates the action of *Rabbit, Run*). Lesser, of course, has his dogged sense of vocation; Rabbit has only his ticky-tacky house in a low-cost suburb, his passionless marriage, his long-haired adolescent son whom he does not understand.

In each of the two novels, a black man insinuates himself into the dwelling place of the white. Each of the Harrys sees his black visitor, spun out of the inferno of the ghetto, as a wild, hostile, threatening figure who also somehow manages —through the white man's guilt?—to exercise a weird attraction. Both Angstrom and Lesser become willing if profoundly ambivalent hosts to their black guests, entering into a relationship of teacher and disciple, though in *Rabbit Redux* it is the white man who is the disciple. In each novel, there is a white woman sexually shared, in rather different ways, by the black and the white man. In each case, the protagonist's persistence in the role of host becomes a crazed acquiescence in his own destruction. "My God, Lesser," cries Levenspiel, the distraught landlord, finding his tenant in bloody battle with Willie, "look what you have done to yourself. You're your own worst enemy, bringing a naked nigger into this house. If you don't take my advice and move out you'll wake up one morning playing a banjo in your grave." Much the same advice is given Angstrom by his two menacing neighbors, Brumbach and Showalter, who come to warn him that he had better get the black man out of his house if he doesn't want serious trouble. Finally, each of the black visitors is involved in an act of fiery destruction toward the conclusion of the action. Willie burns Lesser's novel, the anguished work of ten years, so that the Jewish writer sees himself "buried in ashes," while Updike's Skeeter flees the Angstrom house in a suspect midnight blaze that destroys most of Rabbit's material possessions as well as the pathetic girl Rabbit had not quite managed to love.

Cautiously, one might draw certain general inferences from these similarities of plot. The sustained assertion of black militancy, a decade after James Baldwin's "The Fire Next Time," seems to conjure up for white literary imaginations a recurrent vision of—quite literally—the fire *this* time.

Angry blacks force upon white consciousness the bitter knowledge of their collective pain and degradation; in the novels, Willie does this through his writing, Skeeter through his nightly lectures in Rabbit's living room on black history. The white man responds with guilt, a concomitant feeling of obligation, and, above all, with an apocalyptic fear that such suffering must issue in a destructive rage of unimaginable proportion and effect. The female character shuttling between races in each of the novels embodies a renewed insight into the profoundly sexual nature of the guilt, fear, and attraction that exist between the two races. In both books, the principal characters carry out bizarrely altered reenactments of the historical sexual exploitation of blacks by whites. In *The Tenants*, the white man "emasculates" the black, takes his woman from him, though she is in this case white, first attracted to her lover by his blackness. In *Rabbit Redux*, the white girl, Jill, is forced by Skeeter to assume the historical role of the black woman in a sinister psychodrama where he plays the "white" male, sadistically exploiting her, humiliating her before her lover, making her worship his sex.

Finally, a central awareness most clearly shared by both novels is a white failure of nerve; or at least a flagging sense of white identity, in the face of black assertiveness. Rabbit and Jill, a generation apart, are in their different ways both rudderless people, caught in the powerful undertow of the black man's vehement self-affirmation, and the same is true of Irene in *The Tenants*. Even Lesser, with his habit-bound commitment to the writer's vocation, has only a vague sense of identity, unmoored in the world of experience outside his manuscript, and his black visitor's certainty about self, however manic, exerts its magnetism on him. Willie makes this general point succinctly in describing his relationship with Irene: "She had nothing she believed in herself. I straightened her out in the main ways because I gave her an example, that I believed in my blackness." The white man's fading belief in himself and in his inherited values is brought forth with comic poignancy in one of Lesser's dreams, where, clad in raffia skirt and anklets, he dances before the thatched huts of an African village. Suddenly his decrepit father appears:

"You should be ashamed to dance like a *shvartzer,* without any clothes on."

"It's a ceremonial dance, papa."

"It's my own fault because I didn't give you a Jewish education."

The old man weeps.

Although these tentative generalizations about the common implications of the two novels may have a degree of validity, a closer examination of the imaginative texture of each book will suggest that the two writers make very different use of the same racial preoccupations. In order to convey this difference in texture, I would like to set end-to-end two descriptions of city scenes that occur at the beginnings of the two novels. In each case, we see an older neighborhood in an Eastern city scarred by the characteristic contemporary blight of demolition and parking lots. Here is Lesser, stepping outside his apartment building:

In front of the decaying brown-painted tenement, once a decent house, Lesser's pleasure dome, he gave it spirit—stood a single dented ash can containing mostly his crap, thousands of torn-up screaming words and rotting apple cores, coffee grinds, and broken eggshells, a literary rubbish can, the garbage of language become the language of garbage. . . . Next building on the left had long ago evaporated into a parking lot, its pop-art remains, the small-roomed skeletal scars and rabid colors testifying former colorless existence, hieroglyphed on Levenspiel's brick wall; and there was a rumor around that the skinny house on the right, ten thin stories from the 1880's (Mark Twain lived there?) with a wrought-iron-banistered stoop and abandoned Italian cellar restaurant, was touched for next. Beyond that an old red-brick public school, three stories high, vintage of 1903, the curled numerals set like a cameo high on the window-smashed façade, also marked for disappearance. In New York who needs an atom bomb? If you walked away from a place they tore it down.

To this one might usefully compare Updike's initial description of downtown Brewer:

Now in summer the granite curbs starred with mica and the row houses differentiated by speckled bastard sidings and the hopeful small porches with their jigsaw brackets and gray milk-bottle boxes and the sooty ginkgo trees and the baking curbside cars wince beneath a brilliance like a frozen explosion. The city, attempting to revive its dying downtown, has torn away blocks of buildings to create parking lots, so that a desolate openness, weedy and rubbled, spills through the once-packed streets, exposing church facades never seen from a distance and generating new perspectives of rear entryways and half-alleys and intensifying the cruel breadth of the light. The sky is cloudless yet colorless, hovering blanched humidity, in the way of these Pennsylvania summers, good for nothing but to make green things grow. Men don't even tan; filmed by sweat, they turn yellow.

The obvious difference between Updike's omniscient overview and Malamud's rendering of the scene through his character's point of view has broad ramifications in the way each novel handles its larger subject. What engages us in the passage from *The Tenants* is the manner in which it catches the special inflections of Lesser's thought and, at the very end, of his speech as well. This means, however, that we get nothing of the outside world that does not somehow mirror the struggling novelist's peculiar predicament. Indeed, the world outside his writer's refuge is first seen simply as a dumping-ground for his physical and literary wastes. The only details he picks up of the cityscape around him are reminders that his own fifth-floor hermitage stands under the shadow of the wrecker's ball. The external reflections, in fact, of his own plight are even more specific. A demolished building leaves a hieroglyphic testimony of its colorless existence—which is about what can be expected from Lesser's life, from his career as a writer. A neighboring tenement is lingered over momentarily partly because Lesser thinks it once may have given shelter to a novelist, Mark Twain. One even suspects that the condemned old school with the smashed windows echoes a sense the protagonist has of his own anachronistic bookishness in a landscape of urban violence, ascetic devotee of a Flaubertian concept of the writer's craft in a high-decibel age where activism passes for art.

In the Updike passage, on the other hand, there is a pervading sense of the city scene, the houses and streets with their human population, even the weather, as a coherent ensemble expressing a whole mode of life at a particular time and place. The informing authorial intelligence, personifying porches and cars, sunlight and open space, has an emphatic interpretive view which gives the scene its sharpness of definition, makes it mean something as a moment in social history. Thus, the final observation about people turning yellow instead of tanning hovers somewhere between plausible fact and literary conceit but serves as a firmly cinching summary of the feel of existence in this lifeforsaken town.

Updike has a keen eye for those minute details which remind us just how such a milieu looks, which suggest how its parts fit together—the granite curbs starred with mica, the sooty ginkgo trees, the speckled sidings on the row houses, the jigsaw brackets and gray milk-bottle boxes on the porches. The Malamud passage does have two analogous details —the curled numerals on the school façade and the wrought-iron banister of the tenement stoop—but these are not part of a panorama or descriptive catalogue, and in any case they show a degree of specification quite untypical of the novel as a whole, which is notable for its abstractness. Although urban "renewal" is going on in *The Tenants*, pot is smoked at parties, and blacks are talking of revolution, Lesser's tenement dwelling, scantily furnished and sketchily rendered, is virtually interchangeable with Manischevitz's flat in "Angel Levine" (1952) or Harry Cohen's in "The Jewbird" (1963); and Lesser himself, essentially unmarked by history, could serve as a stand-in for S. Levin, Fidelman, Henry Freeman, Leo Finkle, any of those hapless, stranded Malamud protagonists vaguely longing for a new life, for achievement, and above all for love.

By contrast, *Rabbit Redux* is that rare thing, a convincing sequel, largely because the Harry Angstrom of the Eisenhower years portrayed in *Rabbit, Run* (1960) reappears here thoroughly a creature of his changed time, caught in its social crises, shaped by his class and surroundings as they have evolved into the late 1960s. For this reason, the frequent allusions to current news events are genuinely functional, unlike the lamentable *Couples*, where an unintegrated use of the same device seems a mere affectation of historical realism. Bringing to bear an old-fashioned novelist's instinct for the defining details of ambience, Updike places the thirty-six-year-old Rabbit in a precise social context linked to the recent years of relative affluence, deepening national malaise, and mass-produced inauthenticity. For example, the contents of Rabbit's living room, surveyed in the early morning light, have a "Martian" look: "an armchair covered in synthetic fabric enlivened by silver thread, a sofa of air-foam slabs, a low table hacked to imitate an antique cobbler's bench, a piece of driftwood that is a lamp, nothing shaped directly for its purpose, gadgets designed to repel repair, nothing straight from a human hand, furniture Rabbit has lived among but has never known, made of substances he cannot name, that has aged as in a department store, worn out without once conforming to his body." Elsewhere, the novel is punctuated with reminders of a national era vanished, the most remarkable of these being a virtuoso description of a sparsely-attended baseball game, the magic of an American ritual turned into an empty charade because "the poetry of space and inaction is too fine, too slowly spun" for this crowd of the late sixties, and "the old world of heraldic local loyalties" recalled in the team insignias has become alien, almost forgotten.

Updike, it seems to me, is at his best when he is being a rather traditional kind of novelist—which means broadly when, as in both *Rabbit* novels, the clarity of his social perceptions is not unduly vexed or obfuscated by stylistic mannerisms. I do not mean to suggest in making this general contrast between *Rabbit Redux* and *The Tenants* that social realism is intrinsically a superior mode of fiction. The thinness and schematism, however, of Malamud's new novel could lead one to infer that his real strength as a writer is in the short story rather than the novel because his vision is too private, too detached from the realities of society, his imagination too inclined to fable and parable, for the needs of novelistic elaboration of character, event, and setting. At any rate, I think none of his five novels equals his best short stories in originality of conception and persuasive force, while *The Tenants* seems to me clearly the weakest volume of fiction he has published. As a fabulist of the frustrated, isolate self, as a wry fantasist of grubby failure, Malamud has invented brilliant things. In *The Tenants*, the insistent presence of the new black militancy impinges upon his imagination, but one senses his limitations here precisely because in the end he can only make of a crisis in national consciousness grist for his private mill.

Willie Spearmint duly recalls for us ghetto squalor and degradation, Southern persecution, black anger and pride, but all this finally dissolves in Malamud's claustrophilia, his fixation on the allures of withdrawal and sordid self-interment, and that preoccupation has no intrinsic connection with the racial situation. Here is Lesser near the end of his sad story: "Nights he lay nauseated in piss-smelling hallways, sick, grieving, the self to whom such things happen a running sore." The nastiness of this has to be explained in terms of the loathing Malamud must feel toward the self-defeating masochistic character he is condemned to invent again and again. It has nothing to do with the conflict between black and white. The running sore of the self—a self unrepresentative in its special neurosis—fills the canvas of the novel, blurring the delineation of racial relations within it. Willie Spearmint, as I intimated earlier, becomes another Lesser, like him withdrawing from the world into a dilapidated trap, cultivating a destiny of self-immolation, wallowing in dirt, and at the end, again like his Jewish mentor, dabbling in excreta (each searches daily through the garbage cans outside to fish out the rejected drafts of the other). The ultimate moment of mutual slaughter is less a novelistic ending than an idea, a means of symmetrically finishing off both self-destructive characters since there is no way out of the claustral morass they have entered. The schematic conception of the ending is reflected in the neatness of the reversal by which the black man, having felt himself threatened with emasculation, castrates the white as the latter smashes the brain of the aspiring black writer. The whole working-out of the plot is so caught up in Malamud's private preoccupations with filth, womb-like enclosure, the inability to love (Lesser hopes to learn that by writing about it), and a writer's fear of losing creative élan, that it is extremely difficult to read it as a resonant prophetic warning about the actual relationship between the races.

With *Rabbit Redux* the case is rather different. Updike exhibits, I think, a certain boldness in placing at the center of a novel about our time an average, unintellectual, politically conservative, working-class figure. By successfully representing the confusions, anxieties, and blind longings of such a character, he manages, in a time-honored tradition of the novel, to bring us the "news" about something going on in our society, enabling us to see a familiar phenomenon more sharply, from within. Indeed, if a German–American laborer (laid off in the end by automation) can be granted title to ethnicity, one might contend that this is the first notable novel about the much-discussed anguish of the neglected ethnic amid the upheavals of the Vietnam years, the revolutions of the young and the black. I find the rendering here of one ordinary American's feelings toward blacks generally persuasive because those feelings are represented without authorial attitudinizing, as a visceral perception of the black's otherness. Harry Angstrom is physically uncomfortable in the presence of blacks yet fascinated by their seemingly impenetrable alienness; hidebound by prejudices of class and race against blacks yet paradoxically open to their suffering because, after all, he cannot entirely muffle his awareness that they are men like himself. "Talking to Negroes makes him feel itchy, up behind the eyeballs, maybe because theirs look so semi-liquid and yellow in the white and sore. Their whole beings seemed lubricated on pain." In the bizarre character of Skeeter, Updike strains the idea of black otherness to the limits, Skeeter at times seeming more a projection of Rabbit's fantasies than an independent personage. For me, however, the strategy finally works through its extremeness: the conventional Angstrom is hypnotized into a trance of passivity by the black man's sheer *outrance,* compelled to a dazed attentiveness quite unlike his ordinary mental habits by the psychological and rhetorical contortions of the utterly alien black.

But this is not, one can be thankful, a homiletic novel about the conversion of a bigot. Rabbit is deeply shaken by his extended encounter with Skeeter, literally and figuratively burned by it, but he plausibly remains more or less what he was. At the end he still supports the war in Vietnam, still has scorn for Americans who defame America, still feels prejudice toward "Spics" (his wife's lover is Greek–American) and others who have dark skins or foreign origins. His loyalty to the idea of America remains, but now, after Skeeter's bitter lectures, it is shot through with doubts about what America has really been. His sense of distance from blacks is almost the same, his fear of them surely enlarged, but he also sees them more clearly as human beings, understands in some way the exigencies of their troubled condition.

What emerges most prominently from Rabbit's confusions is a sense of complicity. He can no longer see the nation altogether as a division between "we" who are all right and "they" who make the trouble, for he has reached some inner knowledge that we all have a hand in the trouble. The result, for better or for worse, is not a resolution but a new kind of confusion, a free-floating guilt that as yet has no proper outlet. Harry Lesser's self-victimization is a matter of individual obsession; Harry Angstrom's self-victimization bespeaks a publicly shared feeling of guilt. Implicated in violent destruction, he thinks of himself as a criminal, wonders why the police don't arrest him, and with his sense of punishment coming to him he has an open ear to Skeeter's new gospel for the defeated: "Chuck, you're learning to be a loser. I love it. The Lord loves it. Losers gonna grab the earth, right?"

His attraction to the fire this time is of a piece with the relief so many frustrated, socially and emotionally trapped Americans must feel in the outlet of violence, in glimpses of an apocalyptic end. "You like any disaster that might spring you free," his sister tells him, and the jibe strikes home not only for the predicament of one Harry Angstrom. In Updike's *Rabbit* novel of the late fifties, the prisoner of family, class, and place could still dream of winning freedom by getting into a car and heading for open country. Now the only way out he can readily imagine is through the burning down of the whole house: "Freedom means murder," Rabbit muses moodily during a visit to a Negro bar, "rebirth means death." Mere flirtation with the apocalypse, however, reinforces feelings of impotence and guilt, and it is on this uncertain note that the novel appropriately concludes. Rabbit is back again with his wife, unable yet to make love to her after their pained separation, unsure what their new relationship will be or what he will do with the terrible shocks of new awareness he has absorbed during the *Walpurgisnacht* of his strange ménage with Skeeter and Jill. The dialogue between him and his wife before they drift into an exhausted sleep is curt, impatient, restive. The first voice is Rabbit's:

"I feel so guilty."
"About what?"
"About everything."
"Relax. Not everything is your fault."
"I can't accept that."

As a way of bringing a novel to a close, this may seem indefinite, hesitant, denying us the satisfactions of a resolution—even an apocalpytic resolution like Malamud's—but it says something that sounds right about where we are now. After all that has passed in political and literary history, it is reassuring that some novels still perform that prosaic but necessary task.

—1972

> *It seems to me often that life in this tiny coun-*
> *try is a powerful stimulant but that only the*
> *devout are satisfied with what they can obtain*
> *within Israel's borders. The Israelis are great*
> *travellers. They need the world.*
>
> —Saul Bellow
> *To Jerusalem and Back*

A Problem of Horizons

One of the most striking qualities of Israeli literature since the beginning of the 1960s and, increasingly, into the 1970s, is that it remains intensely, almost obsessively, national in its concerns while constantly pressing to address itself to universal issues and situations, perhaps to an international audience as well. This dialectic is inherently unstable, and of course its operation will be felt differently in different writers, or in poetry and prose. Nevertheless, one can detect in most contemporary Hebrew writers a high-pitched vibration of nervousness about the national setting which is the principal locus for their imaginative work; and if we can understand the peculiar nature of that nervousness, we may be able to see more clearly why the Israeli literary imagination has adopted certain characteristic modes and even certain characteristic constellations of plot and dramatic setting.

The nervousness I have in mind is not about the specific

problems that confront the state of Israel, grave or abundant as they may be, but rather, to put it bluntly, about the simple fact of being in Israel. I do not mean to suggest, as some observers outside Israel would no doubt like to think, that Israeli writers tend to be covert "anti-Zionists." On the contrary, what particularly characterizes most serious writers in Israel is their surprising combination of chronic disaffection and unswerving commitment. Whatever radical doubts they may on occasion raise in their writing, they are notable for their unwillingness to drop out of or rebel against the troubled national enterprise. High school teachers, university instructors, kibbutzniks, journalists, by profession, they tend politically to gravitate toward small, ineffectual groups of the responsible opposition (usually on the Left); and they seem ever ready to lecture to popular audiences, to join in symposia with Arab intellectuals, to sign manifestoes, to deliver scathing statements on current controversies to the daily press, to picket the office of the prime minister, as the case may require. But it is one thing to be an engaged intellectual and quite another to be an imaginative writer in a constantly beleaguered nation-state the size of Rhode Island, and it is the pressures and constrictions of the latter problematic condition that repeatedly make themselves felt in contemporary Hebrew literature.

In a sense, this tension of attitudes is part of the legacy of classical Zionism and of the antecedent Hebrew literature that flourished in Central and Eastern Europe in the nineteenth and early twentieth centuries. Modern Hebrew literature was born out of the German Enlightenment with a vision of progressive cosmopolitanism, dreaming of a new brotherhood of man in which a renascent Hebrew culture within the European sphere would be accorded the opportunity to play its rightful role. By the end of the nineteenth century, the old cosmopolitan optimism having collapsed under the pressures of a new European era of fierce particularism, the early Zionists nevertheless argued for a nationalism which would somehow be universal in scope. A resurgent Jewish commonwealth, they hoped, would not be a new kind of ghetto on a national scale or simply a "Bulgaria in the Middle East" but a vital center for all world Jewry and, with intricate links both to the best modern culture and to the Jewish past, a small but precious beacon for mankind. One might conceivably argue from the complex facts of Israeli actuality in the seventies that the visionary notions of the Zionist founders were not entirely off the mark, but the discrepancy between vision and reality is obviously enormous, and it is out of the pained consciousness of this discrepancy that Israeli writers tend to shape their work.

When your whole cultural tradition tells you that you should be a universalist, though with a proud particularist base, and when, in this tension of expectations, you find yourself part of a tiny linguistic pocket hemmed in at the eastern end of the Mediterranean by enemy guns and a wall of nonrecognition, striving to maintain connections that sometimes must seem tenuous with the "great world" thousands of miles away, you are quite likely to experience flashes of claustrophobia. The only dependable antidote to this collective sense of cultural entrapment is a strong dose of messianism, for if you believe that the future of mankind rides with the ebb and flow of your nation's destiny, no political or geocultural encirclement, however constricting, can ever cut you off from a realm of larger significance. Old-fashioned messianism, however, is not much in evidence these days among serious writers in Israel. In fact, the only convincing example that comes to mind is the poet Uri Zvi Greenberg, now in his eighties, whose fierce mystic nationalism has produced poetic moments of awesome power but who has not inspired any literary emulators. The overwhelming majority of Israeli writers, for whom national identity is an incontestable fact not an incandescent faith, must settle for scrutinizing the surfaces and depths of their national reality while sometimes secretly longing for a larger world to embrace, perhaps even feeling in some corner of awareness the persistent needle of doubt as to whether, if it were only possible, life might be more fully livable somewhere else.

Somewhere Else, in fact, is the symptomatic title of Amos Oz's first novel, published in 1966 (English translation, *Elsewhere Perhaps*). It is one of several books of the early and mid-sixties that could be taken as points of departure for the so-called New Wave in Israeli fiction. Shimon Sandbank is surely right in proposing a new uncertainty of values as one of the distinguishing traits of the last decade and a half of Israeli writing, but, viewing the transition from another angle, I would like to suggest that the difference is also essentially the difference in the imaginative horizons of the fiction and poetry. I am not using "horizons" in any metaphorical sense; what I am referring to, as I shall try to illustrate through some specific instances of Israeli writing, is the actual geographical limits that define the imagined world of the literary work.

The novelists of the Generation of '48—writers like S. Yizhar, Moshe Shamir, Nathan Shaham, Aharon Megged—created fictional worlds focused on distinctive Israeli social realities like the army, the kibbutz, the socialist youth movement, with horizons that never visibly extended beyond Israel. Europe appeared, if at all, in these works as a bad memory, and America was simply not a presence. The writers may have been, like writers elsewhere, acutely unhappy with what they saw, but it never seems to have occurred to them to imagine or seriously muse over any arena of existence other than this newly independent national one in which they were struggling to articulate an authentic identity.

Somewhere Else is, like earlier books by Shaham, Shamir, and others of the older generation, a novel of kibbutz life (Oz in fact has remained a kibbutz member since adolescence), but it is profoundly different from Hebrew fiction of the forties and fifties not only because of its pronounced symbolism and its plangently lyric style but, more crucially, because its imagined horizons are different, as the very title declares. Oz's kibbutz is not simply an assumed institutional framework within which certain social and moral problems may be explored. Sitting in the shadow of ominous mountains and enemy guns, huddled within the perimeter of its own fences, it becomes a parable of claustrophobic collective existence. All the action takes place within the kibbutz, but all the urgent *pressure* on the action originates "somewhere else"— whether in the dark beyond the Syrian border, where jackals howl and primordial forces lurk, or in the moral quagmire of postwar Germany, which through the agency of a sinister visitor penetrates into the kibbutz. The novel's oppositions

between here and elsewhere tend to be too simple and sometimes melodramatic—Oz was scarcely twenty-six when he
completed the book—but the schematism has the effect of
making the symptomatic aspect of the novel vividly clear:
whatever "somewhere else" may actually be, it embodies a
disturbing, and alluring, depth, complexity, ambiguity quite
beyond the rationalist, optimistic commitment to salubrious
collective endeavor of Israel's tight little island.

Recent Israeli literature, I would contend, galvanized by
these claustrophobic flashes, has tended to swing in rapid
oscillation between two poles: on the one hand, an imaginative
leap outward to Europe and the West; on the other hand, a
return to roots, an attempt to recapitulate the Israeli self in
all its distinctiveness by imaginatively recovering the world
of the writer's childhood. Let me offer a variety of examples
of this dialectic movement in Israeli fiction of the sixties and
seventies. Haim Gouri, an established poet of the Generation
of '48, whose first novel, *The Chocolate Deal* (1964), set in
postwar Germany, was a fable of the moral ambiguities of
Jewish survival, subsequently produced, in a totally different
vein, *The Crazy Book* (1972), an affectionate evocation of
Palestinian life in the Mandatory period when Gouri was
growing up. Hanoch Bartov, a contemporary of Gouri's, returned to his own childhood in *Whose Are You, Son?* (1970),
a subtly convincing recreation of a boy's experience in the
town of Petah Tikvah during the 1930s. His most recent novel,
on the other hand, *The Dissembler* (1975), is set mainly in
England and deals with a mysterious accident victim who
turns out to have three national identities—German, French,
and Israeli—and with them three different, internally coherent personal histories. The plot of *The Dissembler* is actually
a brilliant focusing of the whole problem of horizons, Israel
collapsing into France and Germany, or vice versa, until the
entire structure of national identities seems like a house of
cards, but Bartov's rendering of the psychological dimension
of his situation, as the "serious" conclusion to his whodunit
scheme, is unfortunately lame.

There is often, it seems to me, some problem of artistic
authenticity in Israeli fiction set abroad, for the simple and
obvious reason that the writer can hardly ever know in all

their nuanced variety the foreign milieus he has chosen to evoke: French people in Hebrew novels show a propensity to eat nothing but pâté de fois gras, Englishmen repeatedly consume tea and scones, and so forth. This effect of straining after a European horizon is transparently illustrated by Rachel Eytan's recent book, *The Pleasures of Man* (1974), which in its first half is a competent, more or less feminist novel of conjugal distress and social satire focused on what passes for the glittering circles of Tel Aviv society, but which noticeably loses credibility precisely at the point where the heroine runs off to the south of France with a French lover. The general rule-of-thumb would seem to be that when a Hebrew novelist moves dialectically in his work between fictions of Israeli origins and fictions of foreign horizons, the realm of origins is the one that is most consistently handled with authority and conviction.

Amos Oz, whose first novel gave us our point of departure for defining this whole problematic, provides an instructive instance of how a gifted writer can variously work with the geocultural tensions we have been observing. All his early fiction—the volume of stories, *Jackal Country* (1965) as well as *Somewhere Else*—is obsessed with a claustrophobic sense of constriction, the penned-in kibbutz its recurrent symbol, which in turn is converted into an image of the human condition, hedged in and menaced as Oz conceives it to be by vast and inimical forces that man's self-deceiving schemes of rational order futilely hope to subdue. This essentially symbolic conflict of the early fiction then forms the base for the more probing psychological portraits he begins to do in the later sixties of deeply troubled protagonists who manage to mirror in their mental disturbances certain distinctive focuses of neurosis in Israeli life. After one remarkable novel in this manner, *My Michael* (1968) and a striking novella, *Late Love* (1970), Oz was for once seduced by the beckoning expanses of "somewhere else," and in *Touch the Water, Touch the Wind* (1973), he tried to put together a novel that would embrace past and present, Poland, Russia, Israel, the Western world at large, even time and infinity. The result is unpersuasive, especially when compared to the genuinely hallucinated intensity of his best writing. Finally, in his most recent collection of novellas, *The Hill of Evil Counsel* (1976), Oz has gone back, in his own brooding fashion, to his Jerusalem boyhood, just as Bartov, Gouri, Kaniuk, and others have turned to the Mandatory Palestine of their formative years. In these three utterly compelling stories set in the last years before the establishment of the Jewish state, Oz manages to enjoy the imaginative benefits of Zionist messianism without having actually to believe in it himself. In each of the novellas, there is at least one central character obsessed with the apocalyptic vision of a "Judea reborn in blood and fire." These prophetic delusions of the extreme Zionist Right have a profound subterranean appeal for Oz, an antimilitant man of the Zionist Left, and by re-creating such messianism in his characters the writer partly suspends disbelief and momentarily transforms this minutely particularized Jerusalem setting into a landscape of ultimate significance—just as U. Z. Greenberg, with no such ventriloquistic obliquity, does in his poetry. In these fictions, then, set on the threshold of Jewish statehood, there are no inviting horizons to distract attention from the portentous fullness of this time and place.

The nervous shuttling between home and horizon in Israeli writing is also perceptible in the new prominence it has given to the role of the expatriate. Again, in order to keep biographical and literary facts properly sorted, we should remember that there is scarcely a single Israeli writer of any consequence who has actually emigrated, though most of the writers find repeated occasions to spend a year or more in England, on the Continent, or, most frequently, in America. Expatriation, in fact, never seems to solve anything for the spiritually displaced personae that populate this literature, but the expatriate is now a figure who has to be contended with, empathetically explored, because he tries to follow to the end a personal way out of Israel's landlocked location in history. Hebrew, one should note, has no comfortable neutral way of saying expatriate: the usual term for an emigrant from Israel is *yored*, which literally means "one who goes down," and which has at least some of the pejorative force, depending on who is using the word, of "turncoat" or "renegade" in English. In recent years, writers have tried to see what light this conventionally deplored figure could bring to bear on the perplexities of the Israeli condition in the second generation of national independence.

The earliest Hebrew novel I can recall that focuses on an expatriate is Yoram Kaniuk's *The Acrophile* (1961), which in Hebrew is called, much more pointedly, *Ha-Yored L'Ma'alah* —"the upward *yored*," or "he who goes down upward." Kaniuk himself had been living in New York for an extended period when he wrote this first novel, which deals with the marital and spiritual confusions of an ex-Israeli teaching at a university in New York. Kaniuk's subsequent novels, like their author, returned to the Israeli scene. The terrific tension between home and abroad then became the explicit subject of *Rockinghorse* (1973), a wildly uneven novel about an expatriate who, out of a sense of radical disorientation, returns from New York to Tel Aviv to try to make contact with his earliest origins. Kaniuk's latest book, and in many ways his most appealing one, *The Story of Big Aunt Shlomtziyon* (1976), is, like the novels we noted by Bartov and Gouri, an affectionate imaginative engagement in personal history, working back anecdotally through the outrageously domineering figure of Aunt Shlomtziyon to family beginnings in the pre-Mandatory period. Finally, Kaniuk's story, "They've Moved the House," swings once more to the other pole of the dialectic, following the farcical and pathetic odyssey of two expatriate Israelis through California and Central America in search of a kind of El Dorado, deeply uneasy in a world where houses roll along on trailer-frames instead of sitting on permanent foundations. (Amalia Kahana-Carmon's story, "To Build a House in the Land of Shinar" provides a neatly complementary opposite to Kaniuk's fable of the moving house. Her model Israeli household in a new town, visited by a foreign home economist, is a quietly claustrophobic setting of stale domesticity, and the ironic epic overtones of the title—no national symbolism is intended—alluding to the builders of the tower of Babel in Genesis, intimate that this is not a house which will stand.)

Elsewhere, the *yored* stands at the center of Yehuda Amichai's farcical extravaganza, *Hotel in the Wilderness* (1971), a novel about an Israeli residing permanently in New York who works for a Zionist agency propagandizing Israelis in

America to return to Israel (!), and who eventually finds an outlet for his dormant powers as a long-silent poet in writing advertising copy for ladies' underpants. Bartov's *The Dissembler*, of course, takes as its subject the intriguing impossibility of a man who is simultaneously an *oleh* (immigrant to Israel, "one who goes up") and a *yored*, at once a rooted Israeli and a rootless cosmopolitan. Still more recently, in a collection of poems which the quarterly *Siman-Kriyah* began publishing in installments with its Spring 1976, issue, a gifted new poet (he is in fact an important figure in literary-academic circles in Israel) adopts the persona of "Gabi Daniel"—a Russian-born Israeli living in Amsterdam, who in experimental Hebrew verse of Mandelstamian formal intricacy, ponders the role of his peculiar language and culture in the vast arena of human languages and cultural perspectives. In the dramatic setting of these poems, as in much contemporary Hebrew fiction, the figure of the expatriate is used to put to the test some of the fundamental assumptions of the Israeli national enterprise.

Finally, the value-challenging idea of the *yored* is given an ultimate turn of the screw in a published chapter of a novel in progress by A. B. Yehoshua. Here the expatriate Israeli, having returned to his homeland chiefly to look after a legacy, finds himself caught in the deadly meshes of the October 1973 war, and seeking, like a number of his fictional counterparts, a way out, finds it, paradoxically, through a way in: disguising himself as an ultra-Orthodox Jew, he slips away from the Sinai front to one of the old quarters of Jerusalem, where in the beard, earlocks, and black kaftan of a premodern, pre-Zionist Jew, he is for the moment exempt from duty, exempt from history.

In Hebrew poetry contemporaneous with the New Wave in fiction, the problem of horizons is not usually so transparently evident—except where, as in the case of "Gabi Daniel," there is an elaborated dramatic or narrative context for the poems—for the simple reason that a lyric poem is not under the same obligation as a novel to articulate an imagined geography or a set of characters moving within or against cultural limits. Nevertheless, I would argue that the oscillations we have been observing in Isra-

eli fiction are present in a good deal of recent Israeli poetry, sometimes on the level of explicit theme, sometimes
in the formal shaping of the poem's world.

Though there has been abundant and at times highly interesting activity among younger poets, no new creative figure
—in marked contrast to the situation of the Israeli novel—has
as yet emerged to rival in stature the leading poets who
achieved prominence after 1948, like Yehuda Amichai, Natan
Zach, Amir Gilboa, and, just a few years later, Dan Pagis.
Given this circumstance, shifts in the literary fashionability of
the various established poets become revealing.

The poet par excellence of the so-called Palmach Generation (the war generation of 1948) was Haim Gouri. Though he
is very much alive and writing, his plainspoken style, his
frequent focus on group experience, his nostalgic impulse, his
pervasive "Israeliness," now seem out of date, and his poetry
attracts little attention in serious literary circles. Yehuda
Amichai, in my view the finest poet of this generation, whose
verse combines a colloquial sense of place with rich imagery,
inventive allusiveness, and an easy movement between disparate cultural worlds, has managed to remain a perennial favorite, though at various moments his preeminence has been
partly eclipsed by the very different modernist idioms of Zach
or Gilboa. In the last few years, some younger literary intellectuals seem to have fixed particularly on the poetry of Dan
Pagis, and Pagis's popularity, deserved though it may be on
the genuine merits of the poems, is instructive. For this is a
poetry that visibly, in terms of its optic perspectives, shrinks
the Israeli landscape to one dot out of many on an imagined
global scene. Local allusions are relatively rare, the language
is for the most part meticulously clinical, manifestly a distanc-
ing medium; and beginning with his 1970 volume, *Transformation*, Pagis has frequently favored science-fiction situations (using verse for many of the same ends that Italo
Calvino has used prose) in which terrestrial space and time
are seen at an enormous telescopic remove, from the other
end of evolution, long after a global holocaust, or from the
observation post of a spaceship or alien planet. This peculiar
distanced mode is an authentic development within Pagis's
poetry, and it clearly gives him a means of confronting histori-

cal horror with artistic restraint and intellectual lucidity—a concentration-camp prisoner as a child, demons of disaster haunt his work—but I suspect that the gift of globality the poetry offers is at least one important reason for the attraction it now holds for Israeli readers.

At the other end of Pagis's high-powered telescope, and on the opposite side of this geocultural dialectic, one discovers a poet like Dahlia Ravikovitch, whose imagination has virtually a fixed focus on a palpable Israeli geography that repeatedly becomes a screen for the projection of her personal anguish. A sense of entrapment and a dream of escape are recurrent presences in Ravikovitch's poetry, and though hers is a very private claustral distress, she manages to give it a local place and habitation in her encircled native land. One of her best-known poems, "The Blue West," is in fact an archetypal expression of the problem of horizons that figures so importantly in the Israeli literary imagination. The poem begins (I shall quote from Chana Bloch's fine translation) with an image of ruins which is a distinctive piece of local landscape: "If there was just a road there/ the ruins of workshops/ one fallen minaret/ and some carcasses of machines,/ why couldn't I/ come to the heart of the field?" But there is an opaque impenetrability at the heart of the field, at the heart of the native landscape, so that the attempt to penetrate within only reinforces the poet's sense of desperate entrapment. She then turns at the Mediterranean shore to a "blue west" which is not real, like the landscape around her, but a visionary gleam that can only be imagined on another temporal plane, at the end of days. First, she conjures up a kind of surrealistic extension of Israel's actual beleaguered situation, a desolate coast with unvisited harbors: "If only we could reach/ all the cities beyond the sea—/ And here is another sorrow: a seashore where there are no ships." Then, in the two concluding stanzas of the poem, she shifts into prophetic style, mingling the grandeur of biblical eschatology with the naive fantasy of a fairy tale:

> On one of the days to come
> the eye of the sea will darken
> with the multitude of ships.

In that hour all the mass of the earth
will be spread as a cloth.

And a sun will shine for us blue as the sea,
a sun will shine for us warm as an eye,
will wait until we climb up
as it heads for the blue west.

It would be simplistic, I think, to draw direct political inferences from this underlying tension between homeland and
horizon in Israeli literature. What the tension reflects most
profoundly is the key psychological paradox of an imaginative
literature that feels itself to be a full participant in modern
culture at large and yet is boxed into a tiny corner of geography, linguistically limited to at most a scant two million readers. In this regard, contemporary Hebrew literature provides
a vivid if extreme paradigm for the difficult fate of all small
cultures in an age of vast linguistic-cultural blocs and of
global communications. In order to define the outlines of the
paradigm, I have been stressing points of resemblance in
distinctly different novelists and poets, though of course the
points of divergence among them are at least as prominent,
and in any case writers may do remarkably different things
with the same set of oppositions. Most Israeli writers, it
seems to me, tend to cluster at the end of the spectrum we
have been concentrating on, where the imaginative confrontation of here and elsewhere is felt as a continual distress of
creative consciousness. To avoid any misleading schematism,
however, I would like to offer one final example from the other
end of the spectrum—the poetry of Yehuda Amichai.

For Amichai the West has not been a blue vision calling to
him from beyond the shore but a variegated, concretely perceived intellectual and emotional legacy. His German childhood reverberates through his poetry; Rilke and Auden are as
natural sources for his poetic idiom as Israeli speech and the
Bible; and the various American and European scenes he has
passed through as an adult are evoked with little sense that
they present a challenging or alluring alternative to the Israeli setting in which he has taken root. Indeed, some of Amichai's finest poems over the past ten years, beginning with the
remarkable cycle, "Jerusalem 1967," have been imaginative

realizations of the distinctive Israeli cityscapes and land-scapes where topography, architecture, cultural history, poli- tics, and the record of age-old vision are so extraordinarily interfused.

Amichai is surely as aware as any other Israeli writer of the pull of the great world and of the exiguous dimensions of his national sphere (as his novel, *Hotel in the Wilderness*, makes clear), but the peculiar kind of acerbic, playful, and at times visionary intimacy with the local scene which he has cul- tivated in his poems tends to keep the problem of horizons outside them. It may be that the messianic perspective, which makes one little state an everywhere, still remains, despite the prosaic logic of intellectual history, more available to He- brew writers than I have allowed. In Amos Oz, we observed a ventriloquistic messianism which might reflect the writer's half-willingness to believe, or rather to surrender to, a fiery doctrine of national redemption which he would reject on the grounds of sane political principle. In Amichai, one sees in- stead a wryly nostalgic messianism that reflects a kind of affectionate, self-ironic longing for the flashes of transcenden- tal vision that in the past so repeatedly illuminated the Jerusa- lem landscape in which he lives. The nostalgia does not dis- solve into sentimentality because his attraction to Jerusalem as the seedbed of prophecy is always articulated through an unblinking perception of the terrestrial Jerusalem in all its hodgepodge of noise, stench, dirt, color, and piquant incon- gruity, and always rendered through the flaunted inventive- ness of an imagery that constantly yokes feelings and spiritual entities with the most earthy mechanical accoutre- ments of the workaday world. These characteristics can be observed in lively and significant play in the following untitled poem from *Behind All This a Great Happiness Is Hiding* (1974), Amichai's most recent volume of poetry. (My transla- tion must unfortunately surrender much of the verbal wit and sound-play of the original.) The only real horizon of the poem's Jerusalem, at once a city of the seventies and of the ages, is, in defiance of geography and optics, an absolute vertical above the city: the switch in diction in the last two lines to a virtual nursery lisp expresses not a wish of simple escape, as in Ravikovitch, but a fantasy of assumption, in the theological sense. For three faiths, Jerusalem has been the locus of ascent, the "navel," as rabbinic tradition has it, joining heaven and earth; and even an ironic modern poet cannot put that fact of the spirit's history out of his mind as he muses over the city. It is this awareness that makes the poem intensely local yet, like other instances of Hebrew writing that have come out of Jerusalem, a prism of meaning that focuses a universal dream:

> All these stones, all this sadness, all
> the light, shards of night-hours and noon-dust,
> all the twisted pipework of sanctity,
> wall and towers and rusty haloes,
> all the prophecies that couldn't hold in like old men,
> all the sweaty angel-wings
> all the stinking candles, all the peg-legged tourism,
> dung of deliverance, gladness and gonads
> refuse of nothingness bomb and time,
> all the dust, all these bones
> in the course of resurrection and in the course of the wind,
> all this love, all
> these stones, all this sadness.
>
> To fill with them the valleys around her
> so Jerusalem will be a level place
> for my sweet airplane
> that will come to take me on high.

—1977